Exclusion Clauses

Exclusion Clauses

Second Edition

Richard Lawson LLM PhD

Independent Consultant in Marketing Law
Part-time Senior Lecturer in Law at Southampton University

Oyez Longman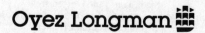

© Oyez Longman Publishing Limited 1983
21/27 Lamb's Conduit Street
London WC1N 3NJ

ISBN 0 85120 729 4

First published   1978
Reprinted with
Scottish supplement 1979
Second edition   1983

Set in Times and Univers by
Vantage Photosetting Co Ltd, Eastleigh and London
and printed in Great Britain by
Biddles Ltd, Guildford, Surrey

Contents

Preface		ix
Table of Cases		xi
Table of Statutes		xvii
Table of Statutory Instruments		xx

Part I: Judicial Control

1 Incorporation of Exclusion Clauses		3
1 Notice		3
(a)	Was the document 'contractual'?	3
(b)	Reasonable sufficiency of notice	5
(c)	Where the clause is unusual	7
(d)	When acceptance cannot be avoided	8
(e)	At or before the time of contracting	9
(f)	The course of dealing	11
(g)	Understanding of the parties and the course of dealing	13
2 Signature		15
(a)	Fraud and misrepresentation	16
(b)	Non est factum	16
2 Interpretation of Exclusion Clauses		19
1 The 'contra proferentem' rule		19
(a)	Strict interpretation of exclusion clauses	21
(b)	Negligence liability	22
2 Some special exclusion clauses		33
(a)	'With all faults'	33
(b)	Excluding or limiting the damages recoverable	33

(c)	Imposing time limits	34
(d)	Excluding the right to reject	34
(e)	Relevance of contract description	35
(f)	Arbitration	35
(g)	Giving an acknowledgement	35
3	Whether exclusion clauses are available to third parties	36

3 Avoidance and Qualification of Exclusion Clauses — 45
1 Onus of proof — 45
2 Liability for fraud — 46
3 Liability for breach of fiduciary duty — 47
4 Liability for breach of rules of natural justice — 47
5 Oral undertakings — 48
6 Misrepresenting the effects of a term — 50
7 Fundamental terms and fundamental breach — 51
  (a) A rule of construction — 53
  (b) The decisions since *Suisse Atlantique* — 55
  (c) Affirmation of the contract — 56
  (d) Total failure to perform — 59

4 Harsh and Unconscionable Bargains — 65
1 Unconscionable bargains — 65
2 Reasonableness — 69

Part II: Legislative Control

5 Unlawful Exclusion Clauses — 77
1 Fair Trading Act 1973 — 77
  Reference 17(1) of 24 April 1974 — 79
2 Consumer Transactions (Restrictions on Statements) Order 1976 — 80
  (a) The first practice — 80
  (b) The forbidden clauses — 80
  (c) The first practice: the other prohibitions — 81
  (d) The second practice — 83
  (e) The third practice — 84
  (f) Offences — 86
  (g) The 'by-pass' provision — 86
  (h) Defences — 87
  (i) Innocent publication of an advertisement — 87
  (j) Trade Descriptions Act 1968 — 88

6 Void and Ineffective Exclusion Clauses 90
  1 Consumer Credit Act 1974 90
  2 Transport 92
  3 Housing 92
  4 Patents 92
  5 Consumer protection legislation 92
  6 Supply of goods and services 93
  7 Unfair Contract Terms Act 1977 94
    (a) Some relevant definitions 94
    (b) Those to whom the Act applies 95
    (c) Negligence liability 95
    (d) Other loss or damage 96
    (e) Assumption of risk 97
    (f) Liability arising in contract 97
    (g) Written standard terms 98
    (h) In the case of breach 99
    (i) In other cases 99
    (j) Sale and supply of goods 101
    (k) Other contracts under which goods pass 102
    (l) Guarantees 104
    (m) Indemnity clauses 105
    (n) Varieties of exemption clause 106
    (o) Anti-avoidance measures 107
    (p) Effect of breach—nullifying *Harbutt's Plasticine* 107
    (q) Dealing as a consumer 108
    (r) Requirement of reasonableness 110
    (s) Misrepresentation 117
    (t) Specified exclusions 121
    (u) Savings for other relevant legislation 122

**Part III: A Practical Guide to Judicial
and Legislative Control**

7 A Practical Guide 129
  1 Liability for negligence 129
  2 Liability for breach of contract 129
  3 Indemnity clauses 130
  4 Void clauses 130
  5 Misrepresentation 130
  6 Guarantees 130

7 Unlawful exclusion clauses   131
8 The status of the parties   131
9 Unequal bargaining power   131

Appendices

1 Unfair Contract Terms Act 1977   133
2 Consumer Transactions (Restrictions on Statements)
   Order 1976   151
3 Council of Europe Resolution [76] 47   155
4 Cases   158
   Hughes v *Hall and Hall*   158
   Woodman v *Photo Trade Processing Ltd*   161
   Southwestern General Property Company Ltd v *Josef
      Marton*   168

Index   175

Preface

Notwithstanding its origins as a Private Member's Bill, the Unfair Contract Terms Act was radical both in intention and effect. Since the first edition of this book, the litigation which has appeared has shown how difficult it is (and this applies both to consumer and business contracts) for the proferens of an exclusion clause to prove its validity. And who can say just how many clauses have been quietly withdrawn, or cases abandoned, when it was realised that the reasonableness test would not be overcome? Enactment of the 1977 Act may also have had another, no less salutary effect, in that strained and artificial constructions of ordinary words are no longer needed to do justice between parties. One may also suspect that the doctrine of fundamental breach has at last been consigned (not without thanks) to something like oblivion. In short, the Act has had, and will continue to have, profound effects throughout the United Kingdom. In recognition of this universality (at least within these isles) the valuable Scottish supplement which was added to the first edition, has now been distributed throughout the main work to form an integral part thereof. For any inaccuracies which may be made in relation to Scotland (and indeed whatever their context) I am, of course, solely responsible.

The book is dedicated to my children who insisted that it should be dedicated to them: but really to their mother.

I have stated the law as at 11 January 1983.

Dr R G Lawson

January 1983

Table of Cases

Adler *v* Dickson [1955] 1 QB 158; [1954] 3 WLR 696; 98 SJ 787; [1954] 3 All
    ER 397; [1954] 2 Lloyd's Rep 267, CA 36
Ailsa Craig Fishing Co Ltd *v* Malvern Fishing Co Ltd [1982] SLT 377 ....31, 33
Albion, The, France Fenwick Tyne and Wear Co *v* Swan Hunter and Wigham
    Richardson. *See* Swan Hunter and Wigham Richardson *v* France Fenwick
    Tyne & Wear Co, The Albion.
Alderslade *v* Hendon Laundry Ltd [1945] KB 189; 1 All ER 244; 114 LJKB
    196; 172 LT 153; 89 SJ 164, CA 28
Alexander *v* Railway Executive [1951] 2 KB 882; [1951] 2 TLR 69; 95 SJ 369;
    [1951] 2 All ER 442 52
Alison (J Gordon) & Co Ltd *v* Wallsend Slipway & Engineering Co Ltd (1927)
    43 TLR 323, CA 21
America Express Co *v* British Airways Board (1982) *The Times*, 25
    November.. 123
Anderson *v* Elsworth (1861) 30 LJ Ch 922; 4 LT 822.. 65
Arcos *v* Ronasasen (E A) & Son [1933] AC 470; [1933] All ER 646; 102 LJKB
    346; 149 LT 98.. 101
Ardennes (SS) (Owner of cargo) *v* Ardennes (SS) (Owners) [1951] 1 KB 55   48
Aron (J) & Co *v* Comptoir Wegimont [1921] 3 KB 435; 90 LJKB 1233.............. 35
Atlantic Shipping and Trading Co *v* Louis Dreyfus & Co [1922] 2 AC 250;
    [1922] All ER 559; 91 LJKB 513; 127 LT 411, CA 34
Baldry *v* Marshall [1925] 1 KB 260; [1924] All ER Rep 155; 94 LJKB 208;
    132 LT 326, CA 20
    132 LT 326, CA 20
Beck & Co *v* Szymanowski & Co [1924] AC 43; [1923] All ER Rep 244; 93
    LJKB 25; 130 LT 387.. 21
Bennett *v* Pontins (1973) unreported.. 96
British Airports Authority *v* British Airways Board (1981) *The Times*, 8
    May 114
British Crane Hire Corporation *v* Ipswich Plant Hire [1975] QB 303; [1974] 2
    WLR 856; (1973) 118 SJ 387; [1974] 1 All ER 1059, CA 14
Burnett *v* British Waterways Board [1973] 1 WLR 700; [1973] 2 All ER
    631 8
Burnett *v* Westminster Bank [1966] 1 QB 742; [1965] 3 WLR 863; 109 SJ 533;
    [1965] 3 All ER 81; [1965] 2 Lloyd's Rep 218 .... 4, 9
Canada Steamship Lines Ltd *v* R [1952] AC 192; 96 SJ 72; [1952] 1 All ER
    305; [1952] 1 Lloyd's Rep 1 PC 23, 30
Chandris *v* Isbrandtsen-Moller Co [1951] 1 KB 240; 94 SJ 534; [1950] 2 All ER
    618; *revsg in part* 94 SJ 303; [1950] 1 All ER 768; 83 L1 L Rep 285............. 52

Chapelton v Barry UDC [1940] 1 KB 532; 109 LJKB 213; 162 LT 169, CA 4, 10

Charterhouse Credit Co v Tolly [1963] 2 QB 683; [1963] 2 WLR 1168; 107 SJ
    234; [1963] 2 All ER 432, CA 53

Clarke v Malpas (1862) 31 LJ Ch 696; 6 LT 596 65

Clifford Davis Management Ltd v WEA Records Ltd [1975] 1 All ER 237 67

Collins v Howell-Jones (1980) 259 EG 331 120

Cosgrove v Horsfall (1945) 175 LT 334; 62 TLR 140 36

Couchman v Hill [1947] KB 554; [1948] 176 LT 278; [1947] 1 All ER 103,
    CA 48, 49

Corfield v Starr [1981] RTR 380.. 88

Coupe v Guyett [1973] 1 WLR 669; 117 SJ 415; [1973] 2 All ER 1058 87

Cremdean Properties Ltd v Nash (1977) 244 EG 547 ....36, 119

Creswell v Potter (1968) unreported.. 65

Curtis v Chemical Cleaning and Dyeing Co [1951] 1 KB 805; 95 SJ 253; [1951]
    1 All ER 631, CA 50, 51

Czarnikow v Roth, Schmidt & Co [1922] 2 KB 478; 92 LJKB 81; 127 LT 824,
    CA 47

Dennis Reed v Nicholls. See Reed (Dennis) v Nicholls.

Director General of Fair Trading v Domestic Appliances (1977) unreported 87

Director General of Fair Trading v Jurgen Krupa (1976) unreported 87

Edwards v Sogat [1971] Ch 354; [1970] 3 WLR 713; 114 SJ 618; [1970] 3 All
    ER 689; 8 KIR 1, CA 47

Eisen and Metall AG v Ceres Stevedoring Co Ltd [1977] 1 Lloyd's Rep 665,
    Quebec, CA 40

Elder, Dempster & Co v Paterson, Zochonis & Co [1924] AC 522; [1924] All
    ER Rep 135; 93 LJKB 625; 131 LT 449 38

Elderslie Steamship Co v Borthwich [1905] AC 93; 74 LJKB 338; 92 LT
    274 19

Enderby Town Football Club v Football Association [1971] Ch 591; [1970] 3
    WLR 1021; (1970) 114 SJ 827; [1971] 1 All ER 215, CA 47

Esso Petroleum Co Ltd v Mardon [1976] QB 801; [1976] 2 WLR 583; 120 SJ
    131; [1976] 2 All ER 5; [1976] 2 Lloyd's Rep 305, CA 16

Evans (J) & Son (Portsmouth) v Merzario (Andrea) [1976] 1 WLR 1078; 120
    SJ 734; [1976] 2 All ER 930; [1976] 2 Lloyd's Rep 165, CA, revsg [1975] 1
    Lloyd's Rep 162 49

Evans v Llewellin (1787) 1 Cox Eq Cas 333; 2 Bro CC 150; 29 ER 1191   65

Everitt v Everitt (1870) LR 10 Eq 405; 39 LJ Ch 777; 23 LT 136 66

Farnworth Finance Facilities v Attryde [1970] 1 WLR 1953; 114 SJ 354; [1970]
    2 All ER 774, CA 55, 58

Firestone Tyre and Rubber Co v Vokins & Co [1951] 1 Lloyd's Rep 32.......... 59

Foley Motors Ltd v McGhee [1970] NZLR 649 69

Fry v Lane (1888) 40 Ch D 312; 58 LJ Ch 113; 60 LT 12...............................65, 67

Gallie v Lee [1971]. See Saunders (formerly Gallie) v Anglia Building Society.

Geier (orse Braun) v Kirawa, Weston and Warne Bros (Transport) Weston
    (Third Party); Warne Bros (Transport) (Third Parties) [1970] 1 Lloyd's
    Rep 364 6

George Mitchell (Chesterhall) Ltd v Finney Lock Seeds Ltd [1982] 3 WLR
    1036, CA; [1981] 1 Lloyd's Rep 476 ....60, 116

Gibaud v Great Eastern Railway Co [1921] 2 KB 426; 90 LJKB 535; 125 LT
    76; [1921] All ER 35; [1920] 3 KB 689.. 71

Gillespie Bros & Co v Bowles (Roy) Transport; Rennie Hogg (Third Party)
    [1973] 1 QB 400; [1972] 3 WLR 1003; 116 SJ 861; [1973] 1 All ER 193;
    [1973] 1 Lloyd's Rep 10 ....29, 30, 69

Gluckstein v Barnes [1900] AC 240; 69 LJ Ch 385; 82 LT 393; 16 TLR 321; 7
    Mans 321, HL 47
Grand Trunk Railway Company of Canada v Robinson [1915] AC 740; 84 LJ
    PC 194; 113 LT 350 70
Grealish v Murphy [1946] IR 35 68
Green (RW) v Cade Bros Farms [1978] 1 Lloyd's Rep 602.................................... 115
Hadley v Baxendale (1854) 9 Ex 341; [1843–60] All ER 461; 23 LJ Ex 179; 23
    LTOS 69 9
Harbutts 'Plasticine' v Wayne Tank and Pump Co [1970] 1 QB 447; [1970] 2
    WLR 198; 114 SJ 29; [1970] 1 All ER 225; [1970] 1 Lloyd's Rep 15,
    CA 56, 58, 59, 107, 108
Harrison v Guest (1855) 6 De G MG 426; (1860) 8 HLC 481 68
Harrison v National Bank of Australasia Ltd (1928) 23 Tas LR 1............. 68
Haseldine v CA Daw & Son Ltd [1941] 3 All ER 156; [1941] 2 KB 343; 111
    LJKB 45; 165 LT 185.. 40
Haverly v Brooks & Brooks [1970] IR 214.. 68
Hedley Byrne & Co v Heller & Partners [1964] AC 465; [1963] 3 WLR 101;
    107 SJ 454; [1963] 2 All ER 575; [1963] 1 Lloyd's Rep 485, HL...............16, 97
Heilbut, Symons & Co v Buckleton [1913] AC 30; [1911–13] All ER 83; 82
    LJKB 245; 107 LT 769.. 49
Henderson v Stevenson (1875) LR2 Sc & Div 470; 32 LT 709; 39 JP 596,
    HL... 5
Herrick v Leonard & Dingley Ltd [1975] 2 NZLR 566...................................... 40
Hollier v Rambler Motors (AMC) Ltd [1972] 2 QB 71; [1972] 2 WLR 401;
    (1971) 116 SJ 158; [1972] 1 All ER, CA.. 12, 15, 26, 28
Hollingworth v Southern Ferries [1977] 2 Lloyd's Rep 70 10
Hood v Anchor Line (Henderson Bros) [1918] AC 837 5
Houghton v Trafalgar Insurance Co [1954] 1 QB 247; [1953] 3 WLR 985; 97 SJ
    831; [1953] 2 All ER 1409; [1953] 2 Lloyd's Rep 503, CA 20
Howard Marine & Dredging Co Ltd v Ogden (A) & Sons (Excavations) [1978]
    QB 574; [1978] 2 WLR 515; [1978] 2 All ER 1134 ....16, 117
Hughes v Hall. See Appendix 4 ....82, 158–160
Hunt & Winterbotham (West of England) v British Road Services (Parcels)
    [1962] 1 QB 617; [1962] 2 WLR 172; 105 SJ 1124; [1962] 1 All ER 111;
    [1961] 2 Lloyd's Rep 422, CA 46
Industrie Chimiche Italia Centrale v Nea Ninemia Shipping Co (1982)
    Financial Times, 11 November.. 32
Jacques v Lloyd D George & Partners [1968] 1 WLR 625; (1968) 112 SJ 211;
    [1968] 2 All ER 187, CA...50, 51
Jarvis v Swans Tours Ltd [1973] 1 QB 233; [1972] 3 WLR 954; 116 SJ 822;
    [1973] 1 All ER 71, CA 106
Johnson Matthey & Co v Constantine Terminals and International Express Co
    [1976] 2 Lloyd's Rep 215 39
Joseph Marton v Southwestern Property Co Ltd (1982) unreported..................... 118
Junior Books Ltd v The Veitchi Co Ltd [1982] 3 WLR 477; [1982] 3 All ER
    201, HL 97
Karsales (Harrow) v Wallis [1956] 1 WLR 936; 100 SJ 548; [1956] 2 All ER
    866, CA 52, 53
Kendall (Henry) & Sons (A Firm) v Lillico (William) & Sons; Holland Colombo
    Trading Company v Grimsdale & Sons; Grimsdale & Sons v Suffolk Agricul-
    tural Poultry Producers' Association [1969] 2 AC 31; [1968] 3 WLR 110;
    112 SJ 562; [1968] 2 All ER 444; [1968] 1 Lloyd's Rep 547, HL...............12, 21
Kenyon, Son & Craven v Baxter Hoare & Co [1971] 1 WLR 519; [1971] 2 All
    ER 708; [1971] 1 Lloyd's Rep 232...57, 70

Krawill Machinery Corporation v Robert C Herd & Co Inc [1959] 1 Lloyd's Rep 305; US Sup Ct 38

Lally v Bird (1980) unreported 112

Lamport & Holt Lines Ltd v Coubro & Scrutton (M & I Ltd) and Coubro & Scrutton (Riggers & Shipwrights) Ltd [1981] 2 Lloyd's Rep 659; [1982] 2 Lloyd's Rep 42, CA 13, 23, 24, 25, 29, 30

Lee (John) & Son (Grantham) Ltd v Railway Executive [1949] WN 373; 93 SJ 587; [1949] 2 All ER 581, CA 19, 69

Lee v Showman's Guild of Great Britain [1952] 2 QB 329; [1952] 96 SJ 296; [1952] 1 All ER 1175, CA 47

L'Estrange v Graucob [1934] 2 KB 394 .... 15, 51

Levison v Patent Steam Carpet Cleaning Co [1978] QB 69; [1977] 3 WLR 90; [1977] 3 All ER 498, CA 10, 45, 46, 70, 113

Lloyds Bank v Bundy [1975] QB 326; [1974] 3 WLR 501; 118 SJ 714; [1974] 3 All ER 757; [1974] 2 Lloyd's Rep 366, CA 67, 68

Lowe v Lombank [1960] 1 WLR 196; 104 SJ 210; [1960] 1 All ER 611, CA 35

Ludditt v Ginger Coote Airways [1947] AC 233; [1947] LJR 1067; 177 LT 334; [1947] 1 All ER 328, PC 70

McCawley v Furness Railway Co (1872) LR 8 QB 57 28

McCrone v Boots Farm Sales [1981] SLT 103 98–99

McCutcheon v MacBrayne (David) [1964] 1 WLR 125; 108 SJ 93; [1964] 1 All ER 430; [1964] 1 Lloyd's Rep 16; 1964 SC (HL) 28; 1964 SLT 66 .... 4, 12, 13

Macrae v Dick [1982] SLT 39 116

Mendelssohn v Normand [1970] 1 QB 177; [1969] 3 WLR 139; (1969) 113 SJ 263; [1969] 2 All ER 1215, CA 48, 55, 58

Mersey Shipping and Transport Co v Rea Ltd (1925) 21 Ll L Rep 375 38

Minister of Materials v Steel Bros & Co [1952] WN 114; [1952] 1 Lloyd's Rep 87, CA 22

Morviken, The [1981] 2 Lloyd's Rep 61; (1982) The Times, 27 November 122

New Zealand Shipping Co v Satterthwaite (AM) & Co [1975] AC 154; [1974] 2 WLR 865; 118 SJ 387; [1974] 1 All ER 1015; [1974] 1 Lloyd's Rep 534, PC 39

Niblett v Confectioners' Materials Co [1921] 3 KB 387 22

Norman v Bennett [1974] 1 WLR 1229; [1974] 3 All ER 351 88

Nunan v Southern Railway Co [1924] 93 LJKB 140; [1924] 1 KB 223; 130 LT 131; 68 SJ 138, CA 5

Olley v Marlborough Court Ltd [1949] 1 KB 532; [1949] LJR 360; 93 SJ 40; [1949] 1 All ER 127, CA 9

O'Rorke v Bolingbroke (1877) 2 App Cas 814; 26 WR 239, HL 66

Overbrooke Estates Ltd v Glencombe Properties [1974] 1 WLR 1335; 118 SJ 775; [1974] 3 All ER 511 120

Parker v South Eastern Railway, Gabell v Same (1877) 46 LJQB 768; 36 LT 540 .... 3, 5, 15, 69

Pearson (S) & Son Ltd v Dublin Corporation [1907] AC 351, 77 LJPC 1; 97 LT 645, HL 47

Peek v North Staffordshire Railway (1863) 10 HLC 473; 32 LJQB 241 113

Penton v Southern Railway Co [1931] 2 KB 103 5

Photo Production Ltd v Securicor Transport Ltd [1980] AC 827; [1980] 2 WLR 283; [1980] 1 All ER 556 .... 31, 47, 58, 59, 60, 61, 70, 71, 108, 114

Polemis and Furness Withy, Re [1921] 3 KB 560 33

Pollock v Macrae 1922 SC (HL) 192 53

Pyrene Co v Scindia Navigation Co [1954] 2 QB 402; 2 WLR 1005; 98 SJ 354; [1954] 2 All ER 158; [1954] 1 Lloyd's Rep 321 37

R v Hammertons Cars Ltd [1976] 1 WLR 1243; [1976] 3 All ER 758.................. 88
Raphael, The. See Lamport & Holt Lines Ltd v Coubro & Scrutton (M & I Ltd)
and Coubro & Scrutton (Riggers & Shipwrights) Ltd
Rasbora Ltd v JCL Marine [1977] 1 Lloyd's Rep 645 ....109, 111
Reed (Dennis) v Goody [1950] 2 KB 277; 94 SJ 270; [1950] 1 All ER 919,
CA.. 51
Richardson, Spence & Co v Rowntree [1897] AC 217 [1891–4] All ER 823; 63
LJQB 283; 70 LT 817, HL 5
Rutter v Palmer [1922] 2 KB 87, 92 LJKB 657; 127 LT 419; 66 SJ 576,
CA..24, 27, 29
Saunders (Executrix of the Estate of Rose Maud Gallie) v Anglia Building
Society [1971] AC 1004; [1970] 3 WLR 1078; [1970] 3 All ER 961,
HL.. 16
Schroeder (A) Music Publishing Co Ltd v Macaulay (formerly Instone) [1974] 1
WLR 1308; 118 SJ 734; [1974] 3 All ER 616, HL 66, 113
Scruttons Ltd v Midland Silicones Ltd [1962] AC 446; [1962] 2 WLR 186; 106
SJ 34; [1962] 1 All ER 1 ....31, 36, 37, 38, 39
Shepherd v Kain (1821) 5 B & Ald 240; 106 ER 1180.. 33
Smeaton Hanscomb & Co v Setty (Sassoon I) Son & Co (No 1) [1953] 1 WLR
1468; 97 SJ 862; [1953] 2 All ER 1471; [1953] 2 Lloyd's Rep 580 52
Smith v Lazarus (1981) unreported 53
Smith v South Wales Switchgear [1978] 1 All ER 18; 1 WLR 165.......................6, 30
Southwestern General Property Company Limited v Josef Marton. See Appen-
dix 4 168–174
Spurling (J) Ltd v Bradshaw [1956] 1 WLR 461; 100 SJ 317; [1956] 2 All ER
121; [1956] 1 Lloyd's Rep 392, CA 7, 46
Sugar v London, Midland & Scottish Railway Co [1941] 1 All ER 172; 164 LT
311; 85 SJ 32.. 5
Suisse Atlantique Societe d'Armement Maritime SA v NV Rotherdamsche
Kolen Centrale [1967] 1 AC 361; [1966] 2 WLR 944; 110 SJ 367; [1966] 2
All ER 61; [1966] 1 Lloyd's Rep 533, HL 54, 55, 56, 57, 58, 59, 70
Swan, Hunter and Wigham Richardson v France Fenwick Tyne and Wear Co,
The Albion [1953] 1 WLR 1026; 97 SJ 524; [1953] 2 Lloyd's Rep 82;
[1953] 2 All ER 679, CA 52
Szymonowski & Co v Beck & Co [1923] 1 KB 457, CA 19, 34
Tesco Supermarkets Ltd v Nattrass [1972] AC 153; [1971] 2 WLR 1116; 115 SJ
285; [1971] 2 All ER 127 ....86, 87
The Suleyman Stalskiy [1976] 2 Lloyd's Rep 609, Can 40
Thompson v London, Midland & Scottish Railway Co [1930] 1 KB 41; 98 LJKB
615; 141 LT 382, CA 5, 69
Thornton v Shoe Lane Parking Ltd [1971] 2 QB 163; [1971] 2 WLR 585; (1970)
115 SJ 75; [1971] 1 All ER 686; [1971] 1 Lloyd's Rep 289, CA......... 7, 8, 10, 69
Tullis v Jacson [1892] 3 Ch 441; 61 LJ Ch 655; 67 LT 340; 36 SJ 646 46
U G S v National Mortgage Bank of Greece and National Bank of Greece SA,
107 SJ 552; [1964] 1 Lloyd's Rep 446, CA; affg The Times, 26 July 1962;
[1962] CLY 1148.. 53
Waldron-Kelly v Marshall (1981) unreported... 112
Walker v Boyle [1982] 1 WLR 495; [1982] 1 All ER 634 ....117, 120
Walkers, Winser & Hamm and Shaw, Son & Co, Re [1904] 2 KB 152.................. 35
Wallis, Son & Wells v Pratt & Haynes [1911] AC 394; [1911–13] All ER 989;
80 LJKB 1058; 105 LT 146, HL... 20
Watkins v Rymill (1883) 10 QBD 178; 52 LJQB 121; 48 LT 426; revsg [1910] 2
KB 1003 69
Webster v Higgin [1948] 92 SJ 454; [1948] 2 All ER 127, CA 20

White *v* Blackmore [1972] 2 QB 651; [1972] 2 WLR 296; 116 SJ 547; [1972] 3 All ER 158, CA 3

White *v* Warwick (John) & Co Ltd [1953] 1 WLR 1285; 97 SJ 740; [1953] 2 All ER 1021, CA 23, 25

White Cross Equipment Ltd *v* Farrell (1982) unreported 115

Whittington *v* Seale-Hayne (1900) 82 LT 49; 16 TLR 181; 44 SJ 229 16

Wilkinson *v* Barclay [1946] 1 All ER 387; 115 LJKB 363; 62 TLR 375.............. 34

Wilson *v* Darling Island Stevedoring and Lighterage Co Ltd [1956] 1 Lloyd's Rep 346 38

Woodman *v* Photo Trade Processing Ltd. *See* Appendix 4 .... 111, 112, 161–167

Woolmer *v* Delmar Price Ltd [1955] 1 QB 291; [1955] 2 WLR 329; 99 SJ 112; [1955] 1 All ER 377 46

Yeoman Credit Ltd *v* Apps [1961] 2 QB 508; [1961] 3 WLR 94; 105 SJ 567; [1961] 2 All ER 281, CA 53

Table of Statutes

Arbitration Act 1950—
  s 4(1) 35
Carriage by Air Act 1961 122
Carriage by Air and Road Act
  1979 122
Carriage by Air (Supplementary
  Provisions) Act 1962 122
Carriage by Railways Act 1972 122
Carriage of Goods by Road Act
  1965 122
Carriage of Goods by Sea Act 1924 122
Carriage of Goods by Sea Act 1971 122
Carriage of Passengers by Road
  Act 1974 122
Civil Aviation Act 1982—
  s 65 110
Consumer Credit Act 1974 90–92
  s 8 90
  s 15 90
  s 19 91
  s 90 91
  ss 137–140 65
  s 173(1) 90, 91
    (2), (3) 91
  s 1891) 94
Consumer Protection Act 1961 93
  s 1 92
  ss 2, 3 .... 92, 93
Consumer Safety Act 1978 93
  s 6(1), (2) 93
Criminal Justice (Scotland) Act
  1980 86
Defective Premises Act 1972 ..... 92, 110
  s 1 110
  s 6(3) 92
Fair Trading Act 1973 ..... 77–80, 86, 88
  ss 3, 13 77
  s 14 .... 77, 78

Fair Trading Act 1973—*contd*
  s 17 .... 78, 79
    (2) 78
  ss 21, 22 78
  ss 23, 24 86
  s 25 87
    (3) 87
  s 26 86
  Pt III 86
Housing Act 1961—
  s 32 92
  s 33(6), (7) 92
Housing (Scotland) Act 1966 92
Medicines Act 1968 86
Merchant Shipping Act 1894—
  s 503(1) 123
Misrepresentation Act 1967
    16, 110, 112, 118, 119, 120, 130
  s 2(1), (2) 16
  s 3 .... 110, 117, 120, 130
  s 4(1) 20
Occupiers' Liability Act 1957 96
Occupiers' Liability (Scotland)
  Act 1960 96
Patents Act 1949—
  s 58 92
Patents Act 1977—
  s 45 92
Post Office Act 1969—
  ss 29, 30 123
Powers of Criminal Courts Act
  1973 86
Railway and Canal Act 1854 113
Road Traffic Act 1960—
  s 148(3) 92
  s 151 92
Road Traffic Act 1972—
  s 143 92

Sale of Goods Act 1893 81
  s 11(1)(c) 20
  s 12... 95
    (1)...................................... 52
  s 13........................ 20, 82, 83, 95, 102
  s 14... 102
    (1).................................... 20, 21
  s 15... 102
  s 55(3)................................. 101, 102
    (4)........................ 80, 102, 110
    (5)...................................... 111
    (7)...................................... 80
Sale of Goods Act 1979
        79, 81, 84, 86, 87, 93, 103, 110
  s 12(1).................................... 52
  s 13.............................. 20, 82, 83
  s 14(3).................................. 20, 21
  s 61(1)................................... 94
Supply of Goods and Services
  Act 1982......................... 93, 103, 130
  s 2................................... 93, 94
  s 11(2)................................... 93
  s 16(1)................................... 93
    (3)(a)................................. 93
Supply of Goods (Implied Terms)
  Act 1973............71, 79, 80, 81, 84, 90,
    93, 95, 101, 107, 109, 115, 130
  s 8... 95
  s 9.................................... 95, 102
  ss 10, 11................................ 102
  s 12(2)............................... 101, 102
    (3).............................. 80, 102
    (4)...................................... 111
    (6)...................................... 80
  s 16...................................... 103
Trade Descriptions Act 1968....... 86, 88
  s 1....................................... 88
  s 23...................................... 88
  s 24.................................. 87, 88
  s 25...................................... 88
Trading Stamps Act 1964
        81, 84, 93, 103, 104
  s 4(1).................................. 79
    (c)................................. 80
  s 10..................................... 104
    (1)................................. 80
Unfair Contract Terms Act 1977
  22, 61, 71, 79, 82, 83, 93, 94–123,
    129, 130, 131, 133–150
  s 1(1)................................... 95
    (2)................................. 121
    (3)................................. 95
    (4)................................. 96

Unfair Contract Terms Act 1977—
  contd
  s 2..............83, 95, 98, 104–106, 121,
        129, 131
    (1)................................. 95
    (2)........................ 96, 97, 111
    (3)........................ 97, 100
  s 3.............95, 98, 100, 104, 106, 108,
        116, 121, 129, 130, 131
    (1)................................. 98
    (2)................................. 99
      (b)................ 98, 99, 100
      (ii)............................ 101
  s 4...........95, 103, 105, 108, 121, 130
    (2)................................ 105
  s 5.................95, 104, 106, 130
    (2)(a)........................... 105
      (b)............................ 104
    (3)................................ 104
  s 6...........80, 95, 106, 108, 111, 130
    (1), (2)......................... 102
    (4)................................. 95
  s 7..........95, 102–104, 106, 108, 109,
        111, 121, 130
    (2), (4)......................... 103
    (5)........................ 103, 104
  s 8............................. 117, 130
  s 9.......................... 61, 107, 108
    (1).......................... 107, 108
    (2)................................ 108
  s 10................................ 107
  s 11................................ 117
    (1)................................ 110
    (2)................................ 111
    (3).......................... 110, 114
    (4).......................... 111, 112
    (5)................................ 112
  s 12.......................... 80, 109
    (1)–(3)......................... 108
  s 13................................ 107
    (1).......................... 106, 107
    (2)................................ 107
  s 14.......................... 94, 104
  s 15.......................... 107, 129
    (2)................................ 121
      (a)............................ 109
    (3)(a)(i), (ii)................ 122
      (b)............................ 122
  s 16..........95, 104, 105, 107, 129, 131
    (1)(b)........................... 97
    (3)................................ 97
  s 17.........98, 100, 104, 108, 116, 129,
        130, 131

Unfair Contract Terms Act 1977—
contd
  s 17(1) 98
       (*a*) 99
       (*b*) 99, 100, 101
       (2) 98
  s 18 .... 106, 108, 130
  s 19 .... 104, 107, 130
       (1) 104
       (2)(*a*) 105
  s 20 .... 107, 108, 111, 130
       (1), (2) 102
  s 21 .... 102–104, 107, 108, 111, 130
       (3)(*a*) 103
       (4) 103, 104
  s 22 108
  s 23 107
  s 24(1) 111
       (2), (3) 111, 112
       (4) 112

Unfair Contract Terms Act 1977—
contd
  s 25 .... 94, 109
       (1) 95, 108
       (2) 96
       (3) 106, 107
       (4) 104
       (5) 107
  ss 26–28 122
  s 291)(*a*), (*b*) 122
       (2), (3) 110
  s 30 93
  Sched 1 .... 95, 121, 129
        2 .... 111, 112, 131
        4 .... 101, 123
Water Act 1945—
  s 27 110
Water Act 1973—
  s 7(4) 110
Weights and Measures Act 1963 86

Table of Statutory Instruments

Babies Dummies (Safety) Regulations 1978 [SI 1978 No 836] 92
Carriage of Goods by Air Acts (Application of Provisions) Order 1967
  [SI 1967 No 480] 122
Children's Clothing (Hood Cords) Regulations 1976 [SI 1976 No 2] 92
Children's Furniture (Safety) Order 1982 [SI 1982 No 523] 93
Consumer Transactions (Restriction on Statements) Order 1976 [SI 1976
  No 1813] 80–88, 90, 94, 104, 131
    art 2 84
      (1) 81
    art 3 86
      (a) 80
      (b), (c) 81
      (d) 82
    art 4 83
    art 5 85
Consumer Transactions (Restrictions on Statements) (Amendment) Order
  1978 [SI 1978 No 127] 80
Cooking Utensils (Safety) Regulations 1972 [SI 1972 No 1957] 92
Cosmetic Products (Safety) Regulations 1978 [SI 1978 No 1354] 92
Dangerous Substances and Preparations (Safety) Regulations 1980 [SI 1980
  No 136] 93
Electrical Appliances (Colour Code) Regulations 1969 [SI 1969 No 310] 92
Electrical Appliances (Colour Code) (Amendment) Regulations 1970 [SI 1970
  No 811] 92
Electrical Appliances (Colour Code) (Amendment) Regulations 1977 [SI 1977
  No 931] 92
Electrical Equipment (Safety) Regulations 1975 [SI 1975 No 1366] 92
Electric Blanket (Safety) Regulations 1971 [SI 1971 No 1961] 92
Filament Lamps for Vehicles (Safety) Regulations 1982 [SI 1982 No 444] 93
Glazed Ceramic Ware (Safety) Regulations 1975 [SI 1975 No 1241] 92
Heating Appliances (Fireguards) Regulations 1973 [SI 1973 No 2106] 92
Nightdresses (Safety) Regulations 1967 [SI 1967 No 839] 92
Novelties (Safety) Regulations 1980 [SI 1980 No 958] 93
Oil Heater (Safety) Regulations 1977 [SI 1977 No 167] 92
Oil Lamps (Safety) Regulations 1979 [SI 1979 No 1125] 92
Pencil and Graphic Instruments (Safety) 1974 [SI 1974 No 226] 92
Stands for Carry Cots (Safety) Regulations 1966 [SI 1966 No 1610] 92
Toys (Safety) Regulations 1974 [SI 1974 No 1367] 92
Upholstered Furniture (Safety) Regulations 1980 [SI 1980 No 725] 93
Vitreous Enamel-Ware (Safety) Regulations 1976 [SI 1976 No 454] 92

Part I

Judicial Control

Chapter 1

Incorporation of Exclusion Clauses

The judicial approach to the control of exclusion clauses is broadly similar in England and Scotland. It is the first essence of an exclusion clause that it effectively be incorporated into the contract. If this basic step has not been achieved, the clause will be totally unavailing, however suitable its drafting to contain or limit the relevant damage. Hereunder, we discuss the ways in which a clause can become a contractual term.

1 Notice

Frequently, the putative terms of a contract, including exclusion clauses, are displayed about the premises where the contract is to be made. They may also be printed in a document tendered or delivered by one party to another, or referred to in such a document, the typical case being the bus-ticket referring to the appropriate conditions of transport.

(a) Was the document 'contractual'?

As learned authors have said, in words endorsed by Lord Denning MR in *White* v *Blackmore*,[1] '. . . the court must be satisfied that the particular document relied on as containing notice of the excluding or limiting term is in truth an integral part of the contract'.[2] This has meant that documents or any writing must have been intended to be contractual and not, for example, in the nature of mere receipts. The latter really represent an acknowledgement of a contract, rather than operate as a part of one.

This was explained by Mellish LJ in the course of his important judgment in *Parker* v *South Eastern Railway*.[3] He thought that 'there may be cases in which a paper containing writing is delivered by one party to another in the course of a business transaction,

3

where it would be quite reasonable that the party receiving it should assume that the writing contained in it no condition, and should put it in his pocket unread. For instance, if a person driving through a turnpike gate received a ticket upon paying the toll, he might reasonably assume that the object of the ticket was that by producing it he might be free from paying toll at some other turnpike gate, and might put it in his pocket unread.'[4]

The Court of Appeal relied on this statement in *Chapelton* v *Barry UDC*.[5] Deck-chairs were stacked by a notice, requesting members of the public to obtain tickets from an attendant and retain them for inspection. The plaintiff took the chairs and obtained two tickets which he did not read. One of the chairs collapsed and he was injured. The Court of Appeal held that no reliance could be placed on the exclusion clauses on the tickets. No one would assume that the ticket was anything but a receipt.

This approach was borne out as correct by the House of Lords in *McCutcheon* v *MacBrayne*.[6] The defendants owned steamers operating between the Scottish mainland and the islands. An oral contract was made with the plaintiff for the shipment of a car. On the voyage, and because of the defendants' negligence, both ship and car were lost. The exclusion clauses put up by the defendants on their behalf were contained in twenty-seven paragraphs of small print displayed both inside and outside their office. The terms were also printed on a 'risk-note' which customers were usually, though not on this occasion, asked to sign. In this case, the only document to have been tendered was a receipt stating that 'all goods were carried subject to the conditions set out in the notices'. Neither the plaintiff, nor his agent through whom the contract was made, had read the words of the notices or the receipt. There was, in any case, no contractual document, and judgment was given for the plaintiff.

A final illustration is *Burnett* v *Westminster Bank*.[7] The plaintiff had accounts at branch *A* and branch *B* of the defendant bank. The new cheque book for branch *A* contained a notice that 'the cheques in this book will be applied to the account for which they have been prepared'. No notice of contractual terms had been contained in previous cheque books. The plaintiff attempted to direct a cheque from the new book to branch *B*, but the computer could not read his instructions on the cheque. Branch *A* duly debited his account, even though the plaintiff had placed a stop notice with branch *B*, whither he assumed the cheque was headed. Mocatta J found that the words in the cheque book were not contained in a contractual document and were, therefore, ineffective.

(b) *Reasonable sufficiency of notice*

It was established in *Parker* v *South Eastern Railway*[8] that a term will only become incorporated in the contract if notice of the term has been given and that notice is reasonably sufficient in all the circumstances of the case. This is a question of fact, 'in answering which the tribunal must look at all the circumstances and the situation of the parties'.[9]

In *Parker's* case itself, the plaintiff had deposited a bag in the cloakroom of a railway station belonging to the defendants. He was given a ticket declaring 'See back'; and on the back were conditions including a clause limiting liability to £10. The plaintiff had not read the clause, but was held bound by it. The defendants had done enough to notify the plaintiff of the clause. The ticket, it may be supposed, was a contractual document.

Although each case depends upon its facts, it has almost become a rule of law that failure to state on the front of the ticket 'for conditions see over' (or an equivalent phrase) will render the exclusion clauses ineffective.[10] In *Sugar* v *London, Midland & Scottish Railway*,[11] the words 'For conditions see back' were obliterated when the tickets were stamped with the date. The right conclusion in such cases 'is that the railway company did not take reasonable steps to bring the conditions to the notice of the passenger, for the obvious reason that it is no use printing words in much clearer type than anything else printed on the ticket if the next thing they do is to blot the words out'.[12]

A not dissimilar case in *Richardson* v *Rowntree*.[13] The plaintiff contracted with the defendants to be taken as a passenger on a steamer from Philadelphia to Liverpool. She paid her fare and received a ticket containing a number of terms, one of which limited the liability of the defendants to £100. The ticket was presented to her folded up, the conditions also being obliterated in part by a stamp in red ink. A jury found that the plaintiff knew there to be writing on the ticket although she did not know that the writing contained terms of the contract. The question was thus posed whether reasonably sufficient notice had been given and the decision of the jury was that it had not. The House of Lords declined to interfere with this finding.

Rather special factors come into play where the plaintiff, even if he were inclined so to do, could not read the appropriate conditions, because he was illiterate, blind, or unable to comprehend English. In *Thompson* v *London, Midland & Scottish Railway*,[14] the plaintiff was unable to read. Her niece bought for her a railway ticket which on its face contained the familiar words 'For conditions see back'. The back of the ticket made reference to time-tables and excursion bills. The bills themselves referred to the time-tables, which contained a clause exempting the company from liability in respect of any injury, however caused. The Court of Appeal held that the illiteracy had no effect since enough had been done to bring the terms to the attention of those members of the public to which the plaintiff belonged.

It appears, however, that where the special disability is known to the other party, that will suffice to disapply the particular clauses. The relevant case is *Geier* v *Kujawa*.[15] A notice in English was displayed in a car, stating that passengers rode at their own risk. This was held not to bind one particular passenger who, to the driver's own knowledge, spoke German but little English. If the railway company in the previous case had known of the passenger's illiteracy, and had she on that occasion been unaccompanied, presumably she would not have been bound by the clauses unless told of their existence in general or specific terms.

An interesting variation on the usual problems of incorporation arose in *Smith* v *South Wales Switchgear*.[16] A contractual document provided that the general conditions were available on request. There were three editions, the last being March 1970. No copy was requested, but the 1969 version was sent. This was done because of a misunderstanding over another contract between the same parties. The House of Lords held that the 1970 version had been incorporated into the contract. The meaning reasonably attributed to the reference was that the conditions referred to were the current ones. It was common experience that general conditions of contract were periodically revised. Had a copy been requested, the recipients would reasonably have expected to receive the 1970 edition.

A particular problem which has not yet been litigated arises where a party does indeed ask for copies of conditions, where his attention is drawn to them before the contract is made, only to be told that they are unavailable, for whatever reason. If the party making the request proceeds nonetheless to make the contract, it is not clear whether he is bound by those contract terms. On the assumption that he was free to turn around and decline the contract, there is reason for saying that he must therefore be bound by those terms. Equally, though, the party who invites reference to those terms, but then fails to proffer them when a reasonable request is made, may be said to have lost the chance to incorporate those terms. As a practical matter, it is likely that in the instant case the attitude and reaction of the party seeking a copy of those terms will do much to clarify the position. If his attitude is that 'it does not really matter', the terms will probably be implied against him. If, in contrast, his attitude is that he is proceeding with the contract on the basis of the inapplicability of those terms, then indeed they will surely be inapplicable.

(c) Where the clause is unusual

If the particular condition relied upon by the party seeking exemption is one that is unusual in that class of contract, that party may have to show that he took special measures fairly to bring the condition to the attention of the other party. In *Spurling* v *Bradshaw*,[17] Denning LJ gave it as his view, obiter dicta, that 'the more unreasonable a clause is, the greater the notice which must be given of it. Some clauses which I have seen would need to be printed in red ink on the face of the document with a red hand pointing to it before the notice could be held to be sufficient'.[18] Significantly, neither Morris nor Parker LJJ made any reference to this point.

The second case, *Thornton* v *Shoe Lane Parking*,[19] is more convincing, if not entirely so. A notice outside a car park bore the legend 'All cars parked at owners [*sic*] risk'. When a driver approached the entrance, a ticket emerged from an automatic machine and he would then proceed into the car park. The ticket contained printed wording to the effect that it was issued subject to the conditions displayed on the premises. These conditions were lengthy and included words exempting the defendants not only from liability for damage to cars, but also from liability for any injury to the customer howsoever caused, whilst his car was in the car park.

Lord Denning regarded the clause as 'so wide and so destructive of rights that the court should not hold any man bound by it unless it is drawn to his attention in the most explicit way. . . . In order to give sufficient notice, it would need to be printed in red ink with a red hand pointing to it, or something equally startling'.[20]

Megaw LJ continued with this basic theme. Where the condition relied on involves a restriction not usual in a particular class of contract, a defendant 'must show that his intention to attach an unusual condition of that particular nature was fairly brought to the attention of the other party'.[21] That had not been done here, since there had been no clear indication which would lead an ordinary sensible person to suppose that a term relating to personal injury had been included in the contract. The learned Lord Justice did not think that the stage had yet been reached that such terms were an accepted feature of such contracts as featured in this particular case.[22]

The unequivocal language of this case seems to make it clear that something special is needed by way of notice before an unusual exclusion clause has effect. In principle, this may be hard to uphold. A person who agrees to conditions brought to his attention, without special notice being given of an unusual condition, has nevertheless assented to a contract on those terms. If it is now said that he has not, it is difficult to see just what are the terms upon which he has contracted. It is worth pointing out that in *Thornton* v *Shoe Lane Parking*, counsel did concede that the defendant had not done enough to give the plaintiff notice of the exempting condition.[23]

(d) When acceptance cannot be avoided

In the above case, it was thought by Megaw LJ to be a 'highly relevant factor', in considering whether the matter was fairly brought to the attention of the plaintiff, that the first attempt to bring the conditions to his attention was when it was 'practically impossible' for him to withdraw from the premises. One can well imagine, the Lord Justice continued, the chaos which would ensue should customers, after seeing the reference on the tickets, leave their cars blocking the entrance to the garage 'in order to search for, find and peruse the notices!'[24]

This is the effective introduction of a novel concept. The fact that a party has virtually no option but to proceed with his acceptance of the offer is not to deny of itself that he was even so fully informed of the terms of agreement, or the fact that there were such terms. Impractical though it may have been, the option still lay with the individual not to proceed with the agreement. Indeed, Megaw LJ viewed such matters only as supporting his view that reasonable notice had not been supplied.

Sir Gordon Willmer, however, took a more robust line. In the case of a ticket proffered by an automatic machine, he said, there is something quite irrevocable: 'it seems to be that any attempt to introduce conditions after the irrevocable step has been taken of causing the machine to operate must be doomed to failure'.[25] In the case of tickets proffered by human hand, in contrast, there remains the opportunity to say: 'I do not like your conditions. I will not have this ticket'.[26]

The same basic point had been made by the Court of Appeal in *Burnett* v *British Waterways Board*.[27] The plaintiff in that case was a lighterman in a barge which was part of a convoy being moved forward into a lock. The rope pulling his barge forward snapped, because of the negligence of the defendants, and the plaintiff was injured, for which injury he later brought an action. The defendants maintained that their liability had been excluded by a notice at the entrance to the dock which was held, by the High Court and the Court of Appeal, to contain wording which was apt to cover the damage which had occurred. In the Court of Appeal, agreeing with the court below that the exclusion clause was of no avail, Lord Denning quoted with approval the words of Waller J: 'The plaintiff was not somebody arriving on his own at the entrance to the dock and saying: "Well, I will not go in because of this notice." He was an employee on a barge, part of a train of barges, and by the time he had got to the dock it was certainly beyond his ability to make a choice and not go in'.[28] The learned judge had gone on to say: 'The plain fact, as I see it, is that the plaintiff was not really in a position to exercise a free choice'.[29]

The full implications of this approach have yet to be worked out. Although couched in terms of automatic machines, there is no reason why tickets offered by human hand cannot also come within the above principles. Where tickets are proffered at the head of a lengthy queue, as at a football match or railway booking office, it is essentially impossible not to accept the offered terms. The same might be said of the passenger who has boarded a bus which then moves off.

(e) At or before the time of contracting

It is firm and settled law that no exclusion clause is effective unless adequately brought to the other party's attention before the time the contract is made. The locus classicus hereabouts is *Olley* v *Marlborough Court*.[30] A husband and wife arrived at a hotel and paid for board and residence in advance. They went to the room allotted to them, and on one of the walls was this notice: 'The proprietors will not hold themselves responsible for articles lost or stolen unless handed to the manageress for safe custody'. In their absence, clothing was stolen from the room. The Court of Appeal held that the contract was completed before the guests went up to their room and that no subsequent notice could affect their rights.

The same point was made by Mocatta J in *Burnett* v *Westminster Bank*.[31] The defendants in that case were in effect seeking to alter the terms of a contract already made, quite apart from any question whether the cheque book was or was not a contractual document. It may also be pointed out that had the ticket in *Chapelton* v *Barry UDC*[32] constituted a contractual document, it would have been ineffective in that it had been given to the plaintiff after he had accepted the offer to hire a chair, and hence after the contract was made.

Another useful example is *Hollingsworth* v *Southern Ferries*.[33] *B* booked a passage for *P* and himself on *D*'s vessel, and was later given tickets containing an exclusion clause. It was held that the contract was concluded before the ticket was delivered and, accordingly, *D* could not rely on the exclusion clause.

The unique problem of when a contract is made if done through the agency of a machine was considered by Lord Denning in *Thornton* v *Shoe Lane Parking*.[34] It was his view that the contract was concluded when the money was put into the machine. The whole business could be translated into the dogma of offer and acceptance in this way. The offer 'is made when the proprietor of the machine holds it out as being ready to receive the money. The acceptance takes place when the customer puts his money into the slot. The terms of the offer are contained in the notice placed in or near the machine stating what is offered for the money. The customer is bound by those terms as long as they are sufficiently brought to his notice beforehand, but not otherwise. He is not bound by the terms printed on the ticket if they differ from the notice, because the ticket comes too late. The contract has already been made'.[35]

This approach, while attractive, must be treated with considerable caution. Lord Denning himself also found more traditional grounds for avoiding the exclusion clause (that not enough notice had been given) while both Megaw LJ and Sir Gordon Willmer expressly reserved judgment on this issue.[36]

What this case does highlight, of course, is the clear need to bear in mind the distinction between an offer and an invitation to treat. This also arose (albeit it did not create much difficulty) in *Levison* v *Patent Steam Carpet Cleaning*.[37] Over the telephone, the owner of a carpet had requested that it be picked up and taken away for cleaning. When the cleaning company called for it, the owner was presented with a form, containing exclusion clauses, which he duly signed. The Court of Appeal was unanimous in its decision that the document had been incorporated into the contract, albeit no firm reason was given why. Lord Denning MR felt that the document had become incorporated through the course of dealing between the parties,[38] a matter we shall be pursuing below. Orr LJ felt that the document would have been part of the contract even 'in the absence of any previous dealing between the parties',[39] a view with which Sir David Cairns agreed.[40] In this latter case, one must view the telephone conversation as merely inviting the defendants to come to the plaintiff's house and offer to take away the carpet for cleaning. It may be asked if this is entirely acceptable: the telephone conversation was more specific than that ('can you come and collect and when?—Yes, 17 July')[41] and it may be wondered if the two judges would have held to their view had the defendants arrived in their van only to be turned away because the plaintiff had changed his mind. It is thought that Lord Denning's clear assumption that a contract had been concluded over the telephone is the correct one.

Yet if this had been a binding contract, and one not concluded on the basis of a usual course of dealing, Sir David Cairns still saw a way to incorporate the exclusion clauses. When the telephone conversation had taken place, reference had been made only to the carpet. Yet when the van arrived, a carpet and a rug were tendered and taken away. This allowed Sir David to suggest a novation: 'a fresh contract was made on 17 July when an additional item, a white rug, was offered for cleaning and accepted'.[42] Manifestly, such acceptance was on the basis of the written terms contained in the document.

While this is acceptable on the special facts of the case, there are inherent dangers. If a contract is agreed upon, and subsequently a document containing exclusion clauses is tendered and accepted, this arguably constitutes a novation. The original contract has been replaced by another incorporating the terms of the document. There is more force in this argument, perhaps, when the document is signed. Yet this is probably to take the argument further than it merits. There was no difficulty in this particular case since new goods were added to the contract: where this is not so, very clear evidence indeed will be needed to show that both parties intended to replace one agreement with another.

(f) *The course of dealing*

It may always be the case that, far from being an isolated transaction, the particular agreement between the parties was one of a regular series of such agreements. If, over that period, the parties have regularly incorporated certain exclusion clauses, it needs to be asked what the effect will be when, perhaps by an oversight, the crucial document is not handed over.

One point can easily be dealt with. In an obiter dictum expressed in *McCutcheon* v *MacBrayne*,[43] Lord Devlin had urged that a term could be introduced by a course of dealing only where there was actual knowledge of the content of that term as opposed to knowledge of its existence.[44] This view was comprehensively rejected by the House of Lords in *Henry Kendall & Sons* v *William Lillico & Sons*.[45]

The latter case is also particularly instructive as to when a course of dealing operates to incorporate particular clauses. There had been a verbal contract followed the next day by a 'sold note' which contained an exclusion clause. There had been more than a hundred similar contract notes in a course of dealing stretching back three years. The recipients knew of the existence of the written conditons but had never raised any query or objection, although they had never read them. As Lord Pearce summarised: 'The only reasonable inference from the regular course of dealing over so long a period is that SAPPA were evincing an acceptance of, and a readiness to be bound by, the printed conditions of whose existence they were aware although they had not troubled to read them. Thus the general conditions became part of the oral contract'.[46]

This case can be usefully contrasted with the finding in *McCutcheon* v *MacBrayne*. There, the plaintiff's agent had dealt with the defendants on a number of occasions: sometimes he had signed a risk note containing the relevant exclusion clauses and sometimes he had not. He had not so signed on the relevant occasion. Holding that the clauses were not part of the contract, Lord Pearce maintained that the defendants were 'seeking to establish an oral contract by a course of dealing which always insisted on a written contract. It is the consistency of a course of conduct which gives rise to the implication that in similar circumstances a similar contractual result will follow. When the conduct is not consistent, there is no reason why it should still produce an invariable contractual result'.[47] As Lord Pearce later added: 'The ordinary course of business was therefore no help to the carrier, since the transaction did not follow the ordinary course'.[48]

The same finding was made in the instructive case of *Hollier* v *Rambler Motors*.[49] The plaintiff telephoned the garage of the defendants asking for some repair work to be done. The defendants agreed to attend to the defects in due course. These were the only terms of the agreement. It was established that during the previous five years, the plaintiff on three or four occasions, had had repairs done by the defendants. On the last two of these occasions, the plaintiff signed a note containing exclusion clauses. This had not happened on this latest occasion. Salmon LJ, with whom Stamp LJ and Latey J concurred, found it impossible to find that the exclusion clauses had been incorporated into the latest contract. If it were not possible to rely on a course of dealing in *McCutcheon* v *MacBrayne*, 'still less would it be possible to do so in this case, when the so-called course of dealing consisted only of three or four transactions in the course of five years'.[50]

An unusual example of how terms can be incorporated through the course of dealing came about in *Lamport & Holt Lines* v *Coubro & Scrutton (M & I) and Coubro & Scrutton (Riggers & Shipwrights)*.[51] The second defendants were a subsidiary of the first, the two companies having been separated in 1975 when nationalisation was threatened. The terms and conditions of contract used by the second defendants were exactly the same as those used by the first defendants, with whom the plaintiffs had contracted for many years. The matter was slightly complicated by the fact that, when the stationery for the second defendants was printed, and because of a printer's error, the terms and conditions of contract were not printed on the reverse of the invoices. The evidence showed that, when work was to be done for the plaintiffs, a form of acknowledgement was sent out on the reverse of which were the standard conditions. It was immaterial to the plaintiffs which of the two defendants did the particular work on any occasion, the decision being left to the defendants. If the work was allotted to the second defendants, the acknowledgement was sent out on their form, on the back of which were printed their terms and conditions, these being, as stated above, identical to those of the parent company. The evidence also showed that the plaintiffs had been well aware that the second defendants were being incorporated to do the riggers' and shipwrights' work originally done by the first defendants. By September, 1975, when the contract in question was made, there had been numerous transactions between the plaintiffs and the second defendants when acknowledgements of order were despatched with the latters' terms and conditions printed on the back. Only one of these acknowledgements could now be found, but Goff J concluded that 'on the evidence before the court, I have no doubt that on each occasion they were sent', and that there cannot be the 'slightest hesitation' in holding that the terms and conditions of the second defendants were incorporated into the contract in question.[52] This was not contested in the Court of Appeal.

(g) *Understanding of the parties and the course of dealing*

The 'course of dealing' as an argument for the incorporation of exemption clauses may be supplemented, indeed superseded, by the 'understanding of the parties'. This is well illustrated by *British Crane Hire* v *Ipswich Plant Hire*.[53] Both parties were companies engaged in the hiring out of earth moving equipment. The defendants needed a dragline crane urgently and contacted the plaintiffs by telephone who agreed to supply one on hire. Nothing was said as to the conditions of hire. Subsequently, a printed form containing the appropriate conditions was sent for signature, but it never was signed. From the evidence, it appeared that there had been two previous agreements within the preceding year which had been effected on the basis of the written terms. These transactions were not known to the defendants' manager when he ordered the crane. In the circumstances, Lord Denning doubted 'whether those two would be sufficient to show a course of dealing'.[54]

The evidence further showed, however, that the defendants knew that firms in the trade imposed conditions as to the hire of plant. Indeed, the defendants did so themselves. In such circumstances, Lord Denning did not doubt but that the written conditions had been incorporated into the contract. He 'would not put it so much on the course of dealing, but rather on the common understanding which is to be derived from the conduct of the parties, namely, that the hiring was to be on the terms of the plaintiffs' usual conditions ... it is just as if the plaintiffs had said, "we will supply it on our usual conditions", and the defendants said, "Of course, that is quite understood"'.[55]

Sir Eric Sachs was of like mind. The machine had been damaged, and under the printed conditions the defendants were to indemnify the plaintiffs. The 'business realities of the situation', Sir Eric declared, are 'plain'.[56] If the defendants had declared to the plaintiffs when the contract was made that risk of damage lay with the latter, the reply would have been 'That is nonsense, and you don't get the machine'.[57] Moreover, Sir Eric said, 'to hold that the plaintiffs did take the risk impliedly would be unrealistic and obviously contrary to the mythical officious bystander's view'.[58] In any case, Sir Eric concluded, the matter goes further: both sides knew 'that contracts of this type are normally subject to printed conditions'.[59] Sir Eric made no specific mention of the usual course of dealing.

It must be appreciated that this line of agrument, based on the common understanding of the parties, is a potentially dangerous one. Most consumers, without being unduly cynical, now expect to have whatever rights they have negated by the small print of the agreement and no doubt contract on that assumption, whether or not presented with the appropriate document. The Court of Appeal was certainly alive to this possibility. Lord Denning pointed to *Hollier* v *Rambler Motors*, observing that in contrast to the instant case, the plaintiff 'was not of equal bargaining power with the garage company'.[60] Sir Eric Sachs was also at pains to stress that nothing in his judgment was relevant to the 'position where the owner and user are in wholly different walks of life, as in *Hollier's* case—where one, for instance, is an expert in a line of business and the other is not'.[61]

No authority was cited for these propositions, and it is indeed difficult to accept them at face value. If there is such a thing as a common understanding, it must apply without discrimination. The fact that one party is of inferior bargaining power can scarcely affect his understanding of the contract: indeed, the weaker a party, the more he may suppose that certain terms, especially exclusion clauses, will be inserted into the contract. The plain truth is, of course, that simple morality ordains a more solicitous view when unequal parties make an agreement.

2 Signature

The effect of signing a written document was first indicated by Mellish LJ in *Parker* v *South Eastern Railway*.[62] In the ordinary case, he said, 'where an action is brought on a written agreement which is signed by the defendant, the agreement is proved by proving his signature, and, in the absence of fraud, it is wholly immaterial that he has not read the agreement and does not know its contents'.[63]

This dictum was accepted as correct by the Court of Appeal in *L'Estrange* v *Graucob*.[64] The plaintiff, the owner of a cafe, agreed to buy from the defendants an automatic slot-machine for cigarettes. The agreement was to pay by instalments, and it contained an exemption clause excluding liability for breaches of warranty or condition. The plaintiff signed the agreement without reading its terms. The machine proved faulty, and the plaintiff purported to terminate the contract for breach of condition.

It was held that she could not do so since she was bound by the terms of the exclusion clause. The words of Scrutton LJ were unambiguous: 'In cases in which the contract is contained in a railway ticket or other unsigned document, it is necessary to prove that an alleged party was aware, or ought to have been aware, of its terms and conditions. These cases have no application when the document has been signed. When a document containing contractual terms is signed, then, in the absence of fraud, or, I will add, misrepresentation, the party signing it is bound, and it is wholly immaterial whether he has read the document or not'.[65]

(a) Fraud and misrepresentation

As both Mellish and Scrutton LJJ observed, a party can escape the full consequences of his signature if he can show that the contract was effected with fraud or misrepresentation. In such cases, the innocent party is entitled to rescind the contract and claim damages. Where the misrepresentation is otherwise than fraudulent, the court, acting under s 2(2) of the Misrepresentation Act 1967, may declare the contract subsisting and award damages in lieu of rescission. Where the misrepresentation is entirely innocent (that is, made free of fraud or negligence) it is only under s 2(2) that damages may be awarded.[66] It is now well established that where the misrepresentation constitutes a negligent breach of the duty of care, there is a common law right to rescind the contract and claim damages.[67] Section 2(1) of the 1967 Act also provides such a remedy. The statutory remedy is more amenable to the claim of one who asserts a misrepresentation, since the onus is placed on the defendant of showing that he was not negligent, this being the reverse of the common law position.[68]

It is to be noted that the concept of fraud in Scots law in relation to annulment of obligations is much wider than that in English law. As a learned writer[69] points out, it is used to cover not only what Bell in his 'Principles' called 'a machination or contrivance to deceive',[70] but also conduct inconsistent with *bona fides*.

There is no Misrepresentation Act in Scotland, and so no possibility of damages for an innocent misrepresentation. Whether this is of much moment, given that there is delictual liability for negligent mis-statement, is open to question.[71] It seems unlikely that there will be many cases where the misrepresentation is completely innocent in the sense that neither party is responsible for it. And in such cases it is not unreasonable that an action for damages should not lie.

(b) Non est factum

A final, and brief, word can be said on the plea of non est factum. This arises where a person claims that he so misunderstood a document to which he put his signature, that he has not therefore assented to its terms, and that the agreement is thus void. It now appears from the decision of the House of Lords in *Gallie* v *Lee*[72] that the plea will avail a mistaken party if he satisfies the court that the document is radically different from that which he intended to sign and that his mistake is not due to his carelessness. But as Lord Wilberforce said 'there still remains a residue of difficult cases. There are still illiterate or senile persons who cannot read, or apprehend, a legal document; there are still persons who may be tricked into putting their signature on a piece of paper which has legal consequences different from anything they intended ... to eliminate it [the plea of non est factum] would, in my opinion, deprive the courts of what may be, doubtless, on sufficiently rare occasions, an instrument of justice'.

Where a person signs a document in blank, the plea of non est factum is not strictly applicable. But if a document is so signed, leaving another to fill in the terms in accordance with an oral agreement, no agreement exists if the completed agreement does not accord with that oral agreement.[73]

1 [1972] 3 All ER 158, 167.
2 Cheshire & Fifoot, *Law of Contract* (10th ed) p 139.
3 1877 (2 CPD) 416.
4 *Ibid* at p 422.
5 [1940] 1 KB 532.
6 [1964] 1 All ER 430.
7 [1965] 3 All ER 81.
8 *Supra* note 3.
9 *Hood* v *Anchor Line* [1918] AC 837, 844 *per* Lord Haldane.
10 See *Henderson* v *Stevenson* (1875) LR 2 HL 470.
11 [1941] 1 All ER 172.
12 *Ibid* at p 174 *per* Lord Caldecote CJ. See too *Numan* v *Southern Railway Co* [1924] 1 KB 223; *Penton* v *Southern Railway Co* [1931] 2 KB 103.
13 [1897] AC 217.
14 [1930] 1 KB 41.
15 [1970] 1 Lloyd's Rep 364.
16 [1978] 1 All ER 18.
17 [1956] 2 All ER 121.
18 *Ibid* at p 125.
19 [1971] 1 All ER 686.
20 *Ibid* at p 690.
21 *Ibid* at p 692.
22 *Ibid*.
23 *Ibid* at p 693.
24 *Ibid*.
25 *Ibid*.
26 *Ibid*.
27 [1973] 2 All ER 631.
28 *Ibid* at p 635.

29 [1972] 2 All ER 1353, 1358.
30 [1949] 1 All ER 127.
31 *Supra* note 7.
32 *Supra* note 5.
33 [1977] 2 Lloyd's Rep 70.
34 *Supra* note 19.
35 *Ibid* at p 689.
36 *Ibid* at pp 692 and 693 respectively.
37 [1977] 3 All ER 498.
38 *Ibid* at p 502.
39 *Ibid* at p 506.
40 *Ibid*.
41 See the judgment of Lord Denning, *ibid* at p 501.
42 *Ibid* at p 506.
43 *Supra* note 6.
44 *Ibid* at p 437.
45 [1968] 2 All ER at pp 444, 474 and 481 *per* Lords Guest and Pearce respectively.
46 *Supra* note 6 at pp 439–40.
47 *Henry Kendall & Sons* v *William Lillico & Sons, supra* note 45 at p 481.
48 *Supra* note 45 at p 481.
49 [1972] 1 All ER 399.
50 *Ibid* at p 404.
51 [1981] 2 Lloyd's Rep 659; [1982] 2 Lloyd's Rep 42.
52 [1981] 2 Lloyd's Rep at p 661.
53 [1974] 1 All ER 1059.
54 *Ibid* at p 1061.
55 *Ibid* at pp 1062–3.
56 *Ibid* at p 1064.
57 *Ibid*.
58 *Ibid*.
59 *Ibid*.
60 *Ibid* at p 1062.
61 *Ibid* at p 1064.
62 *Supra* note 3.
63 *Ibid* at p 421.
64 [1934] 2 KB 394.
65 *Ibid* at p 403.
66 See *Whittington* v *Seale-Hayne* (1900) 82 LT 49. See the discussion in Cheshire & Fifoot, *op cit*, pp 260–6.
67 *Esso Petroleum* v *Mardon* [1976] 2 All ER 5.
68 See *Howard Marine & Dredging* v *Ogden* [1978] 2 All ER 1134.
69 TB Smith, *Short Commentary on the Laws of Scotland* p 833.
70 *Principles* 13.
71 Delictual liability for negligent mis-statement in Scotland almost certainly ante-dated *Hedley Byrne* v *Heller*, See Smith, *op cit*, pp 834–5.
72 [1971] AC at p 1025.
73 See Anson, *Law of Contract* (25th ed) p 318.

Chapter 2

Interpretation of Exclusion Clauses

Given that an exclusion clause has, by whatever means, been incorporated into a particular contract, the next question is whether it is apt to cover the particular loss or damage which has arisen. We also examine the question whether exclusion clauses can benefit those not actually party to the contract.

1 The 'contra proferentem' rule

The so-called 'contra proferentem' rule amounts to this: that a person who, by reference to an exclusion clause, seeks to avoid a liability which otherwise would fall upon him must do so by reference to words which clearly and unequivocally apply to the case in hand. The words of Scrutton LJ in *Szymonowski* v *Beck*[1] are to the point: 'Now I approach the consideration of that clause applying the principle repeatedly acted upon by the House of Lords and by this Court—that if a party wishes to exclude the ordinary consequences that would flow in law from the contract that he is making he must do so in clear terms. As Lord Macnaghten said in one case, 'an ambiguous clause is no protection'.[2]

An excellent example of how this rule is applied exists in *Lee & Son* v *Railway Executive*.[3] The plaintiffs leased a warehouse from the defendants. In the lease was a clause purporting to exempt from liability 'for loss or damage (whether by act or neglect of the company or their servants or agents or not) which but for the tenancy hereby created ... would not have arisen'. Goods in the warehouse were damaged by fire owing to the alleged negligence of the defendants in allowing a spark or some such combustible matter to escape from their railway engines. Applying the contra proferentem rule, the Court of Appeal held that the exclusion clause applied only to liabilities which arose only by reason of the relationship of

19

landlord and tenant created by the lease; this being the impact of the words in the lease 'but for the tenancy hereby created'. Certainly, this clause was capable of bearing a wider interpretation, but it had to be construed against the defendants who were, therefore, not protected.

It is clear from this that the courts will interpret exemption clauses strictly and will, in particular, attribute precise legal meanings to technical expressions. In *Wallis, Son & Wells* v *Pratt & Haynes*,[4] the plaintiff purchased from the defendant certain seed described as 'common English sainfoin'. The seed was in fact a different, lower quality, seed known as 'giant sainfoin'. The contract contained a clause excluding liability for breach of all warranties, whether express or implied. The defendant, of course, was in breach of the condition, implied by s 13 of the Sale of Goods Act 1893 (now repealed and re-enacted by s 13 of the Sale of Goods Act 1979), requiring the goods to correspond with their description. If this had been all, the court could easily have avoided the exclusion clause, since it referred only to warranties, and not to conditions. The problem which arose was that the plaintiff had accepted the goods within s 11 (1) (*c*)[5] and so was compelled to treat the breach of condition as a breach of warranty. Even so, the House of Lords held the sellers disentitled from reliance on the clause. The term in question, although it fell to be treated as a warranty, did not for that reason ever cease from being a condition.

The reasoning of this case was later relied on by the Court of Appeal in *Baldry* v *Marshall*.[6] The signed contract for the sale and purchase of a motor car contained a term excluding 'any other guarantee or warranty express or otherwise'. The purchaser complained that it was not reasonably fit for its purpose, the condition implied by s 14 (1) of the Sale of Goods Act 1893 (now s 14 (3) of the Sale of Goods Act 1979). According to Bankes LJ, if 'there is one thing more clearly established than another it is the distinction between a warranty and a condition'.[7] This particular clause, he affirmed, whether speaking of 'a guarantee' or 'a warranty' speaks of 'nothing but what the law would recognise as a warranty . . . there [is] here no exclusion of any implied condition'.[8] Atkin LJ agreed that it was proper to distinguish a guarantee, or warranty 'as being different from, certainly as not including, a condition'.[9]

Yet further examples can be found. In *Webster* v *Higgins*,[10] a term in a hire purchase contract provided that 'no warranty, condition or description *is* given', it being held that this failed to exclude liability for an undertaking which had *previously* been given. In *Houghton* v

Trafalgar Insurance,[11] a motor insurance policy provided that the insurer was not to be liable 'whilst the car is carrying any load in excess of that for which it was constructed'. Here, it was held that the provision did not serve to exclude liability where the car carried an excess of passengers. Passengers were not embraced by the term 'load'.

(a) Strict interpretation of exclusion clauses

It was said by Scrutton LJ in *Alison* v *Wallsend Slipway & Engineering*[12] that if 'a person is under a legal liability and wishes to get rid of it, he can only do so by using clear words'.[13] The words of the exclusion clause must be apt precisely to cover the liability which is sought to be excluded. Rather than being taken as a separate rule, the question of 'strict interpretation' is best seen as a specific instance of the contra proferentem rule.

An excellent example is afforded in *Henry Kendall & Sons* v *William Lillico & Sons.*[14] The question arose whether a term excluding liability for 'latent defects' sufficed to exclude liability for failure to comply with the term implied by s 14 (1) of the Sale of Goods Act 1983 (now s 14 (3) of the Sale of Goods Act 1979) that goods be reasonably fit for their purpose. Finding that it did not, Lord Morris argued that the word 'defects' related 'prima facie to the quality of goods. Goods might be fit for a known particular purpose and yet have certain defects. Any latent defects covered by the clause are such as do not prevent the goods being reasonably fit for their purpose. As the clause does not refer to the conditions which, being implied, are part of the contract between the parties and as, in my view, the clause does not either expressly or by necessary inference negative or cancel any of the conditions, it must be construed as referring to such latent defects as do not prevent compliance with the conditions'.[15]

This was also the view (as it was indeed of the entire House of Lords) accepted by Lord Pearce. The clause, he said, does not necessarily exclude the implied term. The goods 'might have had defects of quality which did not make them unfit for their purpose. It is to these defects that the clause should be read as applicable. If it was intended to cut down the condition as to fitness in respect of all latent defects, the clause should have said so in clear and unambiguous terms, referring expressly to the condition which it was limiting'.[16]

Two other cases may serve to illustrate the point. In *Beck* v *Szymonowski,*[17] the purchasers had bought 2,000 gross 6-cord sewing cotton thread reels, each reel stated to be 200 yards in length. It was said in the contract that: 'The goods delivered shall be deemed to be in all respects in accordance with the contract, and the buyers shall be bound to accept and pay for the same accordingly, unless the sellers shall within 14 days after the arrival of the goods at their destination receive from the buyers notice of any matter or thing by reason whereof they may allege that the goods are not in accordance with the contract'. The reels had only 188 yards of cotton, not 200 yards, a fact discovered long after 14 days had expired. The House of Lords held that, comprehensive though it appeared, the clause was ineffective. The damages 'are claimed not in respect of the goods delivered but in respect of goods which were not delivered'.[18] In *Minister of Materials* v *Steel Bros*[19] a contract for the sale of goods limited the right to complain as to matters of quality to a period of sixty days. The goods were damaged as a result of defective packing. The Court of Appeal ruled that the clause was ineffective since the ground of complaint was not the quality of the goods. This is a particularly good illustration of judicial hostility to exclusion clauses since in *Niblett* v *Confectioners' Materials*[20] it was held that the quality of goods includes the state of the packing, and that if this is unsatisfactory the goods are not of merchantable quality.

(b) Negligence liability

Nowhere has the animosity of the judges toward exclusion clauses been better displayed than in their attitude to the exclusion of liability for negligence. Of course, and as with so much learning on exclusion clauses, the issue has been drastically affected by the Unfair Contract Terms Act 1977. Yet wide though the impact of this Act is, there will nevertheless remain an area where common law predecent remains paramount. This is because a substantial number of types of contract are excluded from the purview of the Act: and because, even within the Act, certain types of exclusion clause relating to negligence liability remain valid if reasonable. But even if reasonable and hence valid, they will remain to be interpreted, and this explains the continued relevance of much of that was arrived at before the Act.[21]

The special problems relating to negligence liability have been put by learned authorities thus: 'it may happen that, apart from the contract, [the person inserting the clause] may find himself in a situation where the law casts upon him not only a duty of care but also some form of strict liability. In such a case, unless the language of the contract manifestly covers both types of obligation he will be taken to have excluded only the latter'.[22] This is neatly illustrated by *White* v *Warwick*.[23] The plaintiff hired a bicycle from the defendants. It was a term of the agreement that 'nothing in this agreement shall render the owners liable for any personal injuries to the riders of the machine hired.' The saddle tipped over while the bicycle was being ridden and the plaintiff, being dashed to the ground, sustained injuries. He thereupon brought an action, suing alternatively for breach of contract and in tort for negligence. Since liability could be grounded in either negligence or strict liability for breach of contract, the Court of Appeal felt able to hold that the exclusion clause extended only to a claim concerning the latter. Accordingly, the defendants remained liable in negligence.

It must be appreciated that there are limits in the application of this particular case. In *Lamport & Holt Lines* v *Coubro & Scrutton (M & I) and Coubro & Scrutton (Riggers and Shipwrights)*,[24] where reliance was placed by the defendants on the *White* case, Goff J stressed that the earlier case 'was concerned with a clause which exempted the defendant from liability both in contract and in tort, the liability in contract being wider than the liability in tort'.[25] In the *White* case itself, Denning LJ had himself observed that: 'The liability for breach of contract is more strict than the liability for negligence. The owners may be liable in contract for supplying a defective machine, even though they were not negligent ... In these circumstances, the exemption clause must, I think, be construed as exempting the owners only from their liability in contract, and not from their liability in negligence'.[26] When the *Lamport & Holt* case reached the Court of Appeal, Donaldson LJ made the trenchant observation that: 'The basis of the decision was that the contract, on its true construction, would, in the absence of this clause, have imposed a warranty of fitness for the purpose. The clause was therefore held to negative this warranty, while leaving liability in tort unaffected. But I know of no case in which words of exclusion have been held to operate in relation to a liability for breach of an obligation in contract, but not to affect liability for breach of the self-same obligation in tort. Indeed, the whole concept of a hypothetical discussion between two parties, other than law students, which led to such an agreement is patently absurd'.[27]

The general point is also well illustrated by the opinion of the Privy Council in *Canada Steamship Lines* v *The King*.[28] The terms of the lease of a shed provided that the lessee 'shall not have any claim' for damage to goods. An indemnity clause required the lessee to indemnify the lessor against all claims in any manner based upon 'any action taken or things done'. Owing to the negligence of the lessor's servants, a fire broke out, destroying the shed and all its contents. The lessees, and others whose property was destroyed, sought damages from the lessors.

Lord Morton considered that in approaching such clauses as were contained in this particular contract, three principles fell for consideration.[29] First, if the clause contains language expressly exempting a party from the consequences of his negligence, effect must be given to that provision. Second, if there is no such express reference, the court must consider whether, given their natural meaning, the words extend to cover negligence. If the words are sufficiently wide, then, thirdly, the court must consider whether the head of damage may be based on some ground other than that of negligence. Such other ground must not be so fanciful or remote that the party seeking to rely on it cannot be supposed to have sought protection from it. But subject to such a qualification, the existence of a possible head of damage other than that of negligence is fatal even if the words used are prima facie wide enough to cover negligence.

Applying these rules, the following findings were made. The lessors had failed to limit liability in respect of negligence in clear terms and hence the clause was to be construed as relating to a liability not based on negligence. Turning to the indemnity clause, the Privy Council were of the opinion that it also failed to cover negligent acts. It was at least doubtful that the words 'any action taken or things done ... by virtue hereof' could be applied to a negligent act done in the course of carrying out an obligation. But even if they were wide enough, the principle remained that the head of damage might be based on some ground other than that of negligence. Finally, the meaning and effect of the indemnity clause were far from clear, and liability on an indemnity clause must be imposed by clear words. Lord Morton provided the summing-up of the lessor's position when he said that there 'would have been no difficulty in inserting an express reference to negligence' if these clauses had been intended to protect the lessors against the conse-quences of negligence.[30]

We have, at this point, once more to refer to the decision in the *Lamport & Holt* case. What had actually happened there was that a derrick on which certain work was being done was being restowed on the plaintiffs' vessel when the tumbler of the mast topping block carried away or fractured with the result that the derrick damaged a closed hatch cover. At first instance, Goff J turned to consider the principles discussed above as set out by Lord Morton. The clause in dispute had excluded liability 'for any damage ... suffered by you ... and which may arise from or be in any way connected with any act ... of any person or corporation employed by us or by any subcontractors or engaged in any capacity herewith ...' It was contended by the plaintiffs in this case that those words were wide enough to cover heads of liability other than negligence and which were not, as Lord Morton had insisted, too 'fanciful or remote'. The other possible heads were said to be: late delivery of the derrick; restowing it in the wrong position; and, in reliance on *White* v *Warwick*, the fact that there could also be liability in contract. The last possibility was rejected on the grounds referred to above.[31] The first alleged alternative head was rejected for being too 'fanciful', the point being that other clauses in the contract would have applied in the event of breach by late delivery. The remaining contention—that of excluding liability for restowing the derrick in the wrong position, was likewise outside the clause since, on its true construction, 'the condition cannot ... exempt R&S from a simple failure to carry out the works which they had contracted to do. So to apply the condition would be to defeat the very purpose of the contract itself'.[32]

When the *Lamport & Holt* case reached the Court of Appeal, Donaldson LJ was keen to stress that Lord Morton's opinion is likely to mislead 'unless full force is given to his caveat that the "other ground" must not be so fanciful or remote that the proferens cannot be supposed to have desired protection against it'.[33] Before the Court of Appeal, the plaintiffs recast the other possible grounds, the very doing of which 'suggests that it is by no means clear that there is an alternative substantial, ie not fanciful, ground of liability. Late delivery has become the delayed provision of services. Misperformance remains, as does a contractual liability parallel with a tortious liability, but [counsel] now adds nuisance, conversion and detinue'.[34]

The idea of delay being covered by this condition was rejected because other contract terms were more appropriate. Parallel liability in contract and tort was likewise rejected for reasons earlier noted.[35] Misperformance was likewise discounted since there was no obvious reason why, when the clause in dispute was being framed, 'the parties should have been, or be deemed to have been, addressing their minds to contractual neglect rather than tortious neglect or vice versa'.[36] As for the newcomers, nuisance, conversion and detinue: 'Suffice it to say that I am not surprised that [counsel] has only now thought of this. If the officious bystander had raised the point with the parties when they were negotiating the contract, I think that he would still be trying to explain to them what he had in mind'.[37]

There was concern also on the part of May and Stephenson LJJ that a correct understanding be had of the possible other heads of liability argument. According to the former, the court is to discard, when turning its attention to alternative heads of liability outside negligence, any ground to which, on a reasonable assessment 'of all the circumstances at the time the underlying contract was made, it is unlikely that the parties would have addressed their mind ... the excercise upon which the court is engaged in these cases is one of construction, that is one of deciding what the parties meant or must be deemed to have meant by the words they used'.[38] Lord Justice Stephenson agreed that, if there is another head of damage, then the clause will cover that damage, and will not extend to damage resulting from negligence: 'If there is no such head of damage, the court is under no duty to seek out, or think up, remote and far-fetched possibilities in order to defeat the intention, which would otherwise be derived from the plain meaning of the clause, to protect the party relying on it from liability'.[39]

The lengths the courts will go to in finding that an exclusion clause does not extend to cover liability in negligence is nowhere better illustrated than in *Hollier* v *Rambler Motors*.[40] The contentious clause read: 'The Company is not responsible for damage caused by fire to customers' cars on the premises'. While the car was in the garage, a fire broke out as a result of the defendants' negligence which caused substantial damage to the car.

We have seen already that the clause had not, in fact, been incorporated into the contract.[41] The Court of Appeal proceeded, however, to interpret the clause, acknowledging that, as bailees, the defendants' liability could only ever sound in negligence. Salmon LJ imagined that, faced with this particular clause, the ordinary man would say: ' "Well, what they are telling me is that if there is a fire due to any cause other than their own negligence they are not responsible for it." To my mind, if the defendants were seeking to exclude their responsibility for a fire caused by their own negligence, they ought to have done so in far plainer language than the language here used. In my view, the words of the condition would be understood as being meant to be a warning to the customer that if a fire does occur at the garage which damages the car, and it is not caused by the negligence of the garage owner, then the garage owner is not responsible for damage'.[42]

Stamp LJ regarded it as 'settled' law that where there is an exclusion clause open to two constructions, one of which will make it applicable where there is no negligence, the other where there is, it 'requires special words or special circumstances to make the clause exclude liability in case of negligence ... Similarly, I would hold that where the words relied on by the defendant are susceptible either to a construction under which they become a statement of fact in the nature of a warning or to a construction which will exempt the defendant from liability for negligence, the former construction is to be preferred'.[43] The clause in the instant case, he found, was capable of construction as a warning.[44]

Latey J took the same approach. He rejected the argument that, because liability only sounds in negligence, 'no sufficiently clear words are required'. When this is the only source of liability, the law may more readily operate to give sanction to the exclusion clause, but 'the law goes no further than that'. [45]

This approach pushes the law to its limits, indeed, some would say, beyond them. A reviewer has urged that 'in principle it seems improbable that the defendants here, or indeed in any case, intended such a clause to be a warning that they were not liable in the absence of fault. This is the common-sense justification for the well-established principle of construction now virtually discarded by the Court of Appeal'.[46] It is considered prudent to advise against too strong a reliance on this part of the Court of Appeal's judgment. While it is not necessarily obiter dicta (being rather an alternative ground of judgment) it is permissible to regard it in that light.

It is, at any rate, reasonably clear that an exclusion clause is more likely to fulfil its intended role when negligence is the only ground for liability. In *Rutter* v *Palmer*,[47] the owner of a motor car deposited it for sale on commission with the owner of a garage upon the terms of a document containing the condition: 'Customers' cars are driven by your staff at customers' sole risk'. The car was sent out by the owner of a garage in the charge of one of his drivers to be shown to a prospective customer. The car was damaged owing to the negligence of the driver.

The Court of Appeal was unanimous in finding that the exclusion clause was effective. Bankers LJ drew a distinction between those, such as common carriers, who are liable even in the absence of negligence, and other bailees whose liability lies in negligence alone. The former, when drafting an effective exclusion clause, must use words which will include those acts which are negligent: the latter may use more general words, since such words will generally cover negligent acts, although such acts are not specifically mentioned, because otherwise the words would have no effect.[48]

To answer the problem, Scrutton LJ proposed what he called a 'rougher test'. When construing exemption clauses, certain general rules apply. A clause will not exclude liability for negligence unless 'adequate words are used'. Next, the liability of the defendant apart from exempting words must be ascertained; then the particular clause must be considered. If the only liability is grounded in negligence, the clause 'will more readily operate to exempt him'.[49] In *Hollier* v *Rambler Motors*,[50] Salmon LJ accepted these statements by Scrutton LJ, observing only that the Lord Justice did not say, where liability obtained only in negligence, that the exclusion clause would 'necessarily' exempt the negligent party from liability.[51]

The judgments were concurred in by Atkin LJ who drew particular attention to *McCawley* v *Furness Railway*[52]. The crucial clause bore the words 'at his [the passenger's] own risk'. The carrier's liability lay in negligence alone. Atkin LJ cited with approval the words of Cockburn CJ: 'The terms of the agreement under which the plaintiff became a passenger exclude everything for which the company would have been otherwise liable. They would have been liable for nothing but negligence ... But it was agreed that the plaintiff should be carried at his own risk, which must be taken to exclude all liability on the part of the company for any negligence ...'[53]

Bankes and Scrutton LJJ were, however, careful to stress that the exclusion clause, while effective in the present case, was nevertheless subject to limitation. The clause, which read 'Customers' cars are driven by your staff at customers' sole risk', must be taken as referring to the regular driving staff.[54] Second, 'driven' must mean 'driven for the purpose of the bailment'.[55] The clause does not mean, Scrutton LJ concluded, that 'the garage keeper is to be free from liability if a member of his clerical staff takes the car out for pleasure'.[56]

The principles to be deduced from this case were accepted and acted upon in *Alderslade* v *Hendon Laundry*[57] The laundry lost certain articles received for laundering. Reliance was placed by the laundry on a clause which ran: 'The maximum amount allowed for lost or damaged articles is 20 times the charge made for laundering'. It was found that the only relevant liability lay in negligence. Given this, said Lord Green MR, to construe the clause as though it did not cover negligence would be to leave the clause 'without any content at all'.[58] MacKinnon LJ agreed with this, adopting in its entirety the statement of principle given by Scrutton LJ in *Rutter* v *Palmer*.[59]

It is necessary, perhaps, to express a word of caution as to this case. Lord Greene appeared to believe that the clause *must* be construed as covering liability of negligence,[60] an approach certainly endorsed by the Editorial Note.[61] This goes too far: as we have seen, Salmon LJ has pointed out that Scrutton LJ refrained from saying that, where negligence alone founds liability, an exclusion clause necessarily precludes liability.[62] It is rather the case that the clause will 'more readily' have that effect. Exactly this point was made by May LJ in the *Lamport & Holt* case.[63] In Lord Greene's speech, he said, 'the word "must" ... should be read as "should usually" or in some such way consistent with the guide to construction stated by Lord Justice Scrutton in *Rutter* v *Palmer*'.[64]

In the end, whether or not the only ground for liability is negligence, the question whether an exclusion clause avoids there being liability for negligence is essentially a pure matter of construction. This was well illustrated by the decision in *Gillespie Bros* v *Roy Bowles*.[65] The clause in dispute was that one party agreed to indemnify the other 'against all claims or demands whatsoever'.[66] It was stated by Buckley LJ to be 'clearly settled' that liability for negligence may be excluded 'provided that the language or the circumstances are such as to make it perfectly clear that this was the intention of the parties'.[67] The Lord Justice stressed that the intention of the parties must be perfectly clear since it is 'inherently improbable that one party to the contract should intend to absolve the other party from the consequences of the latter's own negligence'.[68]

Since the clause under discussion failed to make express mention of negligence, the question to be decided was whether its language, given its ordinary meaning, was wide enough to cover negligence. If the answer to this were in the affirmative, the clause would effectively exclude liability for negligence if it was not intended to apply to claims derived otherwise than from negligence.[69]

There was no doubt in the Lord Justice's mind that the clause was effective. Buckley LJ recognised that expressions sufficient to avoid liability for negligence were 'however arising' and 'from any cause whatsoever'. Wherever, he continued, the relevant expression is 'any loss' or 'all claims and demands', it is rational to suppose that liability for negligence remained. The crucial factor here was that the exclusion clause contained the word 'whatsoever'. It must, Buckley LJ concluded, have been intended to some purpose and must be given effect to exclude liability for negligence.[70]

Some qualification was placed on this case in *Smith* v *South Wales Switchgear*.[71] Factory owners engaged parties to perform an annual overhaul at the factory. The contract contained terms requiring the latter to indemnify the former against any liability, loss, claim or proceedings arising out of or in the course of the execution of the order. The House of Lords adopted the test put forward by Lord Morton in *Canada Steamship Lines* v *The King*.[72] They disagreed, however, with the view put forward by Buckley LJ in the *Gillespie* case[73] that use of the word 'whatsoever' was an express agreement to except liability for negligence: that required the word 'negligence' or a synonym. The decision in that case, however, was accepted as correct.

The House of Lords held that the clause did not indemnify the factory owners for their own negligence because, on a proper reading, it only applied to liabilities incurred by the factory owners for the acts or omissions of the other parties in connection with the contract work. Furthermore, the clause could also be read as covering the far from fanciful liability of the factory owners in common law for the acts or omissions of the other parties, as occupiers of the factory or as employers. Even if the factory owners would have had a right of relief here, they were still entitled to rely on and use an express indemnity clause rather than raise an action of relief with its attendant hazards.

A clause which was upheld was contained in the *Lamport & Holt* case.[74] That clause ran: 'Except as stated herein we shall not be liable for any damage ... suffered by you ... and which may arise from or be in any way connected with any act ... of any person or corporation employed by us or by any subcontractors or engaged in any capacity herewith ...'. At first instance, Goff J ruled that, on the ordinary meaning of these words, they were wide enough to cover negligence on the part of the servants of the defendants. This was the view also of the Court of Appeal. Donaldson LJ agreed that there was no express reference to negligence, but held that the words 'any act or omission' are 'certainly wide enough to comprehend negligence', particularly when one bore in mind that in *Donoghue* v *Stevenson* itself Lord Atkin had argued that reasonable care must be taken to 'avoid acts or omissions which you can reasonably foresee would be likely to injure your neighbour'.[75] When he interpreted the disputed clause, May LJ was impressed by the fact that the opening words 'Except as stated herein' admitted liability as accepted by the proferens in other clauses of the contract.

This, of course, would predispose one toward accepting it as excluding liability more readily. The learned lord justice noted that the word 'omission' would not of its own be sufficient to exclude liability for negligence, since, in many cases 'the actual negligence giving rise to legal liability comprises a positive act, although the doing of it involves the necessary failure to take care'.[76] On the other hand, he went on to say, the wider phrase 'any act or omission' is 'certainly wide enough on its ordinary meaning to cover negligence on the part of the respondents, their servants or agents'.[77]

Another clause which survived challenge was that to be found in *Ailsa Craig Fishing* v *Malvern Fishing*.[78] It read: 'If . . . any liability on the part of the company shall arise (whether under the express or implied terms of this contract or at common law, or in any other way) to the customer for any loss or damage of whatever nature arising out of or connected with the provision of, the services covered by this contract, such liability shall be limited to the payment by the company of' the sum of £1,000 in respect of any claim arising from a duty assumed by them involving a service not related solely to the prevention or detection of fire or theft. Unanimously, the House of Lords held that this clause was wide enough to cover negligence.[79] Lord Wilberforce stressed that: 'Whether a clause limiting liability is effective or not is a question of construction of that clause in the context of the contract as a whole. If it is to exclude liability for negligence, it must be most clearly and unambiguously expressed . . . But I venture to add at least one further qualification or at least clarification: one must not strive to create ambiguities by strained construction . . . The relevant words must be given, if possible, their natural, plain meaning'.[80] Lord Fraser took the clear view that the clause in question 'is sufficiently clear and unambiguous to receive effect in limiting the liability of Securicor for its own negligence or that of its employees . . . It applies to any liability "whether under the express or implied terms of this contract, or at common law, or in any other way". Liability at common law is undoubtedly wide enough to cover liability, including the negligence of the proferens itself, so that even without relying on the final words "any other way", I am clearly of opinion that the negligence of Securicor is covered'.[81]

The same company were also held to have drafted a clause which covered negligence liability in *Photo Production* v *Securicor Transport*.[82] In the Court of Appeal, Waller LJ held that, even on a strict construction, cover was given against negligence, injurious acts or default which are negligence on the part of the employees of the company by a clause which stated that: 'Under no circumstances shall the company be responsible for any injurious act or default by any employee of the company ... '.[83] A further clause which began: 'If ... any liability on the part of the company shall arise (whether under the express or implied terms hereof or at common law) ...' was so drafted, Waller LJ ruled, that it 'must cover negligence'.[84] The House of Lords agreed that this was so, but little attention was given this point, since other issues required attention.

The position reached in the preceding cases was summarised by Bingham J in *Industrie Chimiche Italia Centrale* v *Nea Ninemia Shipping*.[85] A charterparty provided that a shipowner was to be exempt from repaying moneys to the charterers if the ship were lost through 'errors of navigation'. A question arose as to whether this covered loss or damage brought about by negligent navigation.

According to the learned judge, the general conclusions which emerged from the cases were these. First, the court would not presume that a clause was intended to absolve a party from the consequences of his own negligence 'unless the contrary was shown by clear words or implication'. Second, statements which were made in one case, while they might assist in deciding another, could 'not literally determine the decision. The court's task was one of construction in each case to ascertain the actual or implied intention of the parties'.

The third conclusion which could be drawn from the cases was that, while the test was often what the ordinary literate and sensible person would make of the particular clause, the test would be that of the 'reasonably informed practitioner' where the contract was made in a specialised business by two practitioners in that business. Finally, where the words used were wide enough to cover negligent as well as non-negligent acts or omissions, and the clause would lack 'substance in practical terms if negligence were excluded', then the court might or might not infer that the parties intended negligence to be covered, 'depending on the proper inference to be drawn in the particular case'.

In making his decision on this particular clause, Bingham J declared that it did not matter that a carrier might be held to have no liability for errors of navigation unless they were negligent: 'the important question was whether he could seek protection against the possibility of such liability'. The clause itself contained no reference to negligence nor any synonym therefor. That, said Bingham J, was 'not fatal to the owners' argument, but it did mean that their task was a heavy one'. He noted that 'error' was essentially neutral, and was not 'primarily suggestive of negligence'.

However, he felt incapable of overlooking the fact that the form was amended to exclude the Hague Rules, which provided protection against negligent errors of navigation. It was also the case that the clause specified certain events, such as Act of God or restraint of princes, which were plainly inconsistent with negligence; and none of the specified events was clearly indicative of negligence (fire, dangers and accidents of the seas). The judge also took note of an earlier case where the use of the word 'fire' was held not to cover fire caused by negligence.[86] Fire was a result whereas 'errors of navigation' carried one into the minds of the owners. That made the lack of any express reference to negligence more striking. The inevitable conclusion, therefore, was that the clause was not apt to cover negligence liability.

2 Some special exclusion clauses

(a) 'With all faults'

Where the phrase 'with all faults' has been employed, or some equivalent, the view seems to be that this relates to merchantability or fitness for purpose, and does not offset the duty to supply goods, this being the core of the contract, which correspond with their description. In *Shepherd* v *Kain*,[87] there was a sale of a 'copper-fastened vessel', this being sold 'with all faults, without allowance for any defect whatsoever'. The court held that this did not suffice to protect the seller where what was delivered was not even a copper-fastened vessel.

(b) Excluding or limiting the damages recoverable

Where a clause provides for a precise sum to be recovered by way of damages in the event of a breach, that clause will be enforceable if it is a genuine pre-estimate of the likely loss; but it will be ineffective if it is a penalty clause and was inserted in terrorem, as an intended punishment in the event of breach.[88] On the other hand, a clause which places an upper limit on the damages recoverable (such as £ × thousand or 20 times the contract price) while still to be construed contra proferentem will not be construed quite as strictly as an exclusion clause properly so-called. This was made clear by the House of Lords in *Ailsa Craig Fishing* v *Malvern Fishing*.[89] According to Lord Wilberforce: 'Clauses of limitation are not regarded by the courts with the same hostility as clauses of exclusion: this is because they must be related to other contractual terms, in particular to the risks to which the defending party may be exposed, the remuneration which he receives, and possibly also the opportunity of the other party to insure'.[90] Since it is not entirely clear why such considerations are not relevant when considering clauses of exclusion, perhaps more weight should be given to Lord Fraser's explanation for a more sympathetic view of limitation clauses. He argued that cases expounding principles of strict construction 'are not applicable when considering the effect of clauses merely limiting liability. Such clauses will of course be read contra proferentem and must be clearly expressed, but there is no reason why they should be judged by the specially exacting standards which are applied to exclusion and indemnity clauses. The reason for imposing such standards on these clauses is the inherent improbability that the other party to a contract including such a clause intended to release the proferens from a liability that would otherwise fall upon him'.[91] In this case, there was also the special factor that, as a contract clause itself made clear, the potential losses which could derive from negligence were great in relation to the sum that could be charged by the proferens for its services.[92]

Where the clause excludes any right to damages, the tendency is to restrict it, if possible, to minor matters, or to limit its effect to forbidding rejection or to confining a buyer to claiming a return of the purchase price and nothing beyond. It does seem, however, that if the clause clearly applies to a contractual duty, it will be effective to deny a party any claim to damages.[93]

(c) Imposing time limits

Clauses which require proceedings to be commenced, or defects to be notified, within a certain time are interpreted strictly. In *Atlantic Shipping and Trading* v *Dreyfus*,[94] a clause in a charterparty required a claim to be made, and an arbitrator appointed, within three months of final discharge. This was held only to apply to the express terms of the contract and not to those implied by implication of law. It has been maintained that there is 'no reason why [such clauses] should not be drafted so as to apply to even the most serious breaches, for (unless the period is so short that they effectively bar a right altogether) they do not exclude liability, they simply require that buyers take vigilant steps to finalise transactions'.[95]

(d) Excluding the right to reject

Where clauses purport to exclude an otherwise existing right to reject the goods, it is clear enough that they do not of themselves exclude the right to damages.[96] Since it is for breach of warranty that the right to reject does not exist, it is supposed that the effect of such clauses is to indicate that the terms to which they apply are warranties, not conditions. This is supported by *Re Walkers, Winser & Hamm and Shaw*[97] in which such a clause was said to prevent an implied condition arising, and to render it a warranty instead.

(e) Relevance of contract description

It seems to be established that certain exclusion clauses only operate where goods of the contract description have been supplied. A clause excluding the right to reject the goods 'herein specified' is effective only when the goods 'herein specified' have in fact been supplied, but not when the goods do not conform with their description. In *Aron* v *Comptoir Wegimont*,[98] the clause ran: 'whatever the difference of the shipment may be in value from the grade, type or description specified, it is understood that any such question shall not entitle the buyer to reject the delivery. . . .' It was held that the terms as to shipment were independent and not part of the description so that rejection was still allowed.

(f) Arbitration

Arbitration clauses, since they are essentially procedural, can be ignored, subject to the power of the court to grant a stay under s 4 (1) of the Arbitration Act 1950. This provision, which has no application to Scotland or Northern Ireland, states that any party to an arbitration agreement may, after the commencement of legal proceedings, ask for a stay of proceedings. Such a stay may (not must) be granted if the court is satisfied that the applicant is ready and willing to do all that is necessary for the proper conduct of the arbitration. It is added, however, that where 'a time limit is involved, this aspect of the clause counts as an exemption, unless the time limit only relates to the appointment of the arbitrator and does not bar the right to action'.[99]

(g) Giving an acknowledgement

In the leading case of *Lowe* v *Lombank*,[100] a clause in a hire purchase contract contained an acknowledgement that the goods were examined, found to be free of defects and to be of merchantable quality. It also contained an acknowledgement that the particular purpose for which the goods were wanted had not been revealed to the owner. Such clauses will not be conclusive, unless genuinely representing the intention of the parties. An estoppel might arise against the buyer or hirer, however, even where he had not examined the goods, provided the seller thought on reasonable grounds that he had.[101]

3 Whether exclusion clauses are available to third parties

Questions can, and frequently do, arise as to whether an exclusion clause can operate to protect a person who is not a party to the contract. The basic rule, as might be predicted, is that the notion of privity of contract prevents non-parties from receiving any benefits or burdens which might be terms of an agreement made between others. In *Adler* v *Dickson*,[102] a ticket for a sea voyage contained terms exempting the shipping company from liability. One such term provided that 'the company will not be responsible for any injury whatsoever . . . arising from or occasioned by the negligence of the company's servants'. The plaintiff, having fallen from the gangway, brought an action against the master and boatswain. The Court of Appeal held that reliance could not be placed on the exclusion clause because, on its true construction, it did not purport to offer exemption to these parties. If the clause had on such a construction extended to the master and the boatswain, a majority of the Court were still prepared to hold it unavailing. The 'company's servants', declared Jenkins LJ 'are not parties to the contract'.[103]

A similar finding was made in *Cosgrove* v *Horsfall*.[104] The plaintiff had a free pass for buses run by the London Passenger Transport Board, of which he was an employee. The terms of the pass were that neither the Board nor their servants were to be liable to the holder for injuries however caused. The plaintiff suffered personal injuries as the result of the negligence of the defendant bus driver whom he sued personally. The Court of Appeal held the driver liable. He could not claim the benefit of the exemption clause as he was not a party to the contract.

This strict view eventually received endorsement by the House of Lords in *Scruttons* v *Midland Silicones*.[105] A contract for the carriage of drum chemicals from the United States to the United Kingdom contained a clause limiting the liability of the carriers. When the chemicals were being unloaded, they were damaged through the negligence of a firm of stevedores who were employed by the carriers. Lord Denning considered that the appellant stevedores could claim the benefit of the exclusion clause since the respondents, the consignees, had assented to the limitation of liability; but his was a dissenting judgment. The majority held that the appellants could not claim the benefit of an exclusion clause when they were not parties to the contract. Although 'I may regret it', said Lord Reid, 'I find it impossible to deny the existence of the general rule that a stranger to a contract cannot in a question with either of the contracting parties take advantage of provisions of the contract, even when it is clear from the contract that some provision in it was intended to benefit him'.[106]

A leading authority has pointed out two ways that the strictness of these decisions might be avoided. Between businessmen, the decisions denying third parties the right to the benefit of exclusion clauses can be inconvenient and cause uncertainty. They tend to falsify the assumptions on which the parties are contracting, with special regard to the decision as to the risks against which each should insure.

The first suggestion is that use be made of the concept of agency.[107] It is a historical fact that railway companies in the previous century issued tickets containing exclusion clauses which were held valid against other such companies because the particular company was agent for the other companies or was agent for the passenger.[108] The passenger thus had a direct relationship with the other companies. In *Scruttons*, where the House of Lords left open the question whether the stevedores could have been protected if the carriers had contracted as agents on their behalf, Lord Reid saw a possibility of an agency argument succeeding if '(first) the bill of lading makes it clear that the stevedore is intended to be protected by the provisions in it which limits liability, (secondly) the bill of lading makes it clear that the carrier, in addition to contracting for these provisions on his own behalf, is also contracting as agent for the stevedore that these provisions should apply to the stevedore, (thirdly) the carrier has authority from the stevedore to do that, or perhaps later ratification by the stevedore would suffice, and (fourthly) that any difficulties about consideration moving from the stevedore were overcome'.[109]

The second suggestion relates to an implied contract. The circumstances of the case may indicate that a contract is made with the third parties on the terms of that between the actual parties to the agreement. In *Pyrene* v *Scindia Navigation*,[110] the plaintiffs in England sold goods to parties in India. The latter agreed with the defendants for the carriage of the goods to India. The contract of carriage limited liability to £200. The goods were damaged because of the defendants' negligence. The plaintiffs sued the defendants for £900. Devlin J held that the plaintiffs were bound by the clause.

Although not parties to the contract, they were entitled to its benefits and so must also accept its burdens. Viscount Simonds later said that the decision could be supported 'only upon the facts of the case, which may well have justified the implication of a contract between the parties'.[111] As Anson says, the implied contract was that all three parties intended the plaintiffs to participate in the contract of carriage.

In addition to such methods of avoiding the decision of the House of Lords, yet other authors have pointed to shortcomings in the judgment itself.[112] In particular, the law lords relied on overseas decisions which really rested on the basis that the clauses were inappropriately worded, rather than that the clauses did not extend to third parties.[113]

Most importantly, the decision, say the authors, is 'not easy to reconcile with the earlier decision',[114] that in *Elder Dempster* v *Patterson Zochonis*.[115] Charterers had agreed to carry oil from West Africa to England. They chartered a vessel for this purpose. The bills of lading, made between the plaintiffs and the charterers, contained a term purporting to protect both charterers and shipowners from claims arising out of bad stowage. When the oil was lost because of such stowage, the plaintiffs sued both charterers and shipowners.

It was held by the House of Lords that both parties were protected by the clause. Precisely why the House thought this to be so is unclear: indeed, in *Scruttons* v *Midland Silicones*, no attempt to uncover the ratio was made in view of its very obscurity.[116] Anson states that the most likely ratio appears to be that there was an implied contract between plaintiffs and shipowners, the terms of which incorporated the exclusions and limitations contained in the bill of lading.[117]

An alternative view was that of vicarious immunity, enunciated by Viscount Cave. This approach was to the effect that agents are entitled to any immunity conferred on their principals, and that this applied to the shipowners since they took possession on behalf of, and as agents of, the charterers.[118] Certainly, this line appealed to Scrutton LJ, not the least because he had enunciated this opinion in the Court of Appeal in this case,[119] and which he later repeated, citing the decision of the House of Lords, in *Mersey Shipping* v *Rea*.[120] Where there is a contract, he said, 'which contains an exemption clause, the servants or agents who act under the contract have the benefit of the exemption clause ... they can claim the protection of the contract made with their employers on whose behalf they are acting'.[121]

This particular approach cannot be said to have survived *Scruttons* v *Midland Silicones*. Even so, it now appears that the courts will strive to bring third parties within exclusion clauses and so bring the law closer to the commercial realities of the situation.

This is well evidenced by the majority opinion of the Privy Council in *New Zealand Shipping* v *Satterthwaite*.[122] The consignor loaded goods for carriage to the plaintiff consignee in New Zealand. Carriage was subject to a bill of lading issued by the carrier's agent which contained an exclusion clause purporting to operate, inter alia, for the benefit for the servants, agents and independent contractors of, and employed by, the carriers. After the plaintiff became holder of the bill of lading, the cargo was damaged through the negligence of the defendant stevedores, employed by the carriers to unload the goods in New Zealand. A bare majority of the Privy Council believed that the defendant was entitled to rely on the exclusion clause. The argument was that the exclusion was designed to cover the whole carriage from loading to discharge. The bill of lading brought a bargain into existence, initially unilateral, between the consignor and the defendant, made through the carrier as agent. That became a full contract when the defendant provided services by discharging the goods, for such performance for the consignor was the consideration for the agreement by the consignor that the defendant should have the benefit of the exclusion clause in the bill of lading. It did not matter that the defendant was already obliged to the carrier to perform those services, since the plaintiff thereby received the benefit of a direct obligation which he could enforce. Since Lord Reid had recognised that in this argument there was 'a possibility of success of the agency argument',[123] the Privy Council opinion could be presented as in accord with existing precedent.

That this case is a move away from the spirit of *Scruttons* v *Midland Silicones* is, however, undoubted; and the movement is given further momentum by the decision of Donaldson J in *Johnson Matthey* v *Constantine Terminals*.[124] Very broadly, goods were bailed by *A* to *B* who sub-bailed them to *C*. The goods were stolen. The question arose whether *C* could rely on the exclusion clause in the contract between himself and *B* when sued by *A* in negligence. There was no contractual nexus between *A* and *C*. It was accepted that if *A* could sue without alleging a bailment the decision in *Scruttons* v *Midland Silicones* would prevail; but that if *C*'s duty arose only on the bailment, the whole contract of bailment, including the exclusion clause would prevail.

Donaldson J found that *C*'s duty to *A* arose solely out of the bailment and made it clear that the principle is limited to the special facts of the case. Strictly, therefore, the decision of the House of Lords is unaffected; but it is more truthful to recognise that it has been 'undermined' since the doctrine of privity of contract was 'basic to that decision'.[125]

Further evidence of a movement away from the House of Lords is found in the Canadian decision in *Eisen and Metal AG* v *Ceres Stevedoring*.[126] *P* owned a container filled with scrap and arranged for its delivery to Montreal aboard a vessel owned by *T* under a bill of lading containing a clause protecting the carriers against the negligent acts and defaults of their servants or agents. The container was delivered to *D*, the terminal operators, who left it unguarded and exposed, so that it was stolen. *D* relied on the exclusion clause. Citing the view of Lord Wilberforce, that giving effect to 'the clear intentions of a commercial document' meant giving effect to the exclusion clause, Owen J found that the defendants in the case before him came within this reasoning and hence the clause prevailed.[127]

It is only fair to say, however, that this view has not gone unchecked. In *Herrick* v *Leonard & Dingley*,[128] McMullin J distinguished the opinion of the Privy Council in that the document before him did not purport to include independent contractors, such as the defendant stevedores; and the stevedores had neither authorised nor ratified any attempt by the carrier to limit the former's liability to the plaintiff cargo owner. Again, in *The Suleyman Stalskiy*,[129] Schultz J pointed out that in the case before the Privy Council the authority of the carrier to contract as agent of the stevedore was admitted, whereas it was not in the case before him. It has also been suggested that a stevedore who is ignorant of the terms of a bill of lading until after unloading the goods should not be capable of ratifying a contract made on its behalf by the carrier. In the Privy Council case, the stevedore received the bill two weeks prior to unloading: the stevedore was also the owner of the carrier and habitually did the latter's stevedoring work. A learned reviewer has thus argued that the opinion of the Privy Council was given on a case resting on an 'occasional, and unusual, fact situation'.[130] It is still thought the better view, however, to regard the wish of the courts to accord with commercial realities, and hence to give effect to exclusion clauses, as having the upper hand.

In Scotland, as in England, the primary rule is that only a party to a contract can sue under it. There is an exception to this rule in the law of Scotland where it can be shown that the object of the contract is to benefit a third party. This is the *jus quaesitum tertio*.[131] No direct authority on the application of this principle in the context of exclusion clauses in Scotland exists. The absence of a doctrine of consideration in Scots Law would appear to remove one of the obstacles which may confront third parties seeking judicial support in England for claims to the benefit of exclusion clauses.

1 [1923] 1 KB 457.
2 *Ibid* at p 466. The reference is to *Elderslie Steamship* v *Borthwick* [1905] AC 93, 96.
3 [1949] 2 All ER 581.
4 [1911] AC 394.
5 Since property had passed. This provision was amended by s 4 (1) of the Misrepresentation Act 1967.
6 [1924] All ER Rep 155.
7 *Ibid* at p 158.
8 *Ibid.*
9 *Ibid* at p 160.
10 [1948] 2 All ER 127.
11 [1953] 2 All ER 1049.
12 (1927) 43 TLR 323.
13 *Ibid* at p 324.
14 [1968] 2 All ER 444.
15 *Ibid* at pp 462–3.
16 *Ibid* at p 482.
17 [1924] AC 43. Reference was made earlier to the Court of Appeal decision: *supra* p 19.
18 *Ibid* at p 50.
19 [1952] 1 TLR 499.
20 [1921] 3 KB 387.
21 See generally Chapter 6.
22 See Cheshire & Fifoot, *Law of Contract* (10th ed) pp 145–6.
23 [1953] 2 All ER 1021.
24 [1982] 2 Lloyd's Rep 42; [1981] 2 Lloyd's Rep 659.
25 [1981] 2 Lloyd's Rep 665.
26 *Supra* note 23 at p 1025.
27 [1982] 2 Lloyd's Rep 46.
28 [1952] 1 All ER 305.
29 *Ibid* at p 310. See too *Rutter* v *Palmer* [1922] 2 KB 87, 92 *per* Scrutton LJ.
30 *Ibid* at p 313.
31 *Supra* notes 25, 26.
32 [1981] 2 Lloyd's Rep 665.
33 [1982] 2 Lloyd's Rep 45.
34 [1982] 2 Lloyd's Rep 46.
35 *Supra* notes 25, 26.
36 *Supra* note 34.
37 *Ibid.*

38 [1982] 2 Lloyd's Rep 49.
39 [1982] 2 Lloyd's Rep 51.
40 [1972] 1 All ER 399.
41 See the discussion, *supra* at p 12.
42 *Supra* note 40 at p 406.
43 *Ibid* at p 408.
44 *Ibid*.
45 *Ibid* at p 409.
46 See Barendt, (1972) 35 MLR 644, 646–7.
47 [1922] 2 KB 87.
48 *Ibid* at p 90.
49 *Ibid* at p 92.
50 *Supra* note 40.
51 *Ibid* at p 405.
52 (1872) LR 8 QB 57.
53 *Ibid* at p 59. See Atkin LJ, *supra* note 47, at pp 94–5.
54 *Supra* note 47 *per* Bankes LJ at p 91. See too Scrutton LJ, *ibid*, at p 93.
55 *Ibid* at p 93 *per* Scrutton LJ.
56 *Ibid*.
57 [1945] 1 All ER 244.
58 *Ibid* at p 247.
59 *Ibid*.
60 *Ibid*.
61 Where liability rests on liability alone 'the clause must be construed as extending to that head of damage'—*ibid* at p 244.
62 *Supra* p 28.
63 [1982] 2 Lloyd's Rep 42.
64 *Ibid* at p 49.
65 [1973] 1 All ER 193.
66 Buckley LJ noted that the principles for construing exclusion and indemnity clauses are the same—*ibid* at p 204.
67 *Ibid* at p 203.
68 *Ibid*. See too Stephenson LJ *supra* note 63 at p 51.
69 [1973] 1 All ER 193 at p 204 *per* Buckley LJ.
70 *Ibid* at p 205.
71 [1978] 1 All ER 18.
72 *Supra* p 24.
73 *Supra* note 65 at p 205.
74 [1981] 2 Lloyd's Rep 659; [1982] 2 Lloyd's Rep 42.
75 [1982] 2 Lloyd's Rep 45–6.
76 *Ibid* at p 48.
77 *Ibid*.
78 [1982] SLT 377.
79 Upholding the decision reported at [1981] SLT 130.
80 *Supra* note 78 at p 380.
81 *Ibid* at p 383.
82 [1980] 1 All ER 556; [1978] 3 All ER 146.
83 [1978] 3 All ER 146, 160.
84 *Ibid*.

85 (1982) *Financial Times*, 11 November.

86 *Re Polemis and Furness Withy* [1921] 3 KB 560.

87 (1821) 5 B&A 240.

88 Cheshire & Fifoot, *op cit*, pp 556–9.

89 [1982] SLT 377.

90 *Ibid* at p 380. See the doubts, however, of Lord Denning in *George Mitchell (Chesterhall) Ltd* v *Finney Lock Seeds* [1983] 1 All ER 108, 116.

91 *Ibid* at p 382.

92 *Ibid*.

93 See *Wilkinson* v *Barclay* [1946] 2 All ER 337.

94 [1922] All ER 559.

95 *Benjamin's Sale of Goods* (2nd ed) para 980.

96 *Szymonowski* v *Beck* [1923] 1 KB 457.

97 [1904] 2 KB 152.

98 [1921] 3 KB 435.

99 Benjamin, *op cit*, para 982.

100 [1960] 1 All ER 611.

101 See too *Cremdeam Properties* v *Nash* (1977) 244 EG 547. See too Benjamin, *op cit*. For the best treatment of special exclusion clauses, Benjamin, to which the above is in considerable debt, is the best of texts.

102 [1954] 3 All ER 397.

103 *Ibid* at p 403.

104 (1945) 62 TLR 140.

105 [1962] 1 All ER 1.

106 *Ibid* at p 10.

107 Anson, *Law of Contract* (25th ed) pp 182–3.

108 *Ibid* at p 182.

109 *Ibid* at pp 182–3.

110 [1954] 2 All ER 158.

111 See *Scruttons* v *Midland Silicones, supra* note 105 at p 9.

112 Cheshire & Fifoot, *op cit*, pp 147–151.

113 The cases are: *Krawill Machinery Corporation* v *Herd* [1959] 1 Lloyd's Rep 305 (USA); *Wilson* v *Darling Island Stevedoring* [1956] 1 Lloyd's Rep 346 (Australia).

114 *Supra* note at p 112, 148.

115 [1924] AC 522.

116 Supra note 105 at p 7 *per* Viscount Simonds.

117 *Op cit*, p 180.

118 *Supra* note 115 at p 534.

119 [1923] 1 KB 420, 441–2.

120 (1925) 21 Ll LR 375.

121 *Ibid* at p 378.

122 [1974] 1 All ER 1015.

123 *Scruttons* v *Midland Silicones, supra* note 105, at p 10.

124 [1976] 2 Lloyd's Rep 215.

125 (1977) 40 MLR 706, 708. See too *Haseldine* v *Daw* [1941] 2 KB 343.

126 [1977] 1 Lloyd's Rep 665.

127   *Ibid* at p 671.
128   [1975] 2 NZLR 566.
129   [1976] 2 Lloyd's Rep 609 (Canada).
130   (1977) 40 MLR 709, 711.
131   See T B Smith *Short Commentaries on the Law of Scotland* pp 177 *et seq.*

Chapter 3

Avoidance and Qualification of Exclusion Clauses

In this chapter, we shall be discussing the methods by which the courts seek to avoid giving full effect to exclusion clauses, notwithstanding that the clause has been incorporated into the contract and is apt to cover the damage which has occurred. Particular attention will be paid to the doctrine of fundamental breach.

1 Onus of proof

In *Levison* v *Patent Steam Carpet Cleaning Co*,[1] the terms of a contract for the cleaning of a carpet contained a clause reading 'All merchandise is expressly accepted at the owner's risk'. The carpet was lost, presumably stolen. The defendants, pointing to the exclusion clause, argued that it clearly covered the case in hand because, on the balance of probabilities, the loss was due to their negligence: and that the burden of proof lay on the plaintiffs to prove their case that the carpet had been lost because of a fundamental breach, the latter not being covered by the exclusion clause.

The Court of Appeal held unanimously that the burden of proof in this case lay upon the defendants. A bailee, Lord Denning MR declared, must prove all the circumstances in which the loss or damage occurred. If no explanation is forthcoming, then it is quite likely that the loss or damage was due to a fundamental breach of contract such as theft or delivery to the wrong address. The defendants were in the best position to provide an answer and the onus of proof, which they had failed to discharge, accordingly lay on them.[2]

This was assented to by Orr LJ who found that as a matter both 'of justice and of common sense', the burden properly rested on the defendants who were 'both more likely to know the facts and in a better position to ascertain them than the bailor'.[3] Similarly, it was the view of Sir David Cairns that 'however difficult it may sometimes be for a bailee to prove a negative, he is at least in a better position than the bailor to know what happened to the goods while in his possession'.[4]

In reaching this decision, the court had to face certain difficulties caused by the decision of an earlier Court of Appeal in *Hunt & Winterbottom* v *B R S* (*Parcels*).[5] Goods which had been entrusted to a carrier were lost. It was held that the carrier could rely on a limitation clause without disproving fundamental breach. In *Woolmer* v *Delmer Price*,[6] on the other hand, the defendants had agreed to store a fur coat 'at customer's risk'. The coat was lost in a way not explained and the defendants were held liable as the duty was on them to show that the loss was not due to their fundamental breach.

Some doubt was cast on the correctness of this decision in the *Hunt & Winterbottom* case, although distinguished on the slender ground that it was a case of deposit not carriage.[7] Furthermore, the court there left open the possibility that where fundamental breach was specifically pleaded, as most significantly it was *not* in the *Hunt & Winterbottom* case, the onus falls upon the bailee.[8] Sir David Cairns found this important in *Levison* v *Patent Steam Carpet Cleaning Co*,[9] while Lord Denning MR and Orr LJ found nothing in the *Hunt & Winterbottom* case to prevent them finding as they did. It is significant that Sir David Cairns drew attention to Lord Denning's remarks in *Spurling* v *Bradshaw*[10] where he said: 'A bailor, by pleading and presenting his case properly, can always put the burden of proof on the bailee'.[11] This, the best answer to the problem, is supported by Treitel: 'It may be doubted whether a plaintiff can throw the burden of proof on the defendant by *merely* pleading fundamental breach. But the burden might pass to the defendant if the plaintiff could support his allegation by *some* evidence that the defendant *might* have been guilty of a fundamental breach.'[12] This is just what happened in *Levison's* case.

2 Liability for fraud

It is abundantly clear that the courts will not allow a contracting party to exclude liability for his own fraud. It is true that this has never actually fallen for decision, and that a fractionally obstructive decision exists in *Tullis* v *Jacson*.[13] Here, the parties to a building contract agreed to submit disputes to arbitration, the arbitrator's award to be final, and it was not to be set aside for 'any pretence, suggestion, charge or insinuation of fraud'. An attempt to challenge the award on the ground that it was not made in good faith was defeated because of this term.

This decision was plainly regarded as incorrect by Scrutton LJ in *Czarnikow* v *Roth*[14] and, in any case, plainly does not cover the case of a person seeking to exclude liability for his own fraud. There are, furthermore, the robust observations of the House of Lords in *Pearson & Son* v *Dublin Corporation*.[15] The plaintiffs undertook to execute works for the corporation on the faith of plans supplied by the latter. The agreement provided that the plaintiffs should satisfy themselves as to the accuracy of the plans. It was held that this term would not avail to protect the corporation if the plans were fraudulent. It was said by Lord Loreburn that 'no one can escape liability for his own fraudulent statements by inserting in a contract a clause that the other party shall not rely upon them', though he left open the possibility that an innocent party could guard himself 'by apt and express clauses' from liability for the fraud of his own agents.[16] Lord Halsbury agreed that 'no craft or machinery in the form of contract can estop a person who complains that he has been defrauded from having that question of fact submitted to a jury'.[17] Lord James added that: 'When the fraud succeeds, surely those who designed the fraudulent protection cannot take advantage of it ... As a general principle I incline to the view that an express term that fraud shall not vitiate a contract would be bad in law ...'[18] It is, however, clear that an exclusion clause will, if properly drafted, provide cover against deliberate acts.[19]

3 Liability for breach of fiduciary duty

It is submitted by Treitel that any attempt by a person under a fiduciary duty to contract out of liability for a wilful default in that duty would be ineffective.[20] This argument, surely correct, is based on the fact that the promoter of a company, who is under a fiduciary duty not to profit from the promotion without disclosing it, cannot contract out of that duty.[21]

4 Liability for breach of rules of natural justice

Treitel cites a number of dicta of Lord Denning to the effect that the rules of domestic tribunals purporting to oust the rules of natural justice would be ineffective.[22] Although Treitel offers no comment, it is thought that Lord Denning's views are surely right.[23]

5 Oral undertakings

This method of evading the full impact of exclusion clauses can be usefully introduced by reference to *Couchman* v *Hill*.[24] The catalogue for a sale by auction described certain heifers as 'unserved'. The document also contained an exclusion clause, stipulating that 'all lots must be taken subject to all faults or errors of description (if any) and no compensation will be paid for the same'. Similar terms were contained in the conditions of sale exhibited at the auction rooms. The plaintiff orally requested the defendant to confirm that a particular heifer was unserved, which confirmation was duly given. After the sale, the heifer was found to be in calf and died as a result of carrying a calf too young. It was held that the oral declaration overrode the exclusion clause and that the plaintiff was entitled to damages.[25]

A similar decision was reached in *SS Ardennes* (*Cargo Owners*) v *Ardennes* (*Owners*).[26] The plaintiffs shipped cargo to England from Spain on the defendants' vessel. An oral promise was made by the latter to the effect that the voyage would be direct to England. The written terms of the bill of lading allowed the defendants to reach London 'by any route and whether directly or indirectly'. In fact, the vessel did not proceed directly to London, going instead via Antwerp. It was held that the oral promise was binding.

In both these cases, the oral promise directly contradicted the written exclusion clauses. It is clear, however, that the courts are still prepared to find that an exclusion clause has been overridden by an oral promise, even where that contradiction is not so glaring. A good example is *Mendelssohn* v *Normand*.[27] The plaintiff left his car at a garage owned by the defendants. An exclusion clause disclaimed liability for any loss, however caused: it was further provided that the terms of the agreement could only be varied if made in writing and signed by the management. On the relevant occasion, the attendant told him that the doors were not to be locked and that he, the attendant, would lock them himself. He did not and the luggage was stolen.

It was held that the attendant's promise was not within his actual authority, it nevertheless lay within his ostensible authority, and hence bound his employers, the garage owners.[28] It was held that this rendered the exclusion clauses ineffective. The reason was that 'the oral promise or representation has a decisive influence on the transaction—it is the very thing which induces the other to contract and it would be most unjust to allow the maker to go back on it. The printed condition is rejected because it is repugnant to the express oral promise or representation'.[29] Phillimore LJ observed that the plaintiff 'was clearly concerned about his luggage and ... was induced to leave the car there by the firm promise that it would be locked'.[30] Hence, the printed clauses must fail 'insofar as they are repugnant to the express undertaking'.[31]

For all that these words are robustly put, the element of repugnance is not easily discernible, especially when a comparison is made with *Couchman* v *Hill*. This point emerges even more clearly when we discuss below a more recent case involving these matters.

The particular case is yet another decision of the Court of Appeal, that in *Evans & Son* v *Andrea Merzario*.[32] The plaintiffs imported machines from Italy, habitually using the defendants as forwarding agents. Prior to 1967, transportation of the machines was always done below deck to avoid the problems of rust. In that year, the defendants proposed a changeover to containers. The plaintiffs obtained an oral assurance that the machines would continue to be shipped below deck, and accordingly agreed to containerisation. In the present case, it appeared that, because of an oversight, the machines were shipped above deck and were lost overboard in a heavy swell.

The plaintiffs sued upon the oral promise. The defendants countered that the printed terms of their agreement gave them the right to use whatever method of carriage they desired, that it excluded liability except for wilful neglect or default, and that the amount of damages was also limited by the printed terms. Lord Denning took the view that the oral agreement constituted a collateral contract, the consideration for this being the entry into the transportation contract.[33] There was a clear breach of this oral contract unless, the Master of the Rolls said, the printed exclusion clauses applied. Repeating what he had said in the previous case, that the printed condition is ineffective because repugnant to the oral promise, he found in favour of the plaintiffs.

It is difficult entirely to accept this explanation. If the oral promise is a separate, albeit collateral contract, there should surely be no need to inspect the terms of the printed contract: this is relevant only insofar as it furnishes consideration for the oral promise. In any case, such repugnance as there is surely relates only to the printed term concerning the right of the forwarding agents to ship as they chose, and not to the exclusion and limitation clauses.

Roskill LJ, especially, and Geoffrey Lane LJ, rejected a solution based on a collateral contract. Roskill LJ found there to be one entire contract, partly oral, partly written and partly a matter of conduct. Taken thus, the oral promise must be taken as overriding the exempting conditions, otherwise 'the promise would be illusory'.[34]

Geoffrey Lane LJ regarded the oral agreement as a new term of the agreement. He held that this must override the clause as to the method of carriage as they 'are logically inconsistent with each other' though this scarcely explains why it is the written term which is to be deleted.[35] As for the remaining clauses, they too were ineffective: any other conclusion 'would be to destroy the business efficacy of the new agreement from the day it started'.[36]

It is submitted that the arguments are wholly unconvincing where the two Courts of Appeal are dealing with clauses not wholly antithetical. What in fact we see here is yet another device aimed at avoiding the full impact of an exclusion clause. It is not, further-more, a device yet tested in the House of Lords.

6 Misrepresenting the effects of a term

Where the full effects of an exclusion clause have been misrep-resented, that misrepresentation will be effective to qualify the terms of the clause as it originally stood. This may be looked upon as a species of the oral undertakings discussed immediately above.

The leading case is *Curtis* v *Chemical Cleaning and Dyeing*.[37] The plaintiff took to the defendants' shop a white satin wedding dress for cleaning. She was asked to sign a receipt which contained a clause exempting the defendants from all liability for damage to articles cleaned. She was given a document which she was asked to sign. She asked for an explanation of its contents and was told that it exempted the defendants from certain risks, and, in the present instance, from the risk of damage to the beads and sequins on the dress. The plaintiff then signed the document, which in fact con-tained a clause exempting the defendants from liability for 'any damage, however caused'. When the dress was returned, it was stained: in the subsequent action, the defendants placed reliance on this clause.

The Court of Appeal held that the defendants were liable in damages, and that no regard could be placed on the exclusion clause. According to Somervell LJ, 'owing to the misrepresentation the exception never became part of the contract between the parties'.[38] Denning LJ made the further point that it was quite irrelevant whether the misrepresentation was innocent or fraudulent.

The reasoning of this case was endorsed in *Jaques* v *Lloyd D*

George & Partners.[39] The plaintiff wished to sell his cafe and orally agreed with the defendants, a firm of estate agents, to sell for £2,500 cash. The defendants told the plaintiff that if they found a purchaser and the deal went through, their commission would be £250. The plaintiff signed a printed contract which gave the defendants the right to their commission if the latter found a person 'willing' to sign a contract to purchase. An introduction was made to a willing purchaser but the plaintiff's landlord, finding the references unsatisfactory, declined to proceed. The defendants, relying on the printed terms, claimed the commission.

Finding against the defendants, Lord Denning MR remarked upon the principle that 'an estate agent cannot rely on the printed form when his agent misrepresents the content or effect of the form'.[40] Edmund Davies LJ agreed, pointing to *Curtis* v *Chemical Cleaning and Dyeing*. The same approach could be applied here, he declared: 'Their agent having misrepresented the position, it was not open to them to insist on payment . . .'[41]

The decisions of these two Courts of Appeal represented acceptance of earlier dicta. In *L'Estrange* v *Graucob*,[42] Scrutton LJ had noted that a signed contract was binding on the signatory, regardless of whether he had read its terms or not. This, the lord justice said, applied provided there was no fraud or misrepresentation.[43] Furthermore, Denning LJ had also argued in *Dennis Reed* v *Goody*[44] that if a clause in an estate agent's contract had been misconstrued to the signatory, the courts might well not enforce it.[45]

Predictably, Lord Denning also appears to have attempted considerably to advance the boundaries of this particular principle. In *Dennis Reed* v *Goody*, he appeared to take the view that if a person believes that a contract contains no exceptional clauses when it does, and the other party offers no explanation of the contract, this is tantamount to a misrepresentation of the terms.[46] In *Jaques* v *Lloyd D George & Partners*, Lord Denning made it clear that such indeed was his view. If an estate agent, he said, seeks to depart from ordinary and well-understood contractual terms, he must take care to explain the effect to the client. In the absence of such explanation, the estate agent would be precluded from enforcing a term which is 'unreasonable or oppressive'.[47]

7 Fundamental terms and fundamental breach

It is fair to say that Lord Devlin must be very much regarded as responsible for the introduction into the law of the expressions 'fundamental breach' and 'fundamental term'. In *Chandris* v *Isbrandtsen-Moller*,[48] the claim involved an action for demurrage where a charterer landed a dangerous cargo in breach of contract. Devlin J, as he then was, referred to a breach of 'some fundamental or basic condition of the contract', mentioning also a 'fundamental breach going to the root of the contract'.[49]

A second case was *Alexander* v *Railway Executive*.[50] Devlin J described the actions of a bailee in allowing unauthorised access to the goods as both 'a fundamental breach' and as a 'breach of a fundamental term'.[51]

His lordship's most unequivocal declaration came in *Smeaton Hanscomb* v *Sassoon I Setty*.[52] There he described a fundamental term as something 'narrower than a condition of the contract ... something which underlies the whole contract, so that, if it is not complied with, the performance becomes something totally different from that which the contract contemplates', such as the delivery of pine logs for mahogany logs.[53]

Although the Court of Appeal had indicated in *The Albion*[54] that the concept of breach of a fundamental term should be limited to what are called 'deviation cases',[55] where a vessel has deviated from an agreed route, this was not to be so. Within the ideas of a 'fundamental breach' and 'breach of a fundamental term' have been comprehended unseaworthiness, difference in kind on a sale of goods, and any other term which underlies the whole contract, so that if it were not complied with, the performance would become something totally different from that which was contemplated.[56]

This list of fundamental terms and breaches has been considerably augmented to include the undertakings as to title implied by s 12(1) of the Sale of Goods Act 1893 (now s 12(1) of the Sale of Goods Act 1979),[57] total failure of consideration,[58] and reckless or grossly negligent misconduct.[59]

So great was the attraction of these concepts as a way of avoiding undesirable exclusion clauses that a substantive rule of law virtually emerged to the effect that no exclusion clause was effective where the defendant was in fundamental breach or in breach of a fundamental term. In *Karsales (Harrow)* v *Wallis*,[60] Denning LJ put it this way: 'it is now settled that exempting clauses of this kind, no matter how widely they are expressed, only avail the party when he is carrying out his contract in its essential respects. He is not allowed to use them as a cover for misconduct or indifference or to enable him to turn a blind eye to his obligations. They do not avail him when he is guilty of a breach which goes to the root of the contract. It is necessary to look at the contract apart from the exempting clauses and see what are the terms, express or implied, which impose an obligation on the party. If he has been guilty of a breach of those obligations in a respect which goes to the very root of the contract, he cannot rely on the exempting clauses'.[61] More succinctly, a learned author observed that: 'A party who has been guilty of a fundamental breach of contract cannot rely on an exemption clause inserted in the contract to protect him.'[62]

Several cases illustrate the point. In the *Karsales* case[63] itself, a hire-purchase agreement provided that 'no condition or warranty that the vehicle is roadworthy, or as to its age, condition or fitness for any purpose is given by the owner or implied herein'. The car, in good order when inspected, was a wreck incapable of self-propulsion when delivered. It was held that the buyer was entitled to reject it.

In *Yeoman Credit* v *Apps*,[64] a car, the subject of a hire-purchase agreement, was subject to 'an accumulation of defects which, taken singly, might well have been within the exemption clause, but taken *en masse* constitute such a non-performance or repudiation or breach going to the root of the contract as disentitles the owners to take refuge behind an exception clause intended only to give protection to those breaches which are not inconsistent with and not destructive of the whole essence of the contract'.[65] Compare this decision with that of the Court of Appeal in *Smith* v *Lazarus*.[66] The Court of Appeal, overruling the judge of first instance, held that a car which was 'an almost valueless piece of machinery' was nonetheless a motor car, albeit one 'of very poor quality indeed'. It may be of significance that this was a private sale which did not concern the existence or interpretation of an exclusion clause.

In *Charterhouse Credit* v *Tolly*,[67] it was held that a serious defect in the back axle of a car let on hire-purchase constituted a fundamental breach of an implied term to supply a roadworthy car, so that exclusion clauses in the contract were quite unavailing. This decision probably pushed the doctrine of fundamental breach in England to its farthest point.

Scottish decisions, which in any case preferred the term 'material breach of contract', took the line that everything turned on the construction of the contract, so that liability could always be excluded or limited even in the event of such a breach.[68]

(a) A rule of construction

The doctrine of fundamental breach (which shall hereafter include breach of a fundamental term) has latterly been subject to some re-appraisal. In *UGS* v *National Mortgage Bank of Greece*,[69]

Pearson LJ put it as his view that there was 'a rule of construction that normally an exception or exclusion clause or similar provision in a contract should be construed as not applying to a situation created by a fundamental breach of contract. This is not an independent rule of law imposed by the court on the parties willy-nilly in disregard of their contractual intention. On the contrary it is a rule of construction based on the intention of the contracting parties'.[70]

This statement was unanimously endorsed by the House of Lords in *Suisse Atlantique Societe d'Armement Maritime SA* v *NV Rotterdamsche Kolen Centrale*[71] ('*Suisse Atlantique*' hereafter). A charterparty contained a clause limiting damages to $1,000 a day for each lay day beyond the permitted number of lay days. The number of excess days totalled 150, and liability was admitted in the sum of $150,000. The owners lost a much greater sum by way of profits foregone and so claimed for an amount in excess of $1,000 a day. They argued that the charterers, being in fundamental breach, could not rely on the exclusion clause.

The House of Lords held that the clause, in fact, was an agreed damages provision, and not an exclusion clause. But even if it were an exclusion clause, and assuming there to have been a fundamental breach, it was still held that the clause would have been effective. The main finding was that there was no rule of substantive law by which a fundamental breach, of itself, automatically disentitled a party from reliance on an exclusion clause. The doctrine of fundamental breach is one of construction only. It is simply 'an application of the principle that an exemption clause should not, in the absence of clear words, be construed to apply to breaches which tended to defeat the main purpose of the contract'.[72]

When determining whether an exclusion clause was to apply, Lord Reid insisted that such clauses were to be construed strictly and if ambiguous the narrower meaning was to be taken. Or it may appear that the terms of the clauses are so wide that they cannot be taken literally: that may be because this would 'lead to an absurdity or because it would defeat the main object of the contract or perhaps for other reasons'.[73] He went on to say that a strict construction will not always prevent exclusion clauses from covering a fundamental breach. The resources of the English language, he declared, are not so limited that 'it is impossible to devise an exclusion clause which will apply to at least some cases of fundamental breach without being so widely drawn that it can be cut down on any ground by applying ordinary principles of construction'.[74]

Lord Upjohn agreed, that, in relation to breach of a fundamental term, 'there is a strong, though rebuttable presumption that in inserting a clause of exclusion or limitation ... the parties are not contemplating breaches of fundamental terms ... This result has been achieved by a robust use of a well-known canon of construction, that wide words which in isolation would bear one meaning must be so construed as to give business efficacy to the contract and the presumed intention of the parties, upon the footing that both parties are intending to carry out the contract fundamentally'.[75]

(b) The decisions since Suisse Atlantique

It is not unfair to say that, notwithstanding the decision of the House of Lords, the Court of Appeal has come perilously close to restating the relationship of fundamental breach and exclusion clauses in terms once more of a substantive rule of law.

Consider, first, the case of *Mendelssohn* v *Normand*.[76] When leaving his vehicle at a car park, the owner was told to leave it unlocked. He did so, after receiving a promise from an attendant that the car would subsequently be locked. Certain luggage was stolen from the car.

One reason for ruling that the defendants could not rely on the exclusion clause was the finding that the oral promise of the attendant that he would lock the car, which he did not, took priority over the printed clause of the contract.[77] The other reason stated was that the exclusion clause could not apply because the contract was carried out in a way totally different from that envisaged. Lord Denning MR stated quite bluntly that exclusion clauses only apply when a party is 'carrying out his contract in the stipulated way and not when he is breaking it in a fundamental respect'.[78]

Although this can scarcely be said to be construing the exclusion clause, Lord Denning agreed with *Suisse Atlantique*, declaring that because this was a fundamental breach, the 'clause cannot be construed as extending to it'.[79] This is hardly the way the House of Lords approached the matter, and it is significant that neither of the other lord justices took this point at all.

Precisely the same approach was taken again by Lord Denning in *Farnworth Finance Facilities* v *Attryde*.[80] A motor cycle had been let out on hire purchase. It was supplied 'subject to no conditions or warranties whatsoever express or implied'. The motor cycle suffered a number of defects. Lord Denning cited the remarks of Pearson LJ that 'there is a rule of construction that normally an exception or exclusion clause ... should be construed as not applying to a situation created by a fundamental breach of contract',[81] adding (as was the case) that this had been approved as a statement of principle in *Suisse Atlantique*.[82] Lord Denning then purported to act on this principle, interpreting it to mean that 'we must see if there was a fundamental breach of contract. If there was, then the exempting condition should not be construed as applying to it. . . . If [the terms of the contract] were broken in a fundamental respect, the finance company cannot rely on the exception clauses'.[83] This, of course, is not exactly what Pearson LJ or the House of Lords said. While the lord justice had plainly said that 'normally' an exclusion clause will be inapplicable, Lord Denning has effectively read 'normally' as 'never'.

Fenton Atkinson LJ appeared to base his judgment on more acceptable grounds. He observed that in *Suisse Atlantique* Lord Wilberforce had regarded exclusion clauses as inapplicable when the parties had not contemplated such a mis-performance or could not be supposed to have provided against it without destroying 'the whole contractual sub-stratum'. Without saying so in terms, the lord justice appeared to consider that this met the instant case.[84]

(c) Affirmation of the contract

A substantial effort to re-establish the rule of law approach was made by the Court of Appeal in *Harbutt's 'Plasticine'* v *Wayne Tank and Pump Co.*[85] The defendants designed and installed equipment for storing and dispensing stearine at the plaintiff's factory. Because the defendants had specified an unsuitable material for the piping, a fire broke out on the first night of use, which destroyed the factory. The cost of reinstating the factory was £146,581. The defendants pleaded a clause limiting damages to £2,300.

The Court of Appeal unanimously held that the catastrophe could be adjudged a fundamental breach, notwithstanding that little remedial work would have been needed to cure the defect had it been discovered in time.[86] It was Lord Denning's view that this automatically terminated the contract.[87] Widgery and Cross LJJ preferred to view the contract as having been terminated by the innocent party (in accordance with standard principles of contract) at his option, though recognising that he had little sensible alternative.[88]

Importance was attached to the question of affirmation or termination because of Lord Reid's statement in *Suisse Atlantique*. Where the innocent party has elected to terminate the contract and sue for damages, 'the whole contract has ceased to exist including the exclusion clause, and I do not see how that clause can then be used to exclude an action for loss which will be suffered by the innocent party after it has ceased to exist'.[89] In *Suisse Atlantique* itself, the contract had been affirmed.

The Court of Appeal accepted this reasoning, though Lord Denning pointed out that the contract is terminated, as Lord Reid himself had indicated, only 'for the future'.[90] Yet this raises a problem in itself: for while the cost of building a new factory had been incurred, surely this related to loss caused prior to termination. Lord Reid had illustrated his declaration of principle by reference to the 'loss of profit which would have accrued if the contract had run its full term'.[91] This is a wholly different species of loss compared with the cost of making good damage arising before termination.

If the Court of Appeal is correct in its decision, it would appear to be a rule of law that exclusion clauses are inapplicable where a fundamental breach has been accepted as terminating the contract: those cases where a contract is affirmed despite the breach will be rare indeed.[92] Yet even limiting this principle to such loss as arises after termination of the contract, it can still be regarded as insupportable. As Treitel has pointed out, the disputed clause in *Suisse Atlantique* concerned itself only with damages, not termination: had it excluded the right to terminate on its true construction, repudiation could not have been accepted to put an end to the contract.[93] Anson also argues against there being any general principle that an accepted repudiation must nullify an exclusion clause. Attention is drawn to the remark of Lord Wilberforce that: 'An act which, apart from the exceptions clause, might be a breach sufficiently serious to justify refusal of further performance, may be reduced in effect, or made not a breach at all, by the terms of the clause'.[94] Anson concludes, and this is surely correct, that the operation of an exclusion clause should not be made to depend on affirmation or termination: 'in either case the validity of the clause should be determined by reference to the intention of the parties . . . by considering whether or not the clause, on its true construction, covers the event which has taken place'.[95]

An attempt to achieve a degree of compatibility between the later Court of Appeal decisions and *Suisse Atlantique* was made by Donaldson J in *Kenyon* v *Baxter Hoare*.[96] Warehousemen agreed to store bags of groundnuts. The nuts were placed in a warehouse which, while structurally sound, was not rat-proof. Despite there being clear signs that rats were present, the warehousemen took no positive action. When delivered to their owners, the bags were found to be heavily damaged and substantially contaminated.

The warehousemen relied on a clause excluding liability except where loss or damage arose from wilful neglect or default. Donaldson J pointed to the view put by Lord Wilberforce that a fundamental breach is one of two things: performance 'totally different' from that contemplated, or a breach of such gravity that the victim is at least entitled to refuse performance under the contract.[97] Donaldson J's opinion was that in respect of this second category, the problem was essentially one of construction, the question being whether or not the clause covers the particular breach: if the innocent party has terminated the agreement, the exclusion clause, he said, cannot apply.[98] In the first category, exclusion clauses cannot apply, even though, as a matter of construction, they might cover the particular breach. His lordship qualified this last remark, saying that if the contract was nevertheless affirmed, the clause would apply if it did cover the breach on its true construction.[99]

It has to be said that this approach strains *Suisse Atlantique* and the Court of Appeal decisions to the limit. For one thing, Lord Wilberforce was speaking very much for himself when he defined a fundamental breach, though certainly no exception was taken to his approach by the other law lords. For another, it is difficult to fit the decisions in *Farnworth Finance Facilities* v *Attryde* and *Harbutt's 'Plasticine'* v *Wayne Tank & Pump* into this scheme. Donaldson J maintained that they must come into Lord Wilberforce's first, or 'deviation', category, though this scarcely seems tenable.[100] One which does fall into this category, and which might be explained by Donaldson J's reasoning, is *Mendelssohn* v *Normand*,[101] but this case was not mentioned.

The instant case, Donaldson J decided, was covered by the exclusion clause since performance, while falling short of expectations, 'was not so deficient as to remove the sub-stratum of the contract and did not constitute either wilful neglect or default'.[102]

In any event, the contortions to which Donaldson J was driven in that case, have become of historical interest only in the wake of the ruling of the House of Lords in *Photo Production* v *Securicor Transport*.[103] An employee of a company charged with the task of ensuring the security of a factory deliberately lit a fire which, having got completely out of hand, destroyed the entire premises. In the Court of Appeal, it was held that this conduct, and its consequence, resulted in a fundamental breach which either discharged the contract or rendered it void, so that the exemption clauses only applied to liabilities incurred prior to the breach; or even that the breach destroyed the contract entirely and with it the effectiveness of the exemption clause.

The House of Lords were unanimous in reversing the decision which had been reached in the court below. Lord Wilberforce referred to the judgment of Lord Denning where the latter, referring to *Suisse Atlantique*, had declared that it 'affirms the long line of cases in this court that when one side has been guilty of a fundamental breach of contract ... and the other side accepts it, so that the contract comes to an end ... then the guilty party cannot rely on the exception or limitation clause to escape from liability for his breach'.[104] It was Lord Wilberforce's view that, properly read, *Suisse Atlantique* was 'directly opposed' to any such doctrine and that the effect of the judgments in that case 'was to repudiate it'.[105] For himself, he had no 'second thoughts as to the main proposition that the question whether, and to what extent, an exclusion clause is to be applied to a fundamental breach, or to a breach of a fundamental term, or indeed to any breach of contract, is a matter of construction of the contract'.[106] He was equally certain that *Harbutt's* case was unsound and must be overruled: and the 'ingenious' attempt by Donaldson J to reconcile the cases 'illustrates the contortions which that case has made necessary and would be unnecessary if it vanished as an authority'.[107] Furthermore, and probably finally the Court of Appeal in *George Mitchell (Chesterhall) Ltd v Finney Lock Seeds*[107a] at last accepted defeat and agreed that the question whether or not an exclusion clause covered a fundamental breach fell only to be treated as a matter of construction.

(d) Total failure to perform

In *Firestone Tyre & Rubber v Vokins*,[108] Devlin J stated that 'It is illusory to say—"we promise to do a thing but we are not liable if we do not do it".'[109] In *Suisse Atlantique*, Lord Reid said that an exclusion clause might 'apply to at least some cases of fundamental breach without being so widely drawn that it can be cut down on any ground by applying the ordinary principles of construction'.[110] This clearly indicates that there are some cases where an exclusion clause may not be permitted to apply. Furthermore, Lord Wilberforce declared that parties to a contract cannot contemplate so wide an ambit in an exclusion clause as to deprive the contract of all meaning, so reducing it to a 'mere declaration of intent'. To this extent, Lord Wilberforce concluded, 'it may be correct to say that there is a rule of law against the application of an exceptions clause to a particular type of breach'.[111] Similarly, in the *Photo Production* case, Lord Diplock noted that the parties to a contract are free to modify their obligations to whatever degree they choose 'within the limits that the agreement must contain the legal characteristics of a contract'.[112] As Treitel says, if the court, where there is such a clause, decides nevertheless that there is a contract, the exclusion clause would have to be struck out as repugnant to the purpose of the contract.[113] It is interesting that Donaldson J pointed to the fact that the breach did not destroy the 'sub-stratum' of the contract,[114] the assumption being that if it had no exclusion clause would cover the breach.

This view, that no clause can allow a party effectively to reduce the contract, by the use of an exclusion clause, to a mere declaration of intent, received strong support in *George Mitchell (Chesterhall)* v *Finney Lock Seeds*.[115] In that case, there was a contract for the supply to a farmer of cabbage seeds. The contract contained the following clause: 'In the event of any seeds ... sold ... by us not complying with the express terms of the contract of sale ... or any seeds ... proving defective in varietal purity we will ... refund all payments made to us by the buyer in respect of the seeds ... and this shall be the limit of our obligation ... we hereby exclude all liability for any loss or damage arising from the use of any seeds ... supplied by us and for any consequential loss or damage arising out of such use ... or any defect in any seeds ... supplied by us or for any other loss or damage whatsoever save for ... refund as aforesaid'. What was delivered was so far short of being commercial cabbage seed that it could only be fed to birds. In such circumstances, Parker J felt that he was 'quite unable to construe this clause as covering that situation. This is undoubtedly the delivery of something wholly different in kind from that which was ordered and which the defendants had agreed to supply. It is making commercial nonsense of the contract to suggest that either party can have intended that it was to operate in the circumstances of this case; for to do so would convert the contract ... into nothing but a declaration of intention with nothing more ...'[116] This decision was upheld in the Court of Appeal,[117] though Lord Denning rather unusually thought that the clause did indeed cover the breach which had occurred. Oliver and Kerr LJJ took the view that the clause was not drafted so as to cover the suppliers' negligence; but Oliver LJ was equally clear that Parker J had taken a correct approach when he held that the clause could not be read as covering such a total non-performance. Kerr LJ, on the other hand, thought that a clause could excuse a totally different performance (and disagreed with Parker J's analysis) subject to the proviso that 'the words used do not go so far as, in effect, to absolve one party from any contractual obligation whatsoever, so as to reduce a so called contract to a mere declaration of intent'.

The position would therefore seem to be that while the doctrine of fundamental breach is now largely a matter of history, there remains a category of breach—that of total non-performance—where logic compels that no clause can effectively avoid liability for breach.

The effect of the *Photo Production* case is considerably to reduce the problems once caused by the doctrine of fundamental breach and the way it was applied. Furthermore, the Unfair Contract Terms Act has itself done much to reduce the notion of fundamental breach to a relative insignificance: this was very much Lord Wilberforce's view in the *Photo Production* case when he said that: 'It is not necessary to review fully the numerous cases in which the doctrine of fundamental breach has been applied or discussed. Many of these have now been superseded by the Unfair Contract Terms Act 1977'.[118]

In essence, s 9 of the 1977 Act provides that, regardless of any fundamental breach, and whether or not that breach has been accepted, the sole criterion as to whether the exclusion clause is effective remains the test of reasonableness, if that test would have applied irrespective of any fundamental breach.[119]

1 [1977] 3 All ER 498.
2 *Ibid* at p 505.
3 *Ibid* at p 506.
4 *Ibid* at p 508.
5 [1962] 1 All ER 111.
6 [1955] 1 All ER 377.
7 [1962] 1 All ER 111, 115 *per* Lord Evershed MR.
8 *Ibid* at p 119 *per* Lord Evershed MR.
9 *Supra* note 1 at p 508.
10 [1956] 2 All ER 121.
11 *Ibid* at p 125. See *supra* note 1 at p 508.
12 Treitel, *Law of Contract* (4th ed) p 159. This observation is not made in the fifth edition.
13 [1892] 3 Ch 441.
14 [1922] 2 KB 478, 488.
15 [1907] AC 351.
16 *Ibid* at p 353.
17 *Ibid* at p 356.

18 *Ibid* at p 362.

19 *Photo Production* v *Securicor Transport* [1980] 1 All ER 556, 564 *per* Lord Wilberforce.

20 *Op cit* (5th ed) p 178.

21 See Gower, *Modern Company Law* (4th ed) p 327; *Gluckstein* v *Barnes* [1900] AC 240.

22 Treitel, *Law of Contract* (5th ed) pp 178–9.

23 See Lord Denning in *Lee* v *Showman's Guild* [1952] 1 All ER 1175; *Edwards* v *SOGAT* [1970] 3 All ER 689; *Enderby Town FC* v *The FA* [1971] 1 All ER 215.

24 [1947] 1 All ER 103.

25 *Ibid* at p 105 *per* Scott LJ.

26 [1950] 2 All ER 517.

27 [1969] 2 All ER 1215.

28 *Ibid* at p 1218 *per* Lord Denning MR.

29 *Ibid* at p 1218.

30 *Ibid* at pp 1219–20.

31 *Ibid* at p 1220.

32 [1976] 2 All ER 930.

33 *Ibid* at p 933, citing *Heilbut* v *Buckleton* [1913] AC 30.

34 *Ibid* at p 935.

35 *Ibid* at p 936.

36 *Ibid*.

37 [1951] 1 All ER 631.

38 *Ibid* at p 633.

39 [1968] 2 All ER 187.

40 *Ibid* at p 190.

41 *Ibid* at p 192.

42 [1934] 2 KB 394.

43 *Ibid* at p 403. This case is discussed in Chapter 1 at p 15.

44 [1950] 1 All ER 919.

45 *Ibid* at p 924.

46 *Ibid*.

47 *Supra* note 39 at p 190. The question of reasonableness is discussed in greater detail in Chapter Four.

48 [1951] 1 KB 240.

49 *Ibid* at p 248.

50 [1951] 2 All ER 442.

51 *Ibid* at p 446.

52 [1953] 2 All ER 1471.

53 *Ibid* at p 1473.

54 [1953] 1 WLR 1026.

55 *Ibid* at pp 1030–2 *per* Denning LJ.

56 See *Smeaton Hanscomb* v *Sassoon I Setty, supra* note 52 at p 1473 *per* Devlin J.

57 See Coote, *Exception Clauses* (1st ed) Chapter 4.

58 Coote, *op cit* p 107.

59 Coote, *op cit* pp 107–8. This book is particularly commended as the most scholarly work on exclusion clauses.

60 [1956] 2 All ER 866.

61 *Ibid* at p 868.

62 Guest, 'Fundamental Breach of Contract' (1961) 77 LQR 98.

63 *Supra* note 60.

64 [1961] 2 All ER 281.

65 *Ibid* at pp 289–90 *per* Holroyd Pearce LJ, See too *Pollock* v *Macrae* 1922 SC (HL) 192.

66 Unreported, 23 June 1981.

67 [1963] 2 All ER 432.

68 See *Pollock* v *Macrae* 1922 SC (HL) 192; Alexander Stephen (Forth) Ltd v JJ Riley (UK) Ltd 1976 SC 151

69 [1964] 1 Lloyd's Rep 446.

70 *Ibid* at p 450.

71 [1966] 2 All ER 61.

72 Treitel, *Law of Contract* (5th ed) p 167.

73 *Supra* note 71 at p 71.

74 *Ibid*.

75 *Ibid* at p 89. See too *ibid* at p 93 *per* Lord Wilberforce.

76 [1969] 2 All ER 1215.

77 See Chapter 3.

78 *Supra* note 76 at p 1218.

79 *Ibid*.

80 [1970] 2 All ER 774.

81 *Supra* note 69.

82 *Supra* note 71 at p 88, *per* Lord Upjohn.

83 *Supra* note 80 at p 777.

84 Megaw LJ agreed with the other judgements: *ibid* at p 779.

85 [1970] 1 All ER 225.

86 See Widgery LJ, *ibid* at pp 239–40.

87 *Ibid* at p 233.

88 *Ibid* at pp 240 and 242 respectively.

89 *Supra* note 71 at p 398.

90 *Ibid*.

91 *Supra* note 85 at p 234.

92 *Suisse Atlantique* was one such, although it was there only assumed that the breach was fundamental.

93 Treitel, *Law of Contract* (5th ed) p 173.

94 *Supra* note 71 at p 92.

95 Anson, *Law of Contract* (25th ed) p 169.

96 [1971] 2 All ER 708.

97 *Supra* note 71 at p 91.

98 *Supra* note 96 at p 719.

99 *Ibid*.

100 *Supra* note 96 at pp 719–20.

101 [1969] 2 All ER 1215; *supra*, p 48.

102 *Supra* note 96 at p 721.

103 [1980] 1 All ER 556; [1978] 3 All ER 146.
104 *Harbutt's Plasticine* v *Wayne Tank and Pump* [1970] 1 All ER 225, 235.
105 [1980] 1 All ER 556, 560.
106 *Ibid* at p 561.
107 *Ibid* at p 563.
107a [1983] 1 All ER 108.
108 [1951] 1 Lloyd's Rep 32.
109 *Ibid* at p 39.
110 *Supra* note 71 at p 71.
111 *Ibid* at p 432.
112 [1980] 1 All ER 556, 567.
113 Treitel, *Law of Contract* (5th ed) pp 175–6.
114 *Supra* note 96 at p 721. The wording is that of Lord Wilberforce, *supra* note 71 at p 93.
115 [1983] 1 All ER 108; [1981] 1 Lloyd's Rep 476.
116 [1981] 1 Lloyd's Rep, 476, 480.
117 It was Lord Denning's last case.
118 [1980] 1 All ER 556, 564.
119 See Chapter 6.

Chapter 4

Harsh and Unconscionable Bargains

There is a definite, if slender, line of authority (as far as English law is concerned) showing that an agreement fairly stigmatised as harsh and unconscionable may well be declared unenforceable in the courts. Should this prove too drastic in the individual case, there is nonetheless a degree of precedent, founded principally on certain remarks by Lord Denning, that if an individual clause (more often than not an exclusion clause) is unreasonable it will be struck down. This is in addition to ss 137–140 of the Consumer Credit Act 1974 which permit the reopening of credit agreements where the credit bargain is extortionate.

1 Unconscionable bargains

In the leading case of *Fry* v *Lane*,[1] a claim was made that the sale of a reversionary interest should be set aside. Reviewing the earlier decisions, Kay J observed that three criteria had to be fulfilled before equity would set aside a particular bargain. First, the victim must be 'poor and ignorant'; second, the sale must be at an undervalue; third, the victim must have had no independent advice.[2]

This was up-dated by the judgment of Megary J in *Creswell* v *Potter*.[3] A matrimonial home had been conveyed to a husband and wife as joint tenants, at law and equity. The marriage broke down and the wife was handed a document to execute, described as a conveyance. In fact, it released to the husband all the wife's interest in the home. She received no consideration other than an indemnity against the liabilities under a mortgage of the property. She had believed that the document made it possible for the property to be sold without her rights being affected.

The learned judge assessed the case against the three criteria laid down by Kay J. There was no doubt but that the disposition had been at an undervalue. It was also a fact that the wife had received no independent legal advice. As for the final requirement, that the plaintiff be 'poor and ignorant', Megary J gave this a modern tone. More appropriate terms, he said, would now be 'member of the lower income group' and 'less highly educated'. Furthermore, this latter was to be construed in a relative sense: while the wife needed alertness in her career as a telephonist, in the context of property transactions she could fairly be described as 'ignorant'.

This approach to the third condition clearly gives the courts considerable scope. While the better-off may obtain independent legal advice, they are as capable as the impoverished of believing independent legal advice to be unnecessary. That the law is not confined to the impoverished is readily deducible from those early cases where reversioners of no small means were relieved from the consequences of their improvident agreements.[4] It is better, then, to read the expression 'poor and ignorant' as now meaning 'incapable of coping with the individual transaction without independent legal advice'.[5]

A strong boost to the belief that grossly inequitable contracts are unenforceable was provided by the House of Lords in *Schroeder Music Publishing* v *Macaulay*.[6] The contract was one whereby a young and unknown song-writer entered into an agreement with a music publishing company, whereby the latter engaged his services exclusively for a period of five years. Such was the stringency of the contract in favour of the publishers (they were, for example, under no obligation even to publish any of the song-writer's publications) that it was urged that the contract was void for being an unreasonable restraint of trade.

Lord Reid stressed that this particular contract, one cast in standard form, was not made freely by parties bargaining on equal terms, nor moulded under the pressures of negotiation, competition and public opinion.[7] This being so, he held the agreement unenforceable.

Lord Diplock took a robust line. In such cases, he declared, the court intervenes to protect those 'whose power is weak against being forced by those whose bargaining power is stronger to enter into bargains which are unconscionable'.[8]

His lordship continued by dividing standard form contracts into two categories. One such category related to contracts moulded and produced by parties of equal bargaining power. Here a strong presumption is raised that the contract is fair and reasonable. Such contracts include bills of lading and policies of insurance.[9]

This presumption, Lord Diplock maintained, does not apply to the more modern category of standard contracts of which the nineteenth century ticket cases are probably the best examples. These have not been subject to negotiation between the parties. They have been imposed by parties whose bargaining power enables them to say: 'If you want these goods or services at all, these are the only terms on which they are obtainable. Take it or leave it'.[10] Such cases raise no presumption of unconscionability, but the court must consider all the terms of the agreement to determine the issue of enforceability.[11]

The vital factor to note was that, although this was a case involving an alleged restraint of trade, Lord Diplock pushed the discussion beyond such confines. His clear belief was that any standard form contract imposed upon a party of weaker bargaining power could be void for unconscionability, regardless of the nature of the contract. Indeed, there is no reason to suppose that Lord Diplock would, if pressed, confine himself to standard term contracts. A verbal contract, or a written contract produced for the particular occasion only, can equally be imposed on weaker parties.

This decision of the House of Lords was applied in the not dissimilar case of *Clifford Davis Management* v *WEA Records*.[12] Composers of popular songs signed publishing agreements with music publishers. Amongst the terms of the agreements were clauses assigning copyright in the songs to the publishers and giving the publishers the right to reject any work without payment. Even when a work was retained, the publishers were under no obligation to exploit it.

The present action was for an interlocutory injunction to prevent the composers from breaking the agreement. Since this was the nature of the action, no firm rule of law was required or given. Lord Denning, however, was quick to point to the words of Lord Diplock in the House of Lords. He found it clear on the evidence that the composers had received no independent legal advice: it may well be said that 'there was such inequality of bargaining power that the agreement should not be enforced . . .'.[13] Certainly, the balance of convenience was that the injunction ought to be discharged.[14]

The Court of Appeal had enunciated similar principles in *Lloyds Bank* v *Bundy*.[15] The owner of land had mortgaged his property to support a business venture of his son's. The bank had foreclosed and sought possession of the land. The evidence showed that the owner was an elderly man not well versed in business affairs. Nor did he receive any independent advice.

Reviewing the cases, including *Fry* v *Lane*, Lord Denning found the principle to be that relief is given to one 'who, without independent advice, enters into a contract on terms which are very unfair or transfers property for a consideration which is grossly inadequate, when his bargaining power is grievously impaired by reason of his own needs or desires, or by his own ignorance or infirmity, coupled with undue influences or pressures brought to bear on him by or for the benefit of another.'[16] Sir Eric Sachs was only concerned with the fact that the bank, by failing to ensure that the mortgagor had independent advice, was in breach of its duty to take fiduciary care.[17]

This particular case is astonishingly close to one which it did not cite, the decision of Crisp J in *Harrison* v *National Bank of Australasia*.[18] An elderly woman, without legal advice, gave a bank security over land. The money was to aid her son-in-law in a business venture. She knew that she would be liable should the business fail, although she was completely ignorant of business matters. Crisp J set the agreement aside, noting the court will set aside a bargain entered into 'without due deliberation, without independent advice and not knowing its true effect'.[19]

In *Lloyds Bank* v *Bundy*, Lord Denning recognised that not 'every transaction is saved by independent advice'.[20] This had already been attested to in *Grealish* v *Murphy*.[21] A settlement of land and money was made by a person suffering from some degree of backwardness. He received independent legal advice, but the solicitor neither knew all the facts nor gave the settlor a complete explanation of the nature and effect of the settlement. The solicitor was also unaware of the full extent of the settlor's backwardness. In such circumstances, and despite the independent advice, the court set the agreement aside.[22]

We see from these cases a line of authority, including the House of Lords, willing to accept that contracts may become unenforceable if harsh and unconscionable, particularly where independent advice has not been obtained.[23] Exclusion clauses have not been mentioned in these cases, but only because they were not present in the case at hand. It can be safely said that the measure and extent of any exclusion clause will be a relevant factor in determining whether a contract may be so inequitable as to be unenforceable. Although a decision has never yet had to be cast in such terms, it must be possible that a consumer contract or a business contract for the hire of a television, the purchase of goods, or the leasing of equipment, will be declared void, not least because of the harshness of the exclusion clauses.

2 Reasonableness

As far back as *Parker* v *South Eastern Railway*,[24] there have been obiter dicta (and never anything more) asserting a right in the courts to ignore as void those exclusion clauses which are unreasonable. Bramwell LJ asked himself: 'what if there was some unreasonable condition, as for instance, to forfeit £1,000 if the goods were not removed within 24 hours?' The Lord Justice argued against the clause being binding if the particular individual was told that the conditions were there to be read, but did not in fact read them. I think, he declared, that 'there is an implied understanding that there is no condition unreasonable to the knowledge of the party tendering the document and not insisting on its being read—no condition not relevant to the matter in hand'.[25] It appears that if the contract had been read (or, perhaps, if the one contracting party had ignored the other's insistence) or if the unreasonable terms were relevant to the matter in hand, then the term would have been effective.

This view was supported by the Court of Appeal in *Thompson* v *London, Midlands & Scottish Railway*.[26] Lawrence LJ expressly endorsed the view of Bramwell LJ, saying: 'If there were a condition which was unreasonable to the knowledge of the company tendering the ticket I do not think the passenger would be bound'.[27] Sankey LJ too thought that a 'ridiculous condition' would not be binding: nor, he added, would conditions printed in Chinese.[28]

The most vigorous modern proponent of this view, not unexpectedly, has been Lord Denning. In *John Lee & Son (Grantham) Ltd* v *Railway Executive*,[29] he expressed an opinion that an unreasonably onerous term in a standard form contract would not be enforced in the courts, for 'there is the vigilance of the common law which, while allowing freedom of contract, watches to see that it is not abused'.[30] In *Thornton* v *Shoe Lane Parking*,[31] Lord Denning, when judging a particular clause, did not 'pause to enquire whether the exempting condition is void for unreasonableness',[32] clearly believing there were circumstances where this could be so.

Yet a third example is *Gillespie Bros* v *Roy Bowles Transport*[33] where Lord Denning restated the views first expressed in *John Lee & Son (Grantham) Ltd* v *Railway Executive*: the common law, he reaffirmed, 'will not allow a party to exempt himself from his liability at common law when it would be quite unconscionable for him to do so'.[34]

These various observations are all, however, obiter dicta:[35] more than that, they have on occasions been actively contradicted. In

Grand Trunk Railway Company of Canada v *Robinson*,[36] Viscount Haldane, referring to the implied duty of care incumbent on a railway company, observed that this duty can be superseded by a specific contract which may enlarge, diminish or exclude it. Such a contract, if authorised by the law, 'cannot be pronounced to be unreasonable ... The specific contract, with its incidents either expressed or attached by law, becomes in such a case the only measure of the duties between the parties, and the plaintiff cannot by any device of form [*sic*] get more than the contract allows him'.[37] This was accepted as a statement of general principle by the Privy Council in *Ludditt* v *Ginger Coote Airways*.[38]

A more robust dissent came in the *Gillespie* case itself. It is not, said Buckley LJ, the 'function of a court of construction to fashion a contract in such a way as to produce a result which the court considers that it would have been fair or reasonable for the parties to have intended', although he allowed that, in the event of two possible interpretations, the court should adopt the more reasonable.[39]

An even more substantial blow to the proponents of Lord Denning's view came in *Suisse Atlantique*.[40] There is no indication, said Lord Reid, 'that the courts are to consider whether the exemption is fair in all the circumstances or is harsh and unconscionable or whether it was freely agreed by the customer, ... it appears to me that its solution should be left to Parliament'.[41] This was approved by Donaldson J in *Kenyon, Son & Craven* v *Baxter Hoare*.[42]

Undaunted, Lord Denning restated his beliefs in *Levison* v *Patent Steam Carpet Cleaning Co.*[43] His view was that the exclusion clause was unreasonable, and this was one of his grounds for finding against the defendants.[44] He also held that the doctrine of fundamental breach applies to standard form contracts where there has been an inequality for bargaining power. Where the superior party has imposed an exclusion clause on the weaker party, it will not be valid where he has been guilty of a breach going to the root of the contract.[45] None of the other lord justices discussed the point.

Lord Denning gave his final summing-up on the common law and the test of reasonableness in *Photo Production* v *Securicor Transport*.[46] The point we have now reached, he felt, and one which 'lies behind all our striving' is that 'the court will not allow a party to rely on an exemption or limitation clause in circumstances in which it would not be fair or reasonable to allow reliance on it; and, in considering whether it is fair and reasonable, the court will consider whether it was in a standard form, whether there was equality of bargaining power, the nature of the breach and so forth'.[47] He acknowledged that this was to follow the lead provided by Parliament in the Supply of Goods (Implied Terms) Act 1973, and in the Unfair Contract Terms Act 1977.[48] The judge below had found that the exclusion clause in this case was reasonable. Lord Denning, however, judged that it was not fair and reasonable to allow Securicor to rely on the disputed clause when it was their own patrolman whose deliberate act burned down the factory.[49] Yet again, it had to be reported that none of the other lord justices discussed the point. In the House of Lords, no discussion was given to whether there was an independent common law doctrine of reasonableness to be applied to exclusion clauses. Lord Wilberforce did say, though, that he found the clause to be a reasonable allocation of the risk.[50]

In the *Photo Production* case, Lord Denning had switched from the reasonableness of the clause to the different question as to whether the clause (which could well be reasonable) was one on which it would be fair and reasonable to allow reliance. Either way, however, Lord Denning's views (even after conceding that he has not been altogether alone in what he has had to say) must be treated with considerable circumspection. Indeed, the very existence of the Unfair Contract Terms Act 1977, and its requirement of reasonableness, indicate an omission in the common law. Yet considerable sympathy must still extend to this view, particularly in the form in which it was expressed in *Gibaud* v *Great Eastern Railway*.[51] If, said Bray J, a condition is so 'irrelevant or extravagant' that it must have been known that the recipient never intended to be so bound, his assent to the contract would be deemed to have been obtained by fraud. The mere fact of a condition being unreasonable would not of itself, however, show fraud: indeed, he held that the county court judge erred when holding that the plaintiff was not bound because the clause was unreasonable.[52] Sankey J went slightly further, saying that an extravagant condition (such as having to claim the goods in five minutes) is tantamount to fraud, while irrelevant ones (such as requiring the depositor of goods to become a shareholder in the bailee company) is for that reason not binding.[53] There is much to be said for such a view, which falls short of eliminating clauses which are merely unreasonable. It still remains, however, for the matter to be decided authoritatively.[54]

1 (1888) 40 Ch D 312.
2 *Ibid* at p 322. Amongst the previous authorities were: *Evans* v *Llewellin* (1787) 1 Cox 333; *Anderson* v *Elsworth* (1861) 3 Giff 154; *Clarke* v *Malpas* (1862) 31 Beav 801, (1862) 4 De GF & J 401. See generally

Lawson, 'The Law Relating to Improvident Bargains' (1973) 24 NILQ 171.

3 1968, unreported. See Ross-Martyn (1971) 121 NLJ 1159, 1160.

4 See, for example, *Everitt* v *Everitt* (1870) LR 10 Eq 405.

5 In *O'Rorke* v *Bolingbroke*, Lord Hatherley referred simply to 'uneducated ignorant persons': (1877) LR 2 App Cas 814, 823.

6 [1974] 3 All ER 616.

7 *Ibid* at p 622.

8 *Ibid* at p 623.

9 *Ibid*.

10 *Ibid*.

11 *Ibid* at pp 623 and 624.

12 [1975] 1 All ER 237.

13 *Ibid* at p 240.

14 *Ibid* at p 240.

15 [1974] 3 All ER 757.

16 *Ibid* at p 765.

17 *Ibid* at p 770.

18 (1928) 23 Tas LR 1.

19 *Ibid* at p 8.

20 *Supra* note 15 at p 765.

21 [1946] IR 35.

22 Accepted as correct, but distinguished in *Haverly* v *Brooks & Brooks* [1970] IR 214.

23 Except where the advice was refused: *Harrison* v *Guest* (1855) 6 De GM & G 426, (1860) 8 HLC 481.

24 (1877) 2 CPD 416.

25 *Ibid* at p 428.

26 [1930] 1 KB 41.

27 *Ibid* at p 53.

28 *Ibid* at p 56.

29 [1949] 2 All ER 581.

30 *Ibid* at p 584.

31 [1971] 1 All ER 686.

32 *Ibid* at p 690.

33 [1973] 1 All ER 193.

34 *Ibid* at p 200. See too *Foley Motors* v *McGhee* [1970] NZLR 649, 652 *per* Richmond J.

35 In *Watkins* v *Rymill* (1885) 10 QBD 178, at p 189, Stephen J, referring to the statement of Bramwell LJ, said 'there is no absolute decision on this point'.

36 [1915] AC 740.

27 *Ibid* at p 747.

38 [1947] 1 All ER 328, 331 *per* Lord Wright.

39 *Supra* note 33 at p 205.

40 [1966] 2 All ER 61.

41 *Ibid* at p 76.

42 [1971] 2 All ER 708, 720.

43 [1977] 3 All ER 498.
44 *Ibid* at p 503.
45 *Ibid* at p 504.
46 [1978] 3 All ER 146. He repeated his views in *George Mitchell (Chesterhall) Ltd* v *Finney Lock Seeds* [1983] 1 All ER 108, 115.
47 *Ibid* at p 153.
48 *Ibid*
49 *Ibid* at p 154.
50 [1980] 1 All ER 556, 564.
51 [1920] 3 KB 689.
52 *Ibid* at pp 699–700.
53 *Ibid* at p 703.
54 The case was affirmed on appeal, but the present matters were not discussed: [1921] 2 KB 426.

Part II

Legislative Control

Chapter 5

Unlawful Exclusion Clauses

1 Fair Trading Act 1973

The Fair Trading Act 1973 sets out a procedure for the control of undesirable 'consumer trade practices'. Section 13 defines a consumer trade practice as one carried out in connection with the supply of goods, or services, to consumers, and which relates—

(a) to the terms or conditions (whether as to price or otherwise) on or subject to which goods or services are or are sought to be supplied; or

(b) to the manner in which those terms or conditions are communicated to persons to whom goods are or are sought to be supplied or for whom services are or are sought to be supplied; or

(c) to promotion (by advertising, labelling or marking of goods, canvassing or otherwise) of the supply of goods or the supply of services; or

(d) to methods of salesmanship employed in dealing with consumers; or

(e) to the way in which goods are packed or otherwise got up for the purpose of being supplied; or

(f) to methods of demanding or securing payment for goods or services supplied.

If such a practice can be identified, s 14 gives to the Director General of Fair Trading, to the Secretary of State, or any other Minister, the power to refer to the Consumer Protection Advisory Committee (established by s 3 of the Act) the question whether the particular practice 'adversely affects the economic interests of the consumer'.

Should the Committee find that the consumer is adversely affected, there is nothing in the Act to determine the appropriate consequences. Presumably, armed with the report, representations will be made in the appropriate quarters to have the practice abandoned. Little more can be said, since there have so far been no s 14 references.

There have, however, been four s 17 references to the Committee. These are references made by the Director General under s 14 (and only by the Director General) but where it appears to him that the particular trade practice has, or is likely to have, any of the following effects as set out in s 17(2)—

(a) of misleading consumers as to or withholding from them adequate information as to, or an adequate record of, their rights and obligations under relevant consumer transactions; or

(b) of otherwise misleading or confusing consumers with respect to any matter in connection with relevant consumer transactions; or

(c) of subjecting consumers to undue pressure to enter into relevant consumer transactions; or

(d) of causing the terms and conditions on or subject to which consumers enter into relevant consumer transactions, to be so adverse to them as to be inequitable.

Then the Director General may (not must) attach to his reference proposals recommending to the Secretary of State that the latter use the powers of the Fair Trading Act to control the particular trade practice.

It is the task of the Committee, under the terms of s 21, to report on whether the practice does adversely affect the economic interests of consumers, and whether it does so by reason, or partly by reason, that it has, or is likely to have, one or more of what may be called the s 17 (2) effects. Interestingly, the Committee does not appear to be limited to finding that the s 17(2) effect is one of those specified by the Director General in his original reference.

Should the Committee report positively on these questions, it must further state whether it agrees with the Director General's proposals as set out in the reference, or would agree if modified in a manner specified in the report, or whether it disagrees with the proposals and makes no modifications. In this last case, the proposals for reform may be treated as effectively at an end. But if the Committee has taken either of the two other paths, the issue is then remitted to the Secretary of State under s 22. Where the Committee accepted the Director General's proposals, the Secretary of State may (not must) give effect to the proposals in an order made by statutory instrument. If the Committee has accepted the proposals, but with modifications, the Secretary of State again has an absolute discretion, either to implement the original proposals or the proposals as modified, or, of course, to decline to do anything. An order made by the Secretary of State has to be approved by each House of Parliament. At this stage, the Director General's proposals, in their original or amended form, achieve the force of law.

Reference 17(1) of 24 April 1974

The first of the four s 17 references so far made to the Committee, and the only one relevant to exclusion clauses, has its origins in the provisions of the Supply of Goods (Implied Terms) Act 1973. The familiar provisions of this Act, now contained in the Unfair Contract Terms Act 1977, were to render void those terms in consumer transactions which sought to exclude the implied terms relating to title, fitness for purpose, merchantable quality and correspondence with description, including the terms as to title and merchantable quality implied by s 4 (1) of the Trading Stamps Act 1964.

In his reference, the Director General specified three practices which caused him concern. The first practice concerned the wording of notices displayed on trade premises or vehicles, in advertisements or catalogues, or in documents furnished to consumers acquiring goods, when the wording purports to exclude or restrict the statutory term implied, and rendered inalienable, by the Supply of Goods (Implied Terms) Act. The relevant terms are now, of course, implied by the Sale of Goods Act 1979. The second practice dealt with written statements furnished to consumers by suppliers of goods relating to the consumers' rights against suppliers, but which fail to advise the consumers of the rights implied by law in their favour. The last practice was also concerned with written statements furnished to consumers by suppliers of goods which fail to advise consumers of their implied statutory rights against suppliers. In this case, however, the written statements covered by the practice related to the rights of consumers against third parties, such as manufacturers, or to the obligations of such third parties to consumers. In other words, this practice dealt with what are commonly referred to as manufacturers' 'guarantees'.

The Committee's report contained the conclusion that each 'consumer trade practice specified adversely affects the economic interests of consumers in the United Kingdom, and does so by reason that it has, or is likely to have, the effects ... of misleading consumers as to their rights under relevant consumer transactions or otherwise confusing them as to the terms of the transaction'.[1]

The Committee suggested some modifications to the Director General's proposal, but otherwise gave them complete support. After the lapse of nearly one year, an order contained in a statutory instrument reflecting the modified proposals was laid before, and approved by, each House of Parliament.

2 Consumer Transactions (Restrictions on Statements) Order 1976 SI 1976 No 1813

(a) The first practice

The first practice was covered by a fourfold prohibition. Article 3 (a) rendered it unlawful, as from 1 December 1976, for persons in the course of a business to display at any place where consumer transactions[2] are effected (wholly or partly) a notice containing a statement purporting to apply, in relation to consumer transactions effected there, terms rendered void by s 55 (4) of the Sale of Goods Act 1893 as amended by the Supply of Goods (Implied Terms) Act 1973, or by s 12 (3) of the 1973 Act. In each case, the reference should now be to s 6 of the Unfair Contract Terms Act 1977.[3] The same prohibition applies where the notice purports to exclude the warranty of merchantable quality implied by s 4 (1) (c) of the Trading Stamps Act 1964. Section 6 of the Unfair Contract Terms Act refers to the implied terms of correspondence with description, merchantable quality and fitness for purpose and the implied terms relating to title.

It is worth pointing out that those places are within the prohibition when transactions are only 'partly' effected there. Hence, places are caught when goods are selected from one establishment or store, but the sale is concluded in another. A notice at either place is within the Order.

It should also be remembered that it is enough for the notice to contain a statement which 'purports' to apply to a particular exclusion clause. In other words, a notice drawn insufficiently to the consumer's attention, or one brought to his attention after the contract was made, nevertheless, falls within the Order.

(b) The forbidden clauses

As the Committee's report made clear,[4] the type of statement which most concerned the Director General of Fair Trading was on the following lines: 'We regret no cash refund'; 'We willingly exchange goods but money cannot be refunded, credit notes will be given'. All these terms seek to exclude the rights guaranteed to consumers by the Supply of Goods (Implied Terms) Act 1973, the Trading Stamps Act 1964, and Sale of Goods Act. It has not, however, become unlawful to use such statements as 'Please note we cannot exchange any garment'; 'No articles exchanged'; 'Sale goods cannot be exchanged.' Nothing in the Acts gives any right to exchange goods, even ones that are defective. It was because of this that the Committee modified the original proposals, in that the prohibition would otherwise have extended even thus far.[5]

An offence does not appear to be committed by notices bearing such statements as: 'No money refunded without receipt', since this merely requires an aggrieved consumer to prove that the individual retailer was the appropriate offending party. Even though a consumer may have lost his receipt, but can otherwise supply appropriate proof of purchase yet is refused his statutory remedy, it is not thought that this can retrospectively create a criminal offence out of the notice.

A clothier has been fined £50 at Grimsby Borough Magistrates' Court for continuing to display a sign 'No Cash Refunds' after two warnings. A general store has been fined £5 with £15 costs at Ilkeston Magistrates' Court for displaying a notice relating to umbrellas and containing the void statement 'No returns can be accepted after use'.[6]

(c) The first practice: the other prohibitions

Article 3 (b) makes unlawful the publication of an advertisement,[7] or causing one to be published, when it contains a void exclusion clause or one inconsistent with the term as to merchantable quality implied by the Trading Stamps Act. The 'void exclusion clauses' are here, as they are throughout the Order, those seeking to exclude liability for the implied terms as to title, correspondence with description, fitness for purpose and merchantable quality.

Article 3 (c) forbids the supply to a consumer under consumer transactions of goods bearing, or goods in a container bearing, a statement excluding the above statutory rights. This applies whether or not the exclusion clause is a term of the transaction. In other words, notwithstanding that an exclusion clause is brought to a consumer's attention after the contract has been made, as where goods bearing exclusion clauses are not taken from their container until the consumer has taken them home, a criminal offence is committed.

Pursuant to article 3 (d), it is unlawful to furnish a document including a statement excluding the above rights. This applies to documents supplied to persons likely to enter into a consumer transaction. The wording is apt to cover receipts, invoices and contracts. The provision goes on to affirm, as in those instances already discussed, that statements are within the Order when terms of the transaction, if they were terms of the transaction, or were to become terms of the prospective transaction. Once more, the effect of this approach is to render terms unlawful even when not adequately brought to the consumer's notice and even when no transaction materialises. In *Hughes* v *Hall,*[8] secondhand cars were sold in circumstances in which purchasers were given documents which contained the phrase 'sold as seen and inspected'. The magistrates accepted a submission that this did not offend against the Order, and an appeal was made to the Divisional Court. The essence of their decision, as contained in the case stated, was that the disputed expression would not avoid the legal rights of any consumer 'because the term used is too vague, it does not express clearly what its intention is, and if construed strictly, against the respondent's interests, and without extrinsic evidence, it would not enable the respondent to avoid civil liability. The term would not, therefore, be void by virtue of the [Unfair Contract Terms] Act, and accordingly we upheld the submissions of no case to answer and dismissed the two informations'. In seeking to uphold the decision of the magistrates, the respondents had argued that, if the cars had been sold by description, the clause would not have affected the rights of a purchaser, who would still have been able to rely on the express terms of the contract. It was further argued that the clause in dispute would not have affected any rights of a purchaser to cars which were reasonably fit for their purpose, given that the purchaser had made known the purpose for which the relevant vehicles were wanted. The Divisional Court accepted none of these arguments. A clause such as 'sold as seen and inspected' prima facie, and subject always to the express terms of the contract, would, according to Donaldson LJ, 'negative a sale by description. It would be a sale of a specific object as seen and inspected. That would exclude the implied warranty [*sic*] under s 13 of the Sale of Goods Act, and whether or not or how much it left in the way of an express obligation would depend upon the rest of the contract. For example it would still be open to the purchaser to complain that he got a different car from the one he had seen and inspected. But in my judgment, he would lose some of his rights, even if he might still have other rights'. That, he concluded, would suffice to create an offence under the Order, because 'anything which has that effect would be voided by s 2 of the Unfair Contract Terms Act'. Lord Justice Donaldson added that he was also of the opinion that the clause could not be regarded as too vague. It has to be considered in the context of people who buy and sell secondhand cars, and not in the context of marine insurance brokers. In the context in which it is used, I have no doubt as to what it should be understood as meaning'. The case was thus remitted for the magistrates to continue the hearing.

The result of this decision is virtually to make it impossible ever to sell goods other than by description. That, surely, cannot be what the Order was ever intended to do. Section 13 of the Sale of Goods Act requires correspondence with description only where there is a sale by description. The Unfair Contract Terms Act only renders void, and therefore the Order only renders criminal in effect, clauses which purport to exclude the obligation as to conformity when there is a sale by description in the first place. There is nothing to say, indeed the whole tenor of s 13 points the other way, that a supplier cannot supply other than by description.

(d) The second practice

This practice is not concerned with void terms or with the display of notices on trading premises, but only with written statements furnished by suppliers of goods to consumers which purport to set out the rights and obligations of the parties and which fail to advise consumers of their rights to goods which are of merchantable quality, are reasonably fit for the purpose, and which conform to their description.

Article 4 of the Order provides that in two instances a criminal offence arises unless the relevant statement is qualified by another in close proximity which is clear and conspicuous and to the effect that the relevant statement does not or will not affect the statutory rights of a consumer.

The two instances embodying the relevant statement are as follows. First, the supply to a consumer, pursuant to a consumer transaction, of goods bearing (or goods in a container bearing) a statement about the rights that the consumer has against the supplier or about the obligations to the consumer accepted by the supplier. The article spells out those rights and obligations as those which 'arise if the goods are defective or are not fit for a purpose or do not correspond with a description'. The article also stresses that the offence arises whether or not those rights or obligations are legally enforceable. Yet again, therefore, statements brought to the consumer's notice too late to become a term of the transaction are within the prohibition.

The other instance relates to documents being furnished to a consumer in the course of a business or to persons likely, as consumers, to enter into a consumer transaction, where the documents contain statements as described above. The article also provides that the Order covers documents furnished to consumers likely to enter consumer transactions through the agency of the person supplying the document. The doorstep seller is covered by this provision: so also, one imagines, is the dealer who arranges a hire purchase contract with a finance house.

The universal commercial practice is, in these cases, to add the words: 'This does not affect your statutory rights'. The Order, however, does not make these words mandatory: it states only that there must be a statement that the statutory rights of the consumer are unaffected. Since few consumers will know what these rights are, it may be wondered if such commercial practice is within a fair interpretation of the Order. It certainly more accords with its spirit to interpret the requirement of the Order as meaning that the particular document, goods or container ought to give a summary in some form or other of those statutory rights. Article 2 of the Order actually defines 'statutory rights' as being rights arising under the 1964, 1973 and 1979 Acts, other than the implied terms as to title, and it seems a fair conclusion that this is the way a statement that such rights are unaffected ought to be interpreted.

(e) The third practice

The third practice, in essence, involves manufacturers' guarantees. The Committee cites with approval the following extract from the Moloney Report:[9]

The important general consideration is that the issue of guarantees enables and encourages the retailer to lead the customer into thinking that the manufacturer alone is liable to attend to defects and thus permits him to avoid his responsibilities. We adopt the view that the consumer is widely ignorant of his legal rights and in this state readily accepts that any guarantee reaching him indicates the sum total of the redress he is entitled to claim.

The Committee itself concluded that 'the wording used in "guarantees" and similar undertakings by manufacturers (where no reference is made to the rights of the consumer against the supplier) reinforces these beliefs . . .'[10]

Article 5 tackles this problem by first defining that situation to which the penal provisions are directed. This is the supply of goods in the course of a business to another where, at the time of supply, the goods were intended by the supplier to be, or might reasonably be expected by him to be, the subject of a subsequent consumer transaction. Observe that the supplier is caught even though he did not intend the goods to be the subject of a consumer transaction and did not concern himself with whether they would be. It is enough that, judged objectively, it was reasonable to expect him to foresee a subsequent consumer transaction.

Observe, too, the expression 'subsequent consumer transaction'. It is this which prevents article 5 from applying to retailer-consumer transactions and so limits it to manufacturers' guarantees.

In cases covered by article 5, the supplier must not supply goods which bear, or are in a container which bears, a statement setting out, describing or limiting the obligation accepted by the supplier, or to be accepted by the supplier, in relation to the goods, whether legally enforceable or not. The qualification to this is that no offence arises where there is in close proximity to the above statement another which is clear and conspicuous and to the effect that the statement does not, or will not, affect the statutory rights of a consumer vis-a-vis description, merchantable quality and fitness for purpose.[11] Subject to the same qualification, it is also an offence to furnish a 'document' in relation to goods containing an exclusion or limitation clause as just defined.

Article 5 makes further provision for two cases in which no offence is committed. In the case of goods or containers, no offence arises where the goods have not become the subject of a consumer transaction. It appears from this that no offence arises in the case of goods or containers if they are only likely to be the subject of a consumer transaction, but have not yet so become. Doubtless exclusion clauses in such cases are not usually to be seen until after purchase, but this need not always be so. It is, for instance, quite likely that for display purposes a particular good will stand outside its container.

In the other case, which relates to the furnishing of documents, no offence arises unless the particular goods were the subject of a consumer transaction, or the document was supplied to a person likely to become a consumer, pursuant to the particular transaction.

Guidelines published by the Office of Fair Trading for manufacturers' guarantees suggest that manufacturers should avoid the use of undesirable restrictions in their guarantees. For instance, it would be better if a guarantee were not to require that goods be returned in their original packing; were not to leave it to the guarantor to decide whether or not the goods are defective; and were not to require the return of a guarantee card as a condition of claiming under a guarantee when a reasonable time is not allowed for the return of the registration card. These are, however, only guidelines and no penalty attaches to their breach.

(f) Offences

Enforcement of the Order is charged to the local weights and measures authorities. Section 23 of the Fair Trading Act 1973 prescribes that on breach of an Order a fine not exceeding £1,000 may be imposed on summary conviction. On conviction on indictment, a fine (without limit) may be imposed or a sentence of not more than two years' imprisonment, or both.

Section 26 limits the effect of any breach of an Order by providing that such a breach does not of itself render void or unenforceable the particular contract. The consumer will, however, retain his rights to sue under appropriate legislation, such as the Sale of Goods Act 1979. The consumer will also remain liable to receive compensation awarded by order of a court under the Powers of Criminal Courts Act 1973, or the Criminal Justice (Scotland) Act 1980, for breach of the Order.

(g) The 'by-pass' provision

In common with other legislation such as the Weights and Measures Act 1963, the Medicines Act 1968 and the Trade Descriptions Act 1968, the Fair Trading Act 1973 contains a 'by-pass' provision. Section 24 states that where an offence is committed due to the 'act or default' of some other person, that other may be convicted whether or not proceedings are taken against the person who actually committed the offence. If *Tesco Supermarkets* v *Nattrass*[12] is (as surely it must be) regarded as an authority, a person is only 'some other person' when he is not so high in the company hierarchy as effectively to be part of the controlling mind of, and hence be identified with, the company itself.

It is likely that s 24 will prove popular where a supplier commits an offence under article 3, but the real blame lies with the manufacturer who impressed the void exclusion clauses upon the goods or the containers of the goods.

It is also worth noting in this context the provision of Pt III of the Fair Trading Act. Where a person has persistently infringed an Order made under the Act, or has persistently flouted his obligations under such legislation as the Sale of Goods Act, the Director General of Fair Trading must seek an assurance that such conduct will cease. Where an assurance is breached, action in the Restrictive Practices Court may follow.[13] If that Court makes an order supplementing the previous assurance, breach of the order will be contempt of court, attracting the possibility of a fine and imprisonment.

(h) Defences

Section 25 of the Fair Trading Act 1973 provides a defence modelled on s 24 of the Trade Descriptions Act 1968. The person charged can provide a defence if he can show that the offence was:

(a) due to a mistake, or to reliance on information supplied to him, or to the act or default of another person,[14] an accident or some other cause beyond his control, and

(b) that he took all reasonable precautions and exercised all due diligence to avoid the commission of such an offence by himself or any person under his control.

The use of this defence, where it rests on the act or default of another person or on reliance on information supplied, is restricted: the person seeking to employ the defence shall not, without leave of the court, be entitled to the defence unless, within a period ending seven clear days before the hearing, he has served a notice in writing on the prosecutor, giving such information identifying or assisting in the identification of that other person as was then in his possession.

A word needs to be said on an apparent conflict between s 24 and s 25. It may be put thus: if a person can show a defence under s 25 when an offence is due to another's act or default, how can s 24 ever be employed to charge that other person since s 25 has already effectively provided that, because of that other's default, no offence was committed? The by-pass provision, be it remembered, applies only where an offence *is* committed. The short answer provided in *Coupe* v *Guyett*,[15] a case heard under identical provisions of the Trade Descriptions Act, is that a defence maintained under s 25 is a technical defence only, not one on the merits. For the purposes of s 24, an offence is still committed.

(i) Innocent publication of an advertisement

Where proceedings are brought for an offence arising out of the publication of an advertisement, the person charged has a defence under s 25 (3) of the Fair Trading Act 1973 if he can prove:

    (*a*) it is his business to publish or arrange for the publication of advertisements; and

    (*b*) he received the advertisement for publication in the ordinary course of business; and

    (*c*) he did not know and had no reason to suspect that publication would amount to an offence.

This defence is applicable to the media, radio, television and newspapers: it is not usually available to advertising agencies. It will only be available to agencies when the advertisement was received by them for publication. Since it is, in fact, their task to prepare the advertisement, this will hardly ever happen, if at all.

(*j*) *Trade Descriptions Act 1968*

Section 1 of the Trade Descriptions Act proscribes both the application of false trade descriptions to goods and the supply, or offer to supply, of goods bearing false trade descriptions. In numerous cases, these provisions have been held to apply to cars bearing false mileometer readings. It has also been accepted, though in no case has one ever been held to be effective, that it is possible to 'disclaim' liability for a false mileometer, hence avoiding liability under the Act.[16] Where a note of caution has been sounded in this context is that the disclaimer itself could be an illegal, because false, trade description. As was said by Donaldson LJ in *Corfield* v *Starr*,[17] 'in appropriate cases those whose duty it is to enforce consumer protection legislation may like to consider laying an alternative information based upon the disclaimer itself'.[18] Sections 23–25 of the 1968 Act carry provisions relating to the 'by-pass', available defences and the innocent publication of advertisements which correspond exactly, as has been earlier seen, to the like provisions of the Fair Trading Act.[19]

1 See Rights of Consumers: HC 6 Session 1974/1975: a report by the Consumer Protection Advisory Committee.

2 A 'consumer transaction' is a consumer sale within s 55 (7) of the Sale of Goods Act (now s 12 of the Unfair Contract Terms Act 1977); a hire purchase agreement which is a consumer agreement within s 12 (6) of the 1973 Act (s 12 of the 1977 Act); agreements to redeem trading stamps under a trading stamp scheme within s 10 (1) of the Trading Stamps Act 1964.

3 Consumer Transactions (Restrictions on Statements) (Amendment) Order 1978 (SI 1978 No 127).

4 See para 35 of the report.

5 See paras 35 and 65–9 of the report.

6 Taken from the Office of Fair Trading's Publication *Bee Line* September 1977.

7 An 'advertisement' includes a catalogue and a circular: article 2 (1).

8 See Appendix 4 p 158.

9 Final Report of the Committee on Consumer Protection, Cmnd 1781.

10 See the report at para 52.

11 See *supra* p 84 for, the interpretation of 'statutory rights'.

12 [1971] 2 All ER 127.

13 See *Director General of Fair Trading* v *Jurgen Krupa* 14 February 1976: *Director General of Fair Trading* v *Domestic Appliances* 20 October 1977.

14 See *Tesco Supermarkets* v *Nattrass, supra* note 12.

15 [1973] 2 All ER 1058.

16 See *Norman* v *Bennett* [1974] 3 All ER 351, *R* v *Hammerton Cars* [1976] 3 All ER 758.

17 (1981) 89 Monthly Review 86.

18 *Ibid* at p 87.

19 *Supra* pp 87–88.

Chapter 6

Void and Ineffective Exclusion Clauses

In certain cases, Acts of Parliament have provided that certain exclusion clauses are to be void and of no effect. It must be realised that such legislation does not render the continued use of such clauses unlawful. It merely means that they have no legal validity. It is true, however, that the continued use of void exclusion clauses does mislead those contracting parties who are ignorant of the law into believing that particular claims cannot be maintained. It was because there was evidence of this happening that the Director General of Fair Trading referred to the Consumer Protection Advisory Committee the practice of traders continuing to use those exclusion clauses which had been rendered void by the Supply of Goods (Implied Terms) Act 1973. As we saw and discussed in the previous chapter, this led to the use of certain exclusion clauses being rendered illegal under the terms of the Consumer Transactions (Restrictions on Statements) Order 1976 No 1813.[1]

We turn now to consider those exclusion clauses which Act of Parliament has rendered void and of no effect.

1 Consumer Credit Act 1974

The Consumer Credit Act 1974 contains a considerable number of provisions which can fairly be regarded as inserted into the Act for the protection of the debtor (where the contract relates to the provision of credit) or the hirer (where the contract is one of rental or hire).[2] Section 173(1) of the Act provides that any term in a regulated agreement or linked transaction is void if, and to the extent that, it is inconsistent with a provision 'for the protection of the debtor or hirer or his relative or any surety contained in the Act or in any regulation made under this Act'. It may be usefully noted here that a regulated agreement, by virtue of ss 8 and 15, may be broadly construed as one where the credit provided does not exceed £5,000 or the amount paid for hire does not exceed £5,000.[3] A 'linked transaction', as defined in s 19, is impossible to summarise briefly. The classic example of such a transaction is the maintenance contract which must be entered into under the terms of a television rental agreement.

The subsection bites not only on exclusion clauses contained in regulated or linked agreements. It applies also to clauses in 'any other agreement relating to an actual or prospective regulated agreement or linked transactions'. This appears to be essentially an anti-avoidance device. It means that a separate contract, one which is not itself a regulated agreement, cannot provide that such protective measures as are inserted into the agreement by the Consumer Credit Act are themselves to be excluded. Were it otherwise, the relevant terms of the Consumer Credit Act could easily be avoided.

Section 173 (2) takes the matter further by recognising that a provision of the Act may, in certain circumstances, impose duties or liabilities upon a debtor or hirer, or his relative, or any surety. Where this is so, subsection (2) continues, a term is inconsistent with that provision if it purports 'to impose, directly or indirectly, an additional duty or liability on him in those circumstances'. This is not drafting at its best, since the Act fails to state that, because of such inconsistency, the inconsistent term is void. This is, however, the plain intent of the Act and it will be so interpreted. It may also be taken that the words 'directly or indirectly' are apt to be construed as an anti-avoidance device in the manner just discussed.

The ineffectiveness of clauses to avoid the various provisions of the Consumer Credit Act, while absolute, is not without a degree of qualification. Section 173 (3) provides that notwithstanding s 173 (1), nothing in the Act operates to prevent a person consenting to a thing being done which could otherwise only be done on an order of the court or the Director General. The person's consent according to subsection (3), must be given at the time the particular thing is to be done.

This seemingly abstruse provision means that, for example, a person can consent at the time of repossession, to the repossession of protected goods. The repossessing party is thus relieved of the obligation otherwise imposed on him by s 90 of first obtaining an order of the court. The result is that a clause in the agreement excluding s 90 would be void; but consent to repossession without a court order is effective. Such consent, it must be stressed, is valid only if given at the time of the intended act; repossession, in our example. Consent written into the contract itself, therefore, will be of no effect.

2 Transport

Section 151 of the Road Traffic Act 1960 renders void exclusion clauses purporting to negative or restrict liability for death or personal injury to a passenger in a public service vehicle.

Any antecedent agreement or understanding between the user of a motor vehicle and his passenger(s) which purports to restrict the driver's liability to that passenger in respect of risks for which compulsory insurance cover is required (as to which, see s 143 of the Road Traffic Act 1972) is void under s 148 (3) of that Act.

3 Housing

Section 32 of the Housing Act 1961 implies into certain leases covenants by the landlord to repair. By virtue of s 33 (6) and (7), these terms can be excluded but only by court order made with the consent of the parties. See too the Housing (Scotland) Act 1966.

The Defective Premises Act 1972 imposes a liability on local authorities, their builders, sub-contractors and architects if they fail to build in a professional or workmanlike manner (as the case may be) with proper materials, or fail to ensure that the dwelling is fit for human habitation. By s 6 (3) of the Act, it is not possible to exclude or restrict the operation of such provisions by any agreement.

4 Patents

The Patents Act 1977, s 45, repeats the provisions formerly contained in s 58 of the Patents Act 1949, enabling contracts relating to patents to be determined by either party on three months' notice after the patent or all the patents by which the article or process was protected at the time of the making of the contract has or have ceased to be in force. Contracting out is expressly said to be of no avail.

5 Consumer protection legislation

Section 1 of the Consumer Protection Act 1961 provides for the enactment of regulations to secure the safety of the products specified in those regulations.[4] The supply of goods in contravention of regulations is an offence under s 2; and s 3 gives an action on a breach of statutory duty to any party affected by a breach of the regulations. Section 30 of the Unfair Contract Terms Act 1977 amends the 1961 Act by providing that a term of an agreement is void if it excludes or restricts, or purports so to do, any obligation or liability imposed by ss 2 and 3. However, the 1961 Act is to be repealed from a date yet to be announced under the terms of the Consumer Safety Act 1978. This is true also of s 30 of the Unfair Contract Terms Act. The 1978 Act itself provides for the making of safety regulations[5], and s 6 (1) first provides that a contravention of any such regulations shall be an offence (as will also be supply in contravention of a prohibition notice or prohibition order)[6]: according to s 6 (2) an agreement 'shall be void so far as it would . . . have the effect of excluding or restricting an obligation mentioned in the preceding subsection or liability for a breach of such an obligation'.

6 Supply of goods and services

The Supply of Goods and Services Act 1982 generally relates to contracts for the provision of a service; and to all contracts for the hire of goods and those under which the property in goods is transferred where, in this latter case, the contract is one not subject to the Sale of Goods Act, the Supply of Goods (Implied Terms) Act or the Trading Stamps Act.[7] In the case of contracts for the provision of a service, the terms implied as to time for performance, the price to be paid, and the skill with which the task may be performed may be excluded, according to s 16 (1) of the Act, subject to the provisions of the Unfair Contract Terms Act.[8] Section 16 (3) (a) of the 1982 Act adds that it will be possible in the particular contract for the provider of the service to assume a burden which is stricter than that required by the Act in relation to the time of performance and the skill to be deployed.

In relation to contracts for the hire of goods, s 11 (1) of the 1982 Act states that the terms implied as to title, quality and fitness may be excluded subject to the provisions of the Unfair Contract Terms Act.[9] This is true also of contracts for the supply of goods in which property passes: s 11 (1) provides that exclusion clauses operate subject to the provisions of the Unfair Contract Terms Act,[10] with the significant qualification that, in relation to s 2 of the 1982 Act (which imposes terms as to title, quiet possession and freedom from encumbrances) an amendment to the Unfair Contract Terms Act means that any clauses seeking to exclude or restrict the operation of s 2 are void and of no effect. Note, however, that any such clause will be outside the Consumer Transactions (Restrictions on Statements) Order,[11] and so may be used without criminal penalty, even if the clause is without effect.

7 Unfair Contract Terms Act 1977

The most sweeping and revolutionary changes have been made in the law relating to exclusion clauses by the provisions of the Unfair Contract Terms Act 1977. Before we move to consider its precise terms, we should point out that except where the contrary might be indicated, the discussion of the Act is germane to the whole United Kingdom.

(a) Some relevant definitions

Sections 14 and 25 contain definitions. The most important definition is no doubt that of 'negligence', but that will be examined when we consider negligence liability. For the moment, we draw express attention to 'notice', which 'includes' an announcement, written or not, and any other communication or 'pretended communication'. This last is to cover those notices not actually brought to the attention, for whatever reason, of the relevant party. We also point to 'personal injury' which 'includes' any disease and any impairment of physical or mental condition.

We would also point to two other definitions since they are defined by reference to some other Act of Parliament. 'Goods' is allotted its meaning as in s 61 (1) of the Sale of Goods Act 1979. Here the expression is defined as including 'all personal chattels other than things in action and money, and in Scotland all corporeal moveables except money'. The term includes 'emblements, industrial growing crops, and things attached to or forming part of the land which are agreed to be severed before sale or under the contract of sale'.

A 'hire-purchase agreement' is given the definition provided in s 189 (1) of the Consumer Credit Act 1974, that is to say, 'an agreement, other than a conditional sale agreement, under which—

(a) goods are bailed or (in Scotland) hired in return for periodical payments by the person to whom they are bailed or hired, and

(b) the property in the goods will pass to that person if the terms of the agreement are complied with and one or more of the following occurs—

(i) the exercise of an option to purchase by that person,

(ii) the doing of any other specified act by any party to the agreement,

(iii) the happening of any other specified event'.

(b) Those to whom the Act applies

Quite apart from those specific exclusions contained in Sched 1 to the Act, and which are referred to at the end of this chapter, the precise ambit of the Act in relation to England, Wales and Northern Ireland is limited by the terms of s 1 (3). This states, with the intent of generally removing private transactions from the Act, that ss 2–7, apply only to 'business liability', defined as a breach of obligation or duty arising:

(a) from things done or to be done by a person in the course of his or another's business, (this latter being necessary for vicarious liability); or

(b) from the occupation of premises used for business purposes of the occupier.

Section 1 (3) is made subject to s 6 (4). This states that the liabilities referred to in s 6[12] include not just those referred to in s 1 (3) but also those arising under any contract of sale of goods or hire-purchase agreement. This was made necessary by the fact that terms relating to title and correspondence with description in such contracts and agreements, as laid down in ss 12 and 13 of the Sale of Goods Act and ss 8 and 9 of the Supply of Goods (Implied Terms) Act 1973, apply both to private and to business sales. The Act applies to Scotland as described above.

(c) Negligence liability

The marginal note to s 2, which does not relate to Scotland,[13] speaks of 'negligence liability' while the section is headed 'Avoidance of liability for negligence, breach of contract, etc'. These aids to interpretation give precise indication as to the contents of the section.

The most striking provision is contained in s 2 (1). It is rendered impossible for any person, whether by reference to any contract term or to a notice 'to exclude or restrict his liability for death or personal injury resulting from negligence'. From an abundance of caution, the subsection provides that a notice is equally ineffective whether given to 'persons generally or to particular persons'.

Before discussing the precise impact of s 2 (1), some initial points need making. First, a definition of negligence is provided in s 1 (1).[14] It can be the breach of any obligation to take or exercise reasonable care or skill in the performance of a contract, where the obligation arises from its express or implied terms. Contracts of service will no doubt readily spring to mind here, particularly those relating to installation or repair.

Negligence is also defined as the breach of any common law duty to take or exercise reasonable care or skill, but not any stricter duty. Observe that this definition operates independently of contract. It would extend, therefore, to the activities of surgeons (certainly when acting on NHS patients, since a contract in such cases is not easily located), dentists (again when acting under the health service), and to the provision of free services, such as some local authority car parks. Most important of all since this type of negligence plainly encompasses the tort of negligence itself, it covers manufacturers who negligently commit defective goods to circulation.

The last defined category of negligence is any breach of the common duty of care imposed by the Occupiers' Liability Act 1957 (including that of Northern Ireland); or the Occupiers' Liability (Scotland) Act 1960.

Section 1 (4) and, in Scotland, s 25 (2), stipulate that in determining whether a breach of a duty or obligation has arisen, no notice is to be taken of whether the breach was inadvertent or intentional, or whether liability for any breach arises directly or vicariously. Employers are thus prevented from using exclusion clauses to safeguard themselves from the consequences of an employee's liability. The reference to intention is presumably to ensure that while deliberate infliction of physical injury or even death might not constitute negligence outside the Act, it nevertheless must be so treated for the purposes of the legislation.

Where, therefore, death or personal injury results from negligence, as thus defined, clauses seeking to limit or exclude liability will be absolutely, and without exception, void and of no effect. The importance of this provision is in inverse proportion to its length. Holiday camps, for instance, will henceforth be quite incapable of avoiding liability should a holidaymaker be injured or killed during his holiday because of their negligence.[15] Owners of sports stadia will similarly be unable to avoid the consequences of their negligence which result in death or personal injury. Nor will the manufacturers of goods be able to disclaim responsibility for any negligence of theirs resulting in death or personal injury.

(d) Other loss or damage[16]

Section 2 (2) extends further the ineffectiveness of exclusion clauses, but this time the Act does not operate without qualification.

In the case of other loss or damage resulting from negligence (where the negligence has produced, that is, loss or damage which is not personal injury or death) liability cannot be excluded or restricted '*except in so far as the term or notice satisfies the requirement of reasonableness*'.[17] This particular requirement is central to the Act. For the moment we shall content ourselves with the simple reference, postponing a more detailed discussion until later.[18]

Typical targets of s 2 (2), it is not unfairly supposed, are car parks, dry cleaners and launderers. Henceforth, they will only be able to exclude liability for negligence resulting in damage to property where the exclusion clause is reasonable. Bailees, such as warehouses, will similarly feel the impact of the legislation.

It must not be supposed that 'other loss or damage' necessarily means, and means only, physical loss or physical damage. Economic loss is also within s 2 (2), so that where, for example, a case may be made out under the rule in *Hedley Byrne* v *Heller & Partners*,[19] any exclusion clause is within this particular subsection. It must be remembered though that nothing in the Act creates any right to sue for economic loss where none exists outside the Act: indeed the Act creates no new actions in negligence whatsoever. It merely gives greater, or potentially greater, impact to such rights as already exist.[20]

(e) Assumption of risk

While certain exclusion clauses remain ineffective and not illegal (in which latter case, their use may be presumed to die out) their retention as contract terms or notices could, in theory, outflank Parliament's intentions. This follows from the doctrine of volenti non fit injuria: a person who willingly accepts the risk of injury cannot complain when that injury materialises. An exclusion clause could constitute notification of a risk: subsequent use of the relevant goods or services could thus constitute an acceptance of the risk and hence a denial of any right to sue. Fortunately, this was anticipated by Parliament. Section 2 (3) and, in Scotland, s 16 (3), prescribe that agreement to, or awareness of an exclusion clause is not 'of itself to be taken as indicating [the plaintiff's] acceptance of the risk'. This subsection does not at all obliterate the doctrine of assumption of risk. It merely states that an exclusion clause will not of itself suffice to invoke the doctrine.

(f) Liability arising in contract

The heading to this section is somewhat misleading albeit it is the actual marginal note contained in the Act. It misleads in that its indication is that s 3 alone contains limitations on the exclusion of contract liability, whereas, as we have previously seen, so also does s 2. What is true about s 3 is that it is only concerned with contract liability: s 2 also covers tort and, insofar as it can be regarded separately, occupiers' liability.

Section 3 (1) spells out the precise area of control. The section applies between 'contracting parties where one of them deals as a consumer or on the other's written standard terms of business'.[21]

The double aspect of the subsection must be stressed. Section 3 will not only apply where one of the parties is a consumer: it applies also where both parties are businesses (or, at any rate, 'non-consumers') if they contract on written standard terms.

(g) Written standard terms

Nothing in the Act indicates what we are to understand by 'written standard terms'. Since every business has a beginning, presumably a course of dealing need not be shown. But some less easily answerable questions may be posed. If a contract is drawn up for a specific party (as between businesses this is possible), is this a written contract with standard terms? It may be if presented on a 'take-it-or-leave-it' basis. Again, is it necessary that all the terms be standard? Some terms of the agreement may always be present, others (such as the delivery date or time, amount, or date of payment) may, within limits, be freely negotiated. Then, again, is it necessary that the contract is to be exclusively on standard terms? If the written document is supplemented by orally agreed terms or even by terms implied at law, is the agreement still within the Act? One supposes that in this last case, the answer must be clear: an agreement need only be in part on standard terms to be within the Act. Were it otherwise, the Act would easily be evaded. The same considerations, it is thought, mean that only part of a contract entirely in writing need be on standard terms.[22]

Considerable support has been lent to these arguments by the decision of the Outer House in *McCrone* v *Boots Farm Sales*.[23] Section 17 of the Unfair Contract Terms Act, which applies only to Scotland, does not refer to 'contracts on written standard' terms, but instead to 'standard form contracts'. However, since s 17 (2) speaks of a 'customer' under such a contract as one 'who deals on the basis of written standard terms of business', there is plainly no material difference between s 3 and s 17 in this regard, and the *McCrone* case is thus to be treated as an authority on each. The view of Lord Dunpark expressed in the case was that it was:

plain that the section is designed to prevent one party to a contract from having his contractual rights, against a party who is in breach of contract, excluded or restricted by a term or condition, which is one of a number of fixed terms or conditions invariably incorporated in contracts of the kind in question by the party in breach, and which have been incorporated in the particular contract in circumstances in which it would be unfair and unreasonable for the other party to have his rights so excluded or restricted. If the section is to achieve its purpose, the phrase 'standard form contract' cannot be confined to written contracts in which both parties use standard forms. It is, in my opinion, wide enough to include any contract, whether wholly written or partly oral, which includes a set of fixed terms or conditions which the proponer applies, without material variation, to contracts of the kind in question.[24]

It appears from this that the exclusion clause must itself be one of the fixed terms, which was no doubt the intention of Parliament. This may be fair in the case of contracts negotiated between parties at arm's length, but will be otherwise where the parties are of unequal bargaining power. A consumer contract, of course, remains subject to the Act irrespective of whether the agreement is in standard form or on written standard terms.

(h) In the case of breach

Section 3 (2) and, in Scotland, s 17 (1) (a), deal with that case where A is in breach of his contract with B. In the event of such breach by A, each subsection provides that no contract term incorporated in a contract which is within s 3 (1) or 17 (1) will be effective to exclude or restrict any liability of his in respect of the breach, except insofar as the contract term satisfies the requirement of reasonableness. The type and origin of the breach is not spelled out and is irrelevant. It does not matter if the breach is wilful or innocent; derived or did not derive from negligence; or whether the broken obligation was or was not absolute. Subject to the possibility that the term may be reasonable, a party in default cannot exclude or restrict his liability for his breach of contract. It must be realised, as was pointed out earlier, that no new right to sue or measure of damages is created. The position under the Act is that *Hadley* v *Baxendale*[25] remains the arbiter of what the victim of a breach may claim: that is to say, the wrongdoer is liable for all such loss as he ought to have contemplated as arising from the breach. The Act operates, potentially, to remove some bars from his claim.

(i) In other cases

Section 3 (2) (b) and, in Scotland, s 17 (1) (b), operate regardless of any breach of contract. Subject once more to the possibility that the particular term might be reasonable, the Act provides that as against the consumer, or the party contracting on written standard terms (a standard form contract in Scotland), the other party to the contract may, neither:

(i) claim to render a performance substantially different from that which was reasonably expected of him, nor

(ii) claim to be entitled, in respect of the whole or any part of his contractual obligation, to render no performance at all.

The limitation in paragraph (i) would catch those holiday contracts which, while entered into with a specific holiday in mind, give the tour operators or holiday companies the right in defined or general circumstances to substitute for the promised holiday one of equivalent value.

The use of the phrase 'reasonably expected', which is quite a separate issue from whether the relevant term is reasonable, may cause problems. Note that what matters is the reasonable expectation; that is, the objective standard of a reasonable man, not the perhaps unreasonable assumptions of a particular individual. If a person signs a document containing a right to substitute one performance for another, how far can it then be said that the performance accepted as the principal aim of the contract is any longer reasonably expected? Whereas in s 2 (3) and s 16 (3) as already observed, Parliament was careful to spell out that an exclusion clause did not of itself import an assumption of risk, no equivalent precaution is taken with regard to s 3 or 17. The problem is more acute when the relevant term is distinguished by appearing in block capitals, or is placed in a red box, or is otherwise highlighted, as by appearing in a conspicuous notice effectively incorporated into the contract. In such cases, it is arguably less reasonable to expect a particular performance, and hence more reasonable to accept as a clear possibility the provision of a different performance. It may be that the effect of this part of the two sections is going to mean a less specific content in contracts, thus giving greater scope for arguing that a particular performance is not reasonably expected.

The precise terms of ss 3 (2) (b) and 17 (1) (b) disallow performance of a contract in a way 'substantially different' from that reasonably expected. Just when a performance may be so described is not specified. Tendering chalk for cheese is no doubt a clear example; but it may not be if the contract was for simulated cheese to be used in a stage production. Then again, is a thirteen day holiday in Benidorm 'substantially different' from one lasting fourteen days? Or is a flight to Munich 'substantially different' from a journey by rail, if the same time is allotted to the stay in Munich?

The list of variations where problems may be caused is endless. We know from *Arcos Ltd* v *Ronaasen*[26] that in sales of goods practically any deviation from the contract description will produce a breach of contract even if the goods remain unaffected in their suitability for their intended purpose. Since it is all a matter of reasonable expectation, the correct test to apply, although it will hardly remove every difficulty, is to ask after the essence of the agreement as the reasonable man would see it. Viewed thus, a thirteen day holiday is 'substantially different' from one lasting a fortnight: but being seated with four people instead of two is not so different.

A term is not totally ineffective even though couched in the widest terms. It is merely ineffective to permit a 'substantially different' performance. That same term may still be used to permit insignificant divergences.

Finally, ss 3 (2) (*b*) (ii) and, in Scotland, 17 (1) (*b*) (where the clauses subject to control are run together) impose the reasonableness test on terms which seek to allow no performance at all in respect of the whole or any part of the defendant's contractual obligation. This perhaps raises even more profound problems. Since the Act refers to the defendant's 'contractual obligation', it must therefore be to the contract that one must turn to discover the particular obligation. Yet it is that contract which contains the term allowing a party to provide no performance. His obligation therefore includes the right not to perform, and it can hardly be said not to be performing the contract when not performing, in a very real, contractual, sense, is performance of the contract. Presumably, we are meant to ask what the reasonable man would expect from the contract and to disregard anything derogating from what might be called the 'core' of the agreement. Timetables giving the right not to provide the particular train or bus seem very much within the scope of the Act.

(j) Sale and supply of goods

A major change in the law was wrought by the Supply of Goods (Implied Terms) Act 1973. By inserting a new s 55 (3) into the Sale of Goods Act 1893, any term seeking to exclude or restrict the obligations as to title, quiet possession or freedom from encumbrance became void. This was an absolute provision: it applied to consumer and non-consumer sales alike; and there was no saving for reasonable terms. Section 12 (2) of the 1973 Act made the same provision in respect of hire purchase agreements.

The Unfair Contract Terms Act, Sched 4, repeals both s 55 (3) of the Sale of Goods Act, as inserted above, and s 12 (2) of the Supply of Goods (Implied Terms) Act. No change in the law, however, is thereby produced, because s 6 (1) and, in Scotland, s 20 (1) of the 1977 Act provides that the various obligations as to title implied into contracts of sale and hire purchase cannot be excluded or restricted by reference to any contract term.

Sections 13–15 of the 1893 Act implied into contracts of sale conditions as to correspondence with description or sample, merchantable quality and fitness for purpose. A new s 55 (4) inserted into that Act rendered terms excluding or limiting liability in respect of these sections void in the case of consumer sales, but unenforceable in other cases to the extent that it was shown 'not to be fair or reasonable to allow reliance on the term'. As we shall later see,[27] the phrasing of s 55 (4) placed the burden of proof upon the plaintiff: under the Unfair Contract Terms Act, it rests on the defendant. Sections 9–11 of the 1973 Act implied the same conditions into contracts of hire purchase. The provisions of s 12 (3) of that Act were identical to the new s 55 (4) of the Sale of Goods Act.

Here, too, the provisions covering the validity of exclusion clauses were repealed by the Unfair Contract Terms Act. Again, the burden of proof in regard to reasonableness was shifted, but otherwise identical provisions to those first contained in the Supply of Goods (Implied Terms) Act are now to be found in s 6 (2) and, in Scotland, s 20 (2) of the Unfair Contract Terms Act.

(k) Other contracts under which goods pass

Section 7 of the Unfair Contract Terms Act (s 21 in Scotland) is entirely new. It applies to all contracts under which, or in pursuance of which, possession or ownership of goods passes but where the law of sale of goods or hire purchase is not applicable. These provisions will therefore apply to contracts for the hire or lease of goods. They also apply to contracts for the sale of work and materials, and contracts for installing equipment (if it cannot be construed as a contract for the sale of goods). Presumably, contracts of repair and maintenance are similarly within the Act if ownership or possession of goods passes by virtue of the agreement. In this last case, ss 7 and 21 will only apply to such goods as are newly incorporated into the relevant item by virtue of the maintenance or repair.

The precise import of ss 7 and 21 is to render certain exclusion clauses ineffective. It is important to realise that neither section implies into these 'other contracts' any terms relating to title or quality. Whether or not a contract contains such a term is now a matter for the Supply of Goods and Services Act 1982, except in Scotland to which that Act does not extend.

As far as such terms as the contract relate to quality, the terms of ss 7 (2) and 21 (3) (*a*) are unequivocal: as against a consumer liability in respect of correspondence with description or sample, or quality or fitness, cannot be excluded or restricted by reference to any contract term. Where the contract is not with a consumer, the Act provides for the effectiveness of such a term where it satisfies the requirement of reasonableness.

The position with regard to the implied terms as to title is that in relation to the terms implied by the 1982 Act (which correspond with those implied by the Sale of Goods Act 1979) they cannot be excluded or restricted by any contract term insofar as the terms are implied into contracts under which property passes. This absolute declaration of invalidity arises from an amendment to the Unfair Contract Terms Act by the 1982 Act itself. In relation to contracts under which only the possession of goods passes, however, s 7 (4) of the 1977 Act is not altered, and this provides that, inasmuch as terms are implied as to the right to give possession and to assure quiet possession, exclusion clauses shall be valid if reasonable. Since s 7 (4) is entirely silent on any implied term as to freedom from encumbrances, any such term may be excluded or restricted unimpeded by the Unfair Contract Terms Act. The Supply of Goods and Services Act, it has already been pointed out, does not apply to Scotland, so s 21, which is the counterpart of s 7, applies to contracts within its purview without alteration. That is to say, any implied terms as to title can be excluded if the test of reasonableness is satisfied: implied terms as to description, quality or fitness cannot be excluded in consumer contracts, and can only be excluded in other cases subject to the test of reasonableness.

Section 7 (5) excludes from the application of s 7 those goods passing on a redemption of trading stamps within the Trading Stamps Act 1964. The respective provisions applicable to Scotland are ss 21 (4) and 21. This means that s 4 of the Act, as inserted by s 16 of the Supply of Goods (Implied Terms) Act 1973 remains intact. In essence, this provides that upon the redemption of stamps for goods warranties are implied to the effect that the promoter has a right to exchange the goods, that the customer will obtain freedom from encumbrances and quiet possession (except where the customer is forewarned) and that the goods are of merchantable quality (except for disclosed defects or those which an examination, if made, ought to reveal). These terms apply to all redemptions for goods 'notwithstanding any terms to the contrary on which the redemption is made'. Indeed, clauses purporting to exclude the implied terms as to merchantable quality are now unlawful by virtue of the Consumer Transactions (Restrictions on Statements) Order 1976.[28]

Note that ss 7 (5) and 21 (4) only disapply ss 7 and 21 where the redemption is within the Trading Stamps Act. If the trading stamps are part of a scheme not covered by the Act,[29] then ss 7 and 21 will apply.

(*l*) *Guarantees*

A new regime is prescribed in ss 5 and 19 of the Act for what can usefully be called 'manufacturers' guarantees', although these sections use no such term. What ss 5 (3) and 19 (1) (*b*) in fact do is to exclude contracts under or in pursuance of which possession or ownership of the goods passed. In other words, ss 5 and 19 bite only on guarantees provided by third parties, such as manufacturers or wholesalers.

A definition of 'guarantee' is provided in s 5 (2) (*b*). Anything 'in writing is a guarantee', it runs, 'if it contains or purports to contain some promise or assurance (however worded or presented) that defects will be made good by complete or partial replacement, or by repair, monetary compensation or otherwise'. The provisions applicable to Scotland are the same except that there is reference to a 'document' instead of to something 'in writing'.

It is not entirely clear from the wording of s 5 (2) (*b*) whether only written matter can constitute a guarantee. It is hardly important as a practical matter, however, since the third party will rarely be present when the agreement is made and since he will scarcely wish to prove a statement which the law will then render nugatory. On the other hand, a party given a verbal guarantee (which may happen when he calls, or is visited by, the manufacturer or his representative) is as likely to be deceived when later complaining to the guarantor as one given a written guarantee. Furthermore, verbal exclusion clauses do appear to be within s 2 (s 16 in Scotland) and s 3 (s 17 in Scotland), at least as far as the latter concerns dealing with consumers. Sections 14 and 25 (4) include within the definition of 'notice' an 'announcement, whether or not in writing . . .'.

The precise controls exerted by s 5 (and identical, though not identically worded, provisions are contained in s 19) are as follows. Where goods are of 'a type ordinarily supplied for private use or consumption', liability for loss or damage cannot be excluded or restricted by reference to any contract term or notice contained in, or operating by reference to, a guarantee of the goods, where that loss or damage:

>   (a) arises from the goods proving defective while in consumer use; and
>
>   (b) results from the negligence of a person concerned in the manufacture or distribution of the goods.

None of this necessarily means that a claim in negligence will succeed: merely that certain bars to recovery have been removed. The ordinary rules of negligence will thus be quite free to prescribe what can be recovered.

It is to be noted that, unlike ss 2 and 16, no distinction is drawn between injury to person and injury to property. In all cases, the exclusion clause will be ineffective.

Section 5 (2) (a) defines the situation when goods are in 'consumer use'. This is when the person 'is using them' or 'has them in his possession for use', otherwise 'than exclusively for the purposes of a business'. The use of these particular phrases makes it clear that a person who buys or hires an item which he employs both privately and for his occupation (such as an author and his typewriter) is within the section. It also appears that, when goods have this 'mixed function', a person is within the section if the loss or damage arises while the goods are being used for business purposes. This seems to emerge from the phrase 'or has them in his possession for use ...' This also appears to be so in relation to Scotland by virtue of s 19 (2) (a).

(m) Indemnity clauses

A further departure in the Unfair Contract Terms Act is the control exercised over indemnity clauses. Where a person deals as a consumer, no contract term will be effective to compel him to indemnify another person (whether or not that other person is a party to the contract) in respect of liability incurred by the other for negligence or breach of contract. This is subject to the qualification that reliance on such a contract term is permissible where it satisfies the requirement of reasonableness.

This somewhat obscure provision is aimed at the type of contract term which is not infrequently a feature of agreements made with the operators of car ferries. Where A contracts with the operators, he will agree to indemnify the latter should they, while moving his car, damage that of another. That control of such clauses was the aim of Parliament is further evidenced by s 4 (2). Section 4, this subsection provides, applies whether the liability in question is directly that of the person to be indemnified or is incurred by him vicariously (as when the liability of the ferry operators derives from an act of their employees); and whether the liability is to the person dealing as consumer or to someone else (as the operators', for example, to the owner of the car damaged by their negligence or breach of contract). The equivalent Scottish provision is to be found in s 18. Section 18 makes no specific reference to vicarious liability.

(n) Varieties of exemption clause

Not every clause seeking to exclude or restrict a person's liability is of a straightforward kind, such as: 'No liability is undertaken in respect of ...'. Recognising this s 13 (1) (s 25 (3) in Scotland) extends the controls on exclusion clauses in three directions by bringing certain other categories of clause within the controls imposed by the Act. First, clauses are controlled which make that liability or its enforcement 'subject to restrictive or onerous conditions'. This will counter such clauses as require notification within a particular time before a claim will be entertained, or demand several copies of a claim, or require its attestation by certain persons. No definition is provided of 'onerous', but it may fairly be regarded as something beyond that which is fairly expected.

Second, a clause is additionally controlled where it seeks to exclude or restrict any right or remedy in respect of the relevant liability, or to subject a person to any prejudice in consequence of his pursuing any such right or remedy. What manifestly was intended here was to watch over such clauses as forbid recovery of consequential loss or of damages. Some contracts with tour operators have sought to exclude recovery of damages for disappointment.[30] A clause imposing a prejudice would exist where a deposit is forfeited should action of any kind be taken.

Third, the Act also subjects to control such clauses as exclude or restrict rules of evidence or procedure.

Section 13 (1) also provides that to the extent that ss 2 and 5–7 prevent the exclusion or restriction of any liability, they also prevent the exclusion or restriction of liability by reference to terms and notices which exclude the 'relevant obligation or duty'. This is essentially an anti-avoidance provision. It catches the notice which, instead of excluding liability for negligence, simply contains a statement declining to accept a duty of care. Section 3 is omitted since a person is essentially free to make his own bargain. In any case, ss 6 and 7, as we have seen, render the exclusion of certain obligations either void or voidable, and these two sections are within s 13. With regard to Scotland, s 25 (5) is equivalent to this part of s 13 (1): it is important to note that the subsection applies only to ss 15, 16 and 19–21.

Sections 13 (2) and 25 (3) partially qualify the preceding subsection by providing that a written agreement to submit present of future differences to arbitration is not to be treated as excluding or restricting liability. This means that, the English and Scottish provisions cannot bite on arbitration clauses. Given that the codes of practice encouraged by the Office of Fair Trading themselves adopt arbitration, this is hardly a surprise.

(o) Anti-avoidance measures

The marginal notes to ss 10 and 23 refer to 'Evasion by means of secondary contract'. Specifically, they provide that where the Act itself prevents a party from excluding or restricting certain rights which arise under, or in connection with, the performance of one contract, no other contract is effective in prejudicing or taking away those rights. In other words, it is accepted that where, for example, there is a sale of goods under a consumer contract, no exclusion clause in that contract of sale can restrict or exclude the implied terms as to merchantable quality or fitness for purpose. What these sections now say is that no term in any other contract between the same (or indeed different) parties will be effective to exclude or restrict the implied terms of the contract of sale. What cannot be done directly, cannot be done indirectly.

Although an equivalent section appeared in the Supply of Goods (Implied Terms) Act 1973, yet it may still be permissible to argue that these provisions were inserted into the 1977 Act because of excessive caution. Where the secondary contract was made between the same parties, it is assumed that the two contracts would be read as one, thus striking out void exclusion clauses. Alternatively, it can be argued that seeking to avoid the effect of consumer protection legislation is scarcely consonant with even the narrowest view of public policy.

(p) Effect of breach—nullifying Harbutt's Plasticine

Section 9 of the Unfair Contract Terms Act was very clearly drafted with the Harbutt's Plasticine case firmly in mind.[31] Subsection (1) provides that if a term must be reasonable before it is effective, it may be adjudged reasonable and hence effective despite termination by breach or by a party electing to treat it as repudiated.

It was, of course, laid down in the Court of Appeal that where a contract had been terminated by one party so electing after a fundamental breach (though in the particular case the victims of the breach had no realistic alternative) the whole contract, including any exclusion clause, terminated on the election. Section 9 (1) removed this possibility as far as contracts covered by the Act were concerned by providing that termination fails to prevent a term being judged reasonable and interpreted under ordinary principles.[32] Where the innocent party elects to affirm the contract, s 9 (2) provides that such election does not of itself 'exclude the requirement of reasonableness in relation to any contract term'. This again appears to be a provision inserted because of excessive caution. Presumably, it was inserted to counter the argument (certainly a barely tenable one) that affirmation of a contract removes a party's liberty to contest the application of a clause, or even that such affirmation is conclusive of reasonableness. The same provisions are contained in s 22 in relation to Scotland.

In the light of the decision of the House of Lords in *Photo Production* v *Securicor Transport*,[33] it may now be said that the foregoing provisions are virtually of historical interest only. It will be recalled that the House of Lords effectively annulled the decision of the Court of Appeal in *Harbutt's Plasticine*.

(q) *Dealing as a consumer*

Sections 3, 4, 6 and 7 (ss 17, 18, 20 and 21 in Scotland) are all in one way or another governed by the restriction that, before certain exclusion clauses are rendered ineffective, one of the parties must deal as a consumer.

In determining when such dealing occurs, ss 12 (3) and 25 (1) stipulate that it is for those claiming that a party does not deal as a consumer to show that he does not. Sections 12 (2) and 25 (1) provide that in any case a sale by auction or by competitive tender is not to be considered a consumer sale. It may be wondered where this leaves advertisements containing the rubric (or its equivalent) '£x or nearest offer'. This seems an easy and effective way of converting a consumer sale into an auction or competitive tender.

Sections 12 (1) and 25 (1) provide that a party deals as a consumer, or effects a consumer contract, where three conditions are satisfied. Although not expressly said to be so, it is assumed that this definition is exhaustive. The conditions are, first, that the presumptive consumer neither makes the contract in the course of a business nor holds himself out as so doing.[34] The second limb must be carefully watched since it is far from clear when a person is so holding himself out. An individual buying a car might for the sake of his own protection assume some knowledge with the air of being on equal footing with the dealer. Arguably, he holds himself out as buying in the course of a business and so will not fall to be treated as a consumer.

The second condition (which significantly did not appear in the Supply of Goods (Implied Terms) Act 1973 requires that the party dealing with the alleged consumer must himself have contracted in the course of a business.

Third, the goods, where the contract is one of sale, hire purchase or covered by s 7 (in Scotland, s 15 (2) (a)) of the Act, must be of a type 'ordinarily supplied' for private use or consumption. The phrase 'ordinarily supplied' is easily understood but may cause difficulties. What, for example, is the position with an item such as a word-processor, where the great majority of sales are not to private buyers? It would be odd if they could never be the subject of a consumer sale since such items are far from unknown in sales to private people. If the strict wording of the Act is to be defended, it can be on the ground that people able to buy such goods can usually afford to take care of themselves. Yet some items are more expensive, such as cars, but these are certainly capable of being the subject of a consumer sale. Indeed, cars may well be apposite in that such goods may be no more sold to consumers than to those who use them in business. Although it does some violence to ss 12 and 25, it is thought that 'ordinarily supplied' should be taken to mean 'of a type which can fairly be imagined as supplied for private sale or consumption'.

The one authority, heard on the comparable wording of the 1973 Act, is *Rasbora* v *JCL Marine*.[35] A boat was supplied under a contract of construction and sale.[36] A few days after acceptance trials were held of the boat, and an acceptance certificate signed, an incorporated company, wholly owned by the buyer, was substituted as the buyer in an agreed novation of contract. Lawson J held that the initial contract was clearly a consumer sale, and the novation did not affect this. If this were wrong (and it must be viewed with suspicion) he held that the substituted contract was anyway a consumer sale. The new buyer, he said, was wholly owned by the original buyer and was formed for the sole purpose of buying the boat with the intention that it was to be used only by the original buyer or his licensees. There was no intention to charter or hire the boat, or any other, to third parties. The sellers had thus failed to discharge the onus of proving the sale not to be a consumer sale.[37]

(r) Requirement of reasonableness

We have frequently seen that exclusion clauses stand or fall on whether they satisfy the requirement of reasonableness. It is necessary first to note that, by the terms of s 29 (2), a contract is deemed to be reasonable if incorporated or approved by, or incorporated pursuant to a decision or ruling of, a 'competent authority',[38] acting under a statutory jurisdiction or function. The qualification is that the competent authority must not be adjudicating upon a term in a contract to which the authority is a party. Under s 27 of the Water Act 1945, the reasonableness of terms in a contract for the supply of water may be determined by a decision of the minister. The Defective Premises Act 1972 permits a builder to opt out of the duties imposed by that Act[39] if he assumes other obligations prescribed in the House-Buildings Standards Scheme. Like provision may be found in s 7 (4) of the Water Act 1973, and s 65 of the Civil Aviation Act 1982.

The prime rules are laid down in s 11 (1) and (3) and, in Scotland, s 24 (1). Subsection (1) of s 11 provides that, in relation to a contract term, or s 3 of the Misrepresentation Act 1967, reasonableness means that a term 'shall have been a fair and reasonable one to be included having regard to the circumstances which were, or ought reasonably to have been, known to or in the contemplation of the parties when the contract was made'. The Misrepresentation Act does not apply in Scotland. Section 11 (3), which has no Scottish equivalent, and which deals with a notice not having contractual effect, states in corresponding terms that it must be shown that it is 'fair and reasonable' to permit reliance on the notice, having regard to all the circumstances obtaining when the particular liability arose, or would have arisen but for the clause.

It is important to stress that, insofar as ss 11 (1) and 24 (1) are concerned, there has been a subtle, but highly significant, change from the wording found in the now repealed s 3 of the Misrepresentation Act and s 55 (4) of the amended Sale of Goods Act. In these two cases, the crucial wording was that an exclusion clause was unenforceable to the extent that it was shown 'that it would not be fair or reasonable to allow reliance on the term' (Sale of Goods Act) or to the extent that reliance on the clause was not 'fair and reasonable in the circumstances of the case' (Misrepresentation Act).

These provisions clearly contemplated that reasonableness may be judged in the light of events as they turned out: scrutiny is not to be given simply to the position when the contract was made.[40] In *Rasbora* v *JCL Marine*,[41] Lawson J further supported his judgment by holding that it would not be fair or reasonable to rely on the exclusion clause contained in the agreement because the boat, by reason of the electrical engineering defects for which the defendants were responsible, was destroyed just over a day after being handed over. If the clause were to apply, the learned judge decided, the 'buyer would be left without any remedy at all'.[42] If the case had fallen under the Unfair Contract Terms Act, the events subsequent to breach would not have mattered, attention being given only to the situation prevailing when the contract was made.

The court or arbitrator to whom falls the task of deciding whether or not a clause is reasonable is not left unaided. Sections 11 (2) and 24 (2) stipulate that when the matter falls for decision within the terms of s 6 or 7 (s 20 or 21 in Scotland) (that is to say, where the contract is one of sale, hire purchase or some other contract under which the possession or ownership of goods passes) 'regard shall be had' to the matters specified in Sched 2. Apart from some improvements in the wording, these follow the guidelines to be originally found in s 55 (5) of the amended Sale of Goods Act and, in relation to hire purchase, s 12 (4), of the Supply of Goods (Implied Terms) Act.

In fact, the contents of Sched 2 are no more than those factors which would be taken into account in every case in which the issue of reasonableness was in question. In *Woodman* v *Photo Trade Processing*,[43] the case arose under s 2 (2) and therefore there was no requirement that reference be made to the Schedule. The registrar did, however, adopt the contents of the Schedule in considering the issue of reasonableness, an approach which the learned county court judge regarded as legitimate since in 'considering that wide question of what is "fair and reasonable" the "guidelines" set out in Schedule 2 for other types of contract would be among the matters necessarily needing consideration in this case'.

A qualification to ss 11 (2) and 24 (2) of the 1977 Act provides that neither in any way prevent the particular court or arbitrator from holding, in accordance with any rule of law, that a particular exclusion clause is not in fact a term of the contract. This qualification serves to emphasise what the courts would doubtless have held even in its absence: that whether a term is reasonable or not, it cannot begin to be effective unless it is incorporated into the contract.

Nor are the guidelines of Sched 2 the only aid in determining reasonableness. Sections 11 (4) and 24 (3) provide that where a contract term or notice seeks to restrict liability to a 'specified sum' of money, regard shall be had in deciding if such clause is reasonable to:

(a) the resources which the proponent of the clause could expect to be available to meet the liability; and

(b) the availability of insurance.

The respective subsections provide that these terms are without prejudice to the guideline rules contained in Sched 2. Section 11 (4) further provides that its terms apply when the issue of reasonableness arises under the Unfair Contract Terms Act or any other Act. This latter presently appears to apply only to the Misrepresentation Act 1967. No such reference is made in s 24 (3) since the Act of 1967 does not apply in Scotland.

The Act does not define a 'specified sum' and the question arises whether it includes a sum which can be readily ascertained but is not specified. A laundry contract may limit liability to twenty times the cost of laundering the particular goods. It is believed that where the precise sum merely awaits the working out of a prescribed formula, this constitutes a 'specified sum' within the Act.

A final, crucial, point is that under ss 11 (5) and 24 (4), the burden is placed on the proponent of the clause to prove that it is reasonable. An assessment of the cases since the Act came into force shows how extremely difficult, particularly in consumer contracts, it will ever be for the party seeking to uphold the disputed clause ever to discharge the burden of proof. In *Lally* v *Bird*,[44] the plaintiffs were moving house and contracted with the defendants for the storage and onward delivery of their furniture. The night before delivery, the defendants' driver left the furniture van outside his house, from where it was stolen. The contract limited liability to a sum of money per article, and required all claims to be made within a certain period. The judge ruled that these clauses were inapplicable, both because there had been a deviation from the contract and because the terms did not pass the reasonableness test under the Unfair Contract Terms Act. In *Waldron-Kelly* v *Marshall*,[45] a suitcase was delivered at one BR station for onward transmission to another. The contract was made at owner's risk, and contained a clause whereby damage was restricted on a weight basis. The suitcase was lost and BR claimed to restrict their liability to £27 as opposed to the more than £320 which was the actual value of the items missing. The county court judge again ruled that the limitation clause was not a reasonable one.

In *Woodman* v *Photo Trade Processing*,[46] a roll of film was handed over for processing subject to a contract term which limited liability to the replacement cost of the film. When the defendants attempted to invoke this clause, Judge Clarke was considerably influenced by the decision of the house of Lords in *Peek* v *North Staffordshire Railway*.[47] The question in that early case involved the provision in the Railway and Canal Traffic Act 1854 which stipulated that contract terms in a railway company's conditions of carriage were valid only if 'just and reasonable'. The term in dispute limited liability for loss or damage to fragile goods except where these were declared and insured according to their value. By six to five, the House of Lords had decided that the clause failed to pass the test: it excluded liability for mistake as well as negligence, the railway company's monopoly effectively forced customers to accept their terms; and the only insurance cover available was 'exorbitant'.

Judge Clarke was also considerably influenced by the existence of a code of practice for the photographic industry which had been negotiated with the Office of Fair Trading. It recognised that processors could maintain a two-tier system: a cheaper one with full exclusion of liability; and a more expensive one with a greater degree of liability. The defendants offered neither of these alternatives.

Two further cases were referred to by the learned county court judge as also influencing his decision to find that the limitation clause, like those in the previous cases, was unreasonable. In *Levison* v *Patent Steam Carpet Cleaning*,[48] Lord Denning had condemned a clause as unreasonable when the attention of the other party had not been drawn to it by its proferens. This was true also of the instant case. In *Schroeder Music Publishing* v *Macaulay*,[49] Lord Diplock, albeit in the context of restraint of trade, had posed as the test of fairness 'whether the restrictions are both reasonably necessary for the protection of the legitimate interests of the promisee and commensurate with the benefits secured to the promisor under the contract'. Applying that test to the case in hand, Judge Clarke found that, while the defendants had a 'legitimate interest in keeping their costs down', it still could not be regarded as 'reasonably necessary to protect that interest by compelling everybody, including the few who have high value photographs, to take their chance with the PTP mass promotion system. For the majority of customers the lower price, resulting from excluded liability, may be a commensurate benefit, but even then the balance is uncertain because he does not know the extent of the risk he runs to get those lower prices'.

No case has yet been heard on the reasonableness of indemnity clauses but reference may usefully be made to *British Airports Authority* v *British Airways Board*.[50] A clause in the Authority's terms and conditions of use ran thus:

The operator will indemnify the Authority its servants or agents against any claim which may be made against the Authority its servants or agents for loss damage or injury (including fatal injury) incurred by any person using or being in an aircraft however such loss, damage or injury may be caused, including (without prejudice to the generality of the foregoing) any claim arising from the act, omission, neglect or default of the Authority, its servants or agents unless done with intent to cause damage or recklessly and with knowledge that damage would probably result.

Obviously, the arrangement by which airlines could use Authority property could not be classed as a consumer contract, so the Unfair Contract Terms Act was not directly in point. Even so, Parker J observed of the clause that it 'smacks of unreasonableness'.

The learned judge did have cause to apply s 11 (3) of the Act in relation to this clause:

Neither the Authority nor any servant or agent of the Authority shall be liable for loss of or damage to the aircraft, its parts or accessories or any property contained in the aircraft, occurring while the aircraft is on the airport or is in the course of landing or taking off at the airport, or being removed or dealt with elsewhere ... arising or resulting directly or indirectly from any act, omission or default on the part of the Authority its servants or agents unless done with intent to cause damage or recklessly and with knowledge that damage would probably result.

The Judge held in accordance with s 11 (3) that it was 'fair and reasonable' to allow reliance on this clause. He gave no specific reasons but was clearly impressed by the effect the clause would have in enabling the Authority to limit its costs and in freeing it from involvement in disputes and accidents, the facts of which would be almost entirely unknown to it.

The implication of this last case is that it might be less onerous for the burden of proof more easily to be satisfied where the contracting parties are both in the way of business. There was a clear indication that this certainly ought to be so in *Photo Production* v *Securicor Transport*.[51] As Lord Diplock said: 'In commercial contracts negotiated between businessmen capable of looking after their own interests and of deciding how risks inherent in the performance of various kinds of contract can be most economically borne (generally by insurance) it is, in my view, wrong to place a strained construction on words in an exclusion clause which are clear and fairly susceptible of one meaning ...'; in the same case, Lord Wilberforce remarked that, with regard to the Unfair Contract Terms Act, it is 'significant that Parliament refrained from legislating over the whole field of contract. After this Act, in commercial matters generally, when the parties are not of unequal bargaining power, and when risks are normally borne by insurance, not only is the case for judicial intervention undemonstrated, but there is everything to be said ... for leaving the parties free to apportion the risks as they think fit and for respecting their decisions'.[52]

These powerful observations were specifically alluded to and relied on in *White Cross Equipment* v *Farrell*.[53] The contract (which in fact was heard under the reasonableness test contained in the Supply of Goods (Implied Terms) Act 1973) related to the sale of goods between businesses. Referring to the Schedule and the guidelines, the Deputy High Court judge noted first that the parties were of approximately equal bargaining power. They contracted at arm's length and: 'I have no doubt that the defendant could have bargained away the plaintiffs' terms had he so wished. If the plaintiffs had not been willing to give up (the exclusion clause) the defendant could undoubtedly have gone elsewhere'. The Deputy High Court judge also noted that the sellers did in the contract offer a complete six months' guarantee; and noted that it was always possible for such a machine as was concerned in this case to be mis-used: 'Those considerations, in my view, amply justify the plaintiffs saying to a purchaser: "After 6 months you are on your own as far as defects of design or workmanship are concerned".' He concluded by observing that this was not a case where insurance had a role to play: 'So I have viewed this matter simply as a question of allocating risks between two commercial parties of equal bargaining power'. This led inexorably to his conclusion that it was fair and reasonable to allow reliance on the exclusion clause. It seems indisputable that, had the matter arisen for hearing under the 1977 Act, the learned Deputy would have found the clause a reasonable one to incorporate.

Even so, there is precedent to show that even contracts between businesses may be subject to adverse findings under the Act. In *Green* v *Cade Bros Farms*,[54] the contract was for the sale of seed potatoes to a farmer. Included in that contract were terms which insisted on complaints being made within three, or sometimes seven, days; and which also limited damages to the contract price. The judge upheld this latter clause since the contract had been one moulded over the years by trade associations representing both parties, and because the potatoes were somewhat cheaper since they were uncertified. On the other hand, he rejected the first-mentioned clause since no one, at the time the contract was made, would have reckoned it a practical matter to have complained of the particular defect within the prescribed time. This is close indeed to a finding that the clause was not a reasonable one to incorporate under the 1977 Act.

An adverse finding was also recorded in *George Mitchell* v *Finney Lock Seeds*.[55] A contract for the supply to a farmer of cabbage seed had stipulated that: 'In the event of any seeds ... sold ... by us not complying with the express terms of the contract of sale ... or any seeds ... proving defective in varietal purity we will ... refund all payments made to us by the buyer in respect of the seeds ... and this shall be the limit of our obligation. We hereby exclude all liability for any loss or damage arising from the use of any seeds ... supplied by us and for any consequential loss or damage arising out of such use ... or any defect in any seeds supplied by us or for any other loss or damage whatsoever save for the refund as aforesaid'. In finding that this clause was not one upon which it was fair and reasonable to allow reliance (a decision upheld by the Court of Appeal),[56] Parker J stated that: the seedsmen could have insured against the risk; this would not materially have raised the price; the protection of the exclusion clause for the very rare case such as had materialised in this instance was 'not reasonably required'; and it would have been possible for the seed to have been tested before being placed on the market. There seems no doubt at all that this catalogue of objections would have led to a finding of unreasonableness under the Unfair Contract Terms Act.

In only one case, and this operates very much at the margin, has a clause in a consumer contract been upheld as passing the test of reasonableness. In *Macrae* v *Dick*,[57] a dealer sold a Rolls Royce subject to a clause which gave the dealer a right to buy back within twelve months in the event of the buyer wishing to sell. It was said that this clause was one which allowed the supplier to provide a contract performance which was substantially different from that which was reasonably expected within ss 3 and 17. The judge declined to make a finding on this point since he was clear in any case that the clause was reasonable. The point was that the clause had not been part of the contract when first made, and was inserted only with the agreement of the buyer. The buyer could have stood on the contract as it was first drawn up and demanded delivery of the car without the disputed contract term: since the buyer had this option: 'I cannot see how it can possibly be said that it was not fair and reasonable for the pursuers to introduce the obligation into the contract'.

(s) Misrepresentation

Section 3 of the Misrepresentation Act 1967 (the Act having no application to Scotland), which makes clauses excluding liability for misrepresentation subject to a test of reasonableness is repealed and replaced by s 8 of the 1977 Act. The new s 3 is identical to the old, except that the requirement of reasonableness to be satisfied is that contained in s 11 of the 1977 Act. The onus is placed on those insisting that a term is reasonable to prove their case.

The precise nature of the exclusion clauses which are subject to the test of reasonableness is as follows:

  (a) any provision excluding or restricting any liability to which a party to a contract may be subject by reason of any misrepresentation;
  (b) any provision excluding or restricting any remedy available to another party by reason of such misrepresentation.

In *Howard Marine & Dredging* v *Ogden*,[58] a clause provided that '... charterers acceptance of handing over the vessel shall be conclusive that (she is) ... in all respects fit for the intended and contemplated use by Charterers and in every other way satisfactory to them'. The High Court had ruled that it was not fair and reasonable to allow reliance on the clause, an opinion which neither Bridge nor Shaw LJJ were prepared to disturb, though neither expressed any particular view. Lord Denning, however, regarded the clause as upheld by the evidence: the charterers had had full inspection and examination of the barges; their surveyors had given them an 'on-hire condition' survey; and an expert would have given them the information they sought. Their case was not supported by any written representations, and there was in any case a severe conflict of evidence. Lord Denning concluded that it was 'just such conflicts which commercial men seek to avoid by such a clause as this'.[59] Everything Lord Denning said was directed to the test then relevant, namely, whether it was fair and reasonable to allow reliance on the clause in dispute. Whether such a clause would withstand the test of reasonable incorporation must be moot, especially as the majority of the Court of Appeal were not prepared to dissent from the court below.

A case directly in point is *Walker* v *Boyle*.[60] A clause in the National Conditions of Sale (which was altered in the wake of this case) provided that there was no right to rescind the contract for errors, mis-statements or omissions in the preliminary answers, or in the sale plan or Special Conditions, 'nor (save where the error, mis-statement or omission is in a written answer and relates to a matter materially affecting the description or value of the property) shall any damages be payable or compensation allowed by either party, in respect thereof'. Without specifying his reasons, the judge found that the proferens had failed to show that the clause was reasonable: he appears to have been influenced by the fact that the condition would exclude compensation for any oral mis-statement, however grave, even to the extent of being fraudulent.

The general difficulty of ever satisfying the burden of proof is further demonstrated in *Josef Marton* v *Southwestern General Property*.[61] The short facts were that land was bought at auction in reliance on a misrepresentation. The vendors pleaded in their favour the following clauses: 'The property is believed to be and shall be taken as correctly described and any incorrect statement, error or omission found in the particulars or conditions of sale shall not annul the sale or entitle the purchaser to be discharged from his purchase'. A further clause denied the purchaser any right to take any point under town and country planning legislation, requiring him to 'take the properties as they are under the said Acts, rules and regulations'. A further, and final, clause, 'quite obviously designed to avoid the effect of the Misrepresentation Act' ran as follows:

(a) All statements contained in the foregoing particulars are made without responsibility on the part of the auctioneers or the vendor and are statements of opinion and are not to be taken as or implying a statement or representation of fact and any intending purchaser must satisfy himself by inspection or otherwise as to the correctness of each statement contained in the particulars;

(b) The vendor does not make or give any representation or warranty in relation to the property nor has the auctioneer or any person in the employment of the auctioneer any authority to do so on his behalf.

The vendors, seeking to uphold these clauses, said the circumstances of auction sales necessitated their inclusion. The reply from the purchaser was that the misrepresentation concerned matters which came from the vendors themselves which were peculiarly in their knowledge. It was also said that the particulars did stress the need for purchasers to satisfy themselves of the accuracy of the particulars. This was rejected by Croom-Johnson J who answered that 'it might be said that people do attend auctions at short notice, as Mr Marton did, when there is simply not time, as in this case, to make enquiries'. The vendors finally argued that they were not just catering for private buyers, such as the present party, but also for other types, including speculators. At the end of the day, however, the judge pointed to the fact that it is the reasonableness of the particular clause in the particular contract with the particular buyer. He stressed that the facts on which the representation were based were peculiarly within the knowledge of the vendor and related to issues which were 'central to the purchase'. In the end, and repeating that what he had to consider were 'the parties to this contract, and the circumstances in which this contract was made', Croom-Johnson J held that the vendors had failed to show him that the clause was reasonable: if it were otherwise, the vendors would be able to avoid liability 'for a failure to tell more than only a part of the facts which were among the most material to the whole contract of sale'.

A most instructive decision on the effectiveness of exclusion clauses in this context is *Cremdean Properties* v *Nash*.[62] The defendants, against whom it was alleged that a misrepresentation had been made, relied on a clause reading: 'These particulars are prepared for the convenience of an intending purchaser or tenant and although they are believed to be correct their accuracy is not guaranteed and any error, omission or misdescription shall not annul the sale or the grounds on which compensation may be claimed and neither do they constitute any part of an offer of a contract. Any intending purchaser or tenant must satisfy himself by inspection or otherwise as to the correctness of each of the statements contained in these particulars'.

Bridge LJ paraphrased the argument of the defendants in these words: 'the footnote is effective ... to bring about a situation in law as if no representation at all had even been made'.[63] In the more robust wording of Scarman LJ, the defendants were arguing thus: 'a statement is not a representation unless it is also a statement that what is stated is true. If in context a statement contains no assertion, express or implied, that its content is accurate, there is no representation. Ergo, there can be no misrepresentation; ergo, the Misrepresentation Act 1967 cannot apply to it'.[64]

The Court of Appeal were unanimous in finding that this argument was untenable.[65] The language of the exclusion clause, said Bridge LJ 'simply does not, on its true interpretation, have the effect contended for'.[66] Scarman LJ found that, fairly construed, the exclusion clause was a warning to the would-be purchaser to check the facts. Such a warning 'does not destroy the representation;

indeed, it is wholly consistent with the statement being a representation. It is because the statement contains the representation that the warning is given. Since the statement was false, there was a false representation; the Act therefore applies'.[67]

Bridge LJ took the matter further. While finding against the defendants in that the clause could not bear the construction sought to be placed upon it, he felt 'extremely doubtful whether the court' would ever allow s 3 to be thus evaded. Supposing, he said, an exclusion clause was drafted to read: 'notwithstanding any statement of fact included in these particulars the vendor shall be conclusively deemed to have made no representation within the meaning of the Misrepresentation Act 1967'.[68] It was the Lord Justice's opinion that 'this was only a form of words the intended and actual effect of which was to exclude or restrict liability, and I should not have thought that the courts would have been ready to allow such ingenuity in forms of language to defeat the plain purpose at which Section 3 is aimed'.[69] This is surely right: a misrepresentation cannot change its character by simply saying that it is not what it is.[70]

The Court of Appeal, through Bridge LJ, supported in this by Scarman LJ, rejected the idea that for the purposes of the Misrepresentation Act there was a distinction between a 'representation' and statements of opinion, belief or information. The word itself, said Bridge LJ is 'an extremely wide term; I cannot see why one should not be making a representation when giving information or when stating one's opinion or belief ... it would be a retrograde step if the court were to give the word 'representation' where it appears in the Misrepresentation Act 1967, any narrow or limited construction less wide than the perfectly natural meaning of the word'.[71]

The Court left undecided the issue whether or not the clause was reasonable. That was a matter for consideration at the trial. The only issue here was whether the Misrepresentation Act applied at all. The Court also left over until trial the possible impact of the final part of the clause which required intending purchasers or tenants to satisfy themselves as to the correctness of the particulars. This part of the clause, said Bridge LJ, 'may have considerable importance ... as bearing upon the question of fact ... as to whether the plaintiffs relied upon any misrepresentation'.[72] In *Walker* v *Boyle*, Dillon J referred to the small print which appeared above replies on the form of preliminary enquiries: 'These replies on behalf of the vendor are believed to be correct but accuracy is not guaranteed and they do not obviate the need to make appropriate searches, enquiries and inspections'. He concluded that words such as these cannot negative any representation which may in fact have been made.[73]

(t) Specified exclusions

Schedule 1, as implemented by s 1 (2), provides that ss 2–4 and s 7 do not extend to contracts of insurance, contracts relating to the creation, transfer or termination of an interest in land, contracts relating to the creation, transfer or termination of an interest in intellectual property, contracts relating to the formation or dissolution of a company or to its constitution or the rights or obligations of its members, and any contract relating to the creation or transfer of securities or of any right or interest in securities.

It is thought that these exclusions must be strictly construed. In particular, the exception for interests in land must be taken, witness the vital word 'relates', as referring to the contract by which the particular interest is transferred. It is difficult to accept that the exemption should extend to cover estate agents, valuers and surveyors, since their work is one step removed from the actual contract transferring the interest. It is also arguable that the exemption only 'relates' to the contract terms which create, transfer or terminate the interest. That is to say, in a contract for the sale of real property, only the term passing the estate falls outside the Act.

There are also limited exceptions relating to marine salvage or towage, charterparties of ships or hovercrafts, the carriage of goods by ship or hovercraft, contracts of employment, or relating to awards of compensation in respect of pneumoconiosis.

The approach taken differs with regard to Scotland. Only the specified contracts, as enumerated in s 15 (2), are within the Act. Contracts relating to the transfer of ownership or possession are included as are contracts of service or apprenticeship. All contracts of service are included and, without intending to be exhaustive, the 1977 Act specifically mentions contracts of carriage, deposit and pledge, care and custody, mandate, agency, loan and services relating to the use of land. Although contracts for the transfer of heritable property are not included in the Act, the inclusion of contracts to provide services relating to land brings within its scope provisions in leases which relate to the maintenance and repair of premises. Contracts relating to the liability of an occupier of land to persons entering upon or using that land come within the scope of the 1977 Act, as do grants of any right or permission to enter upon or use land not amounting to an estate or interest in land.

Some contracts that fall within these categories are in fact specifically excluded. Section 15 (3) (a) (i) excludes contracts of insurance including annuities on human lives. Contracts relating to the formation, constitution or dissolution of companies, partnerships and unincorporated associations are, by virtue of s 15 (3) (a) (ii), outside the 1977 Act. Certain marine contracts are only partially within its scope; and these include contracts of marine salvage or towage, charterparties of ships or hovercrafts, and contracts for the carriage of goods by ship (s 15 (3) (b)).

In addition, s 26 restricts the impact of the Act in certain international supply contracts.

The essence of s 27 is that parties should be allowed to select as the proper law of their contract any country of their choosing. However, this will not be possible where the contract is with a consumer who was habitually resident in the United Kingdom and when the 'essential steps necessary for the making of the contract' were taken in the United Kingdom. The Act will also apply where any clause in a contract to the contrary was inserted wholly or mainly simply for evading the operation of the Act. The effect of s 28 is to implement the Athens Convention on the Carriage of Passengers and their Luggage by Sea 1974. This contains limits on the liability of the carrier in relation to death, personal injury, or loss or damage to luggage.

(u) Savings for other relevant legislation

Where a contractual provision is authorised or required by the express terms or necessary implication of an enactment, s 29 (1) (a) provides that nothing in the Unfair Contract Act Terms removes, restricts or prevents reliance upon that provision. Paragraph (b) also provides that contractual provisions remain valid where made pursuant to an international agreement to which the United Kingdom is a party. This has particular relevance to enactments concerned with the carriage of passengers or goods, many of which have their origin in international agreements. The following implement conventions which relate to the international carriage of passengers or goods and which contain restrictive provisions as to the amounts which may be claimed and the time limit for making claims: Carriage of Goods by Sea Act 1924; the Carriage by Air Act 1961; the Carriage by Air (Supplementary Provisions) Act 1962; the Carriage of Goods by Road Act 1965; the Carriage by Air Acts (Application of Provisions) Order 1967; the Carriage of Goods by Sea Act 1971;[74] the Carriage by Railways Act 1972; the Carriage of Passengers by Road Act 1974; the Carriage by Air and Road Act

1979. Section 503 (1) of the Merchant Shipping Act 1894 limits the liability of shipowners in regard to injury, death or damage to property without their 'actual fault or privity'. This is now required by the International Convention relating to the Limitation of the Liability of the Owners of Sea-Going Ships (1957) and is unaffected by the Unfair Contract Terms Act. In this latter case, the particular provision must not operate more restrictively than is contemplated by the agreement.

As a final note, it is worth pointing out that Parliament removed from Sched 4, the list of repeals, ss 29 and 30 of the Post Office Act 1969 which appeared in the Bill. This means that the Post Office is still exempt from liability in tort.[75]

1 See Chapter 5, pp 80–5.
2 For a consideration of such provisions, reference is best made to the appropriate texts, the best of which are Goode, *Consumer Credit Act* (loose-leaf); Bennion, *Consumer Credit Control* (loose-leaf); Lawson, *Consumer Credit Act* (cassette); Lawson, *Consumer Credit.*
3 The Government has announced its intention to raise the limits to £15,000.
4 See: Stands for Carry-Cots (Safety) Regulations 1966/1610; Night-dresses (Safety) Regulations 1967/839; Electrical Appliances Colour Code Regulations 1969/310, 1970/811; Electric Blanket (Safety) Regulations 1971/1961; Cooking Utensils (Safety) Regulations 1972/1957; Heating Appliances (Fireguards) Regulations 1973/2106; Pencils and Graphic Instruments (Safety) Regulations 1974/226; Toys (Safety) Regulations 1974/1367; Glazed Ceramic Ware (Safety) Regulations 1975/1241; Electrical Equipment (Safety) Regulations 1975/1366; Children's Clothing (Hood Cords) Regulations 1976/2; Vitreous Enamel-Ware (Safety) Regulations 1976/454; Oil Heater (Safety) Regulations 1977/167; Electrical Appliance (Colour Code) (Amendment) Regulations 1977/931; Babies Dummies (Safety) Regulations 1978/836; Cosmetic Products (Safety) Regulations 1978/1354; Oil Lamps (Safety) Regulations 1979/1125.
5 See Dangerous Substances and Preparations (Safety) Regulations 1980/136; Upholstered Furniture (Safety) Regulations 1980/725; Novelties (Safety) Regulations 1980/958; Filament Lamps for Vehicles (Safety) Regulations 1982/444.
6 The only Order still in force is the Children's Furniture (Safety) Order 1982/523.
7 See generally Lawson, *The Supply of Goods and Services Act.*
8 *Infra* p 97.
9 *Infra* p 102.
10 *Infra* p 102.
11 *Supra* pp 80–5.
12 *Infra* pp 101–2.

13 The equivalent provisions having application to Scotland are to be found in s 16.

14 Section 25 (1) in Scotland.

15 In *Bennett* v *Pontins* (unreported, 1973) where damages were refused when, even though negligence was proved, a widow failed to recover for the death of her husband in a swimming pool since negligence was within an exclusion clause.

16 This is separate from the question of guarantees dealt with on p 104.

17 Section 16 (1) (*b*) in Scotland.

18 See pp 110–21.

19 [1963] 2 All ER 575.

20 It would appear that pure economic loss generally is now recoverable: *Junior Books* v *The Veitchi Company* [1982] 3 All ER 201.

21 Or, in Scotland, pursuant to a 'standard form contract': s 17 (1).

22 See p 99 for the position under s 3 (2) (*b*).

23 [1981] SLT 103.

24 *Ibid*, at p 105.

25 (1854) 9 Ex 341.

26 [1933] All ER 646.

27 *Infra* p 110.

28 *Supra* pp 80–5.

29 Trading Stamps Act 1964, s 10.

30 A measure of damage now available under *Jarvis* v *Swans Tours* [1973] 1 All ER 71.

31 See *Harbutt's Plasticine* v *Wayne Tank & Pump Co* [1970] 1 All ER 225, discussed *supra* p 56.

32 Section 9 (and s 22 in Scotland) are presumably to be read as applying only where the test of reasonableness is required under the terms of the Unfair Contract Terms Act, and not in the case of a (possible) requirement at common law: see pp 61–71.

33 [1980] 1 All ER 556.

34 The definition of a 'business' is considered *supra* p 95.

35 [1977] 1 Lloyd's Rep 645.

36 It was apparently accepted that the contract was one of sale.

37 *Supra* note 36 at p 651.

38 Defined in s 29 (3) as meaning any court, arbitrator or arbiter, government department or public authority.

39 To perform work in a 'workmanlike or ... professional manner, with proper materials and so that as regards that work the dwelling will be fit for habitation ...': s 1.

40 It might be thought, where a misrepresentation was concerned, that it would have been more appropriate to consider events as at the time of misrepresentation.

41 *Supra* note 35.

42 *Ibid* at p 651.

43 See Appendix 4.

44 Unreported, 23 May 1980.

45 Unreported, 17 March 1981.

46 *Supra* note 43.
47 (1863) 10 HLC 493.
48 [1977] 3 All ER 498.
49 [1974] 3 All ER 616.
50 Unreported, 7 May 1981.
51 [1980] 1 All ER 556.
52 *Ibid* at pp 568, 561 respectively.
53 Unreported, 22 March 1982.
54 [1978] 1 Lloyd's Rep 602.
55 [1981] 1 Lloyd's Rep 476.
56 [1983] 1 All ER 108.
57 [1982] SLT 39.
58 [1978] 2 All ER 1134.
59 *Ibid* at p 1143.
60 [1982] 1 All ER 634.
61 Unreported, 6 May 1982: see appendix.
62 (1977) 244 EG 547.
63 *Ibid* at p 549.
64 *Ibid* at p 551.
65 Thus upholding the decision of Fox J: (1977) 241 EG 837.
66 *Supra* note 62 at p 551.
67 *Ibid.* It was assumed for the purposes of the action that a misrepresenta-
    tion had been made.
68 *Ibid.*
69 *Ibid.*
70 But the court agreed with *Overbrooke Estates* v *Glencombe Properties*
    [1974] 1 WLR 1355 that s 3 does not qualify the right of a principal to
    limit his agent's authority: *ibid*, at p 549 per Bridge LJ. The *Overbrooke*
    case was also endorsed by the Court of Appeal in *Collins* v *Howell-
    Jones* (1980) 259 EG 331.
71 *Ibid* at p 551.
72 *Ibid* at p 549.
73 *Supra* note 60 at p 640.
74 A clause in a bill of lading which specified the Netherlands as a forum
    for the settlement of disputes could not be relied on when Dutch law
    imposed a maximum liability on carriers for negligence or breach of
    contract less than the maximum provided for in the Hague-Visby Rules
    scheduled to the 1971 Act: *The Morviken* (1982) *The Times*, 27
    November.
75 See *American Express Co and Another* v *British Airways Board* (1982)
    The Times, 25 November.

Part III

A Practical Guide to Judicial and Legislative Control

Chapter 7

A Practical Guide

In the paragraphs which follow, some of the more likely problem areas are isolated and the appropriate head of law indicated.

1 Liability for negligence

As from 1 February 1978, the exclusion of liability for negligence is exclusively the preserve of ss 2 and 16 of the Unfair Contract Terms Act 1977. No distinction is drawn in the Act hereabouts between consumers and other contracting parties: they are all treated on the same footing. The only distinction drawn in these sections is between negligence resulting in death or personal injury, and negligence producing any other kind of loss or damage. In the former case, exclusion clauses are quite ineffective: in the latter, all hinges on the question of reasonableness.

It is essential to remember that not every species of agreement is covered by the Act. A complete list of the exemptions (as contained in Sched 1 to the Act) in relation to England, Wales and Northern Ireland is to be found in the Appendix. With regard to Scotland, the contracts within the Act are spelled out in s 15.

2 Liability for breach of contract

Once more, and again subject to the exemptions found in s 15 and Sched 1, the Unfair Contract Terms Act 1977 is the dominant factor. This, however, under the terms of ss 3 and 17, will only be so where the party against whom a clause is sought to be enforced is a consumer or is dealing on the other's written standard terms (or, in Scotland, on a standard form contract). In other words, contracts between businesses will also fall within the protection of the Act where dealing is on such standard terms or contract.

It is important to realise that the relevant sections cover not only those clauses which exclude or restrict liability for breach of contract, but also those clauses seeking to allow a variation of performance or no performance at all.

Where ss 3 and 17 do not apply, which will only be where the relevant party is neither a consumer nor one contracting on written standard terms (or on a standard form), the question to be answered is whether any of the common law controls, such as unreasonableness, incorporation or interpretation, cover the issue.

3 Indemnity clauses

Sections 4 and 18 of the Unfair Contract Terms Act 1977 deal only with consumers, providing the relevant contracts are within the Act. Where the Act does not apply, only the common law controls are relevant.

4 Void clauses

Sections 6 and 7 (ss 20 and 21 in Scotland) of the Unfair Contract Terms Act 1977 contain the original provisions of the Supply of Goods (Implied Terms) Act 1973 relating to clauses excluding liability for failure to pass a good title or supplying defective goods. Sections 7 and 21 create new law in extending this to all other contracts under which goods pass. Both sections cover consumers and businesses alike, although the level of control differs. An amendment to the 1977 Act renders void attempts to exclude the implied terms as to title contained in the Supply of Goods and Services Act 1982.

5 Misrepresentation

The Misrepresentation Act 1967 is unaffected by the Unfair Contract Terms Act 1977 except that the provisions of s 3 of the earlier Act relating to the exclusion of liability for misrepresentation are now contained in s 8 of the later Act. The 1967 Act does not apply to Scotland.

6 Guarantees

Sections 5 and 19 of the Unfair Contract Terms Act 1977 impose controls on the use of guarantees, but only where they seek to exclude liability for damage arising through negligence, and only when the goods are in consumer use. It must also be remembered that, under the terms of the Consumer Transactions (Restrictions on Statements) Order 1976, the use of guarantees in consumer transactions is a criminal offence unless required wording is used.

7 Unlawful exclusion clauses

Specific controls are imposed on exclusion clauses by the Consumer Transactions (Restrictions on Statements) Order 1976. These controls, however, only apply to contracts made with consumers. It is worth pointing out that the use of clauses rendered void by the Unfair Contract Terms Act 1977 is not an offence, except where they are coincidentally those clauses covered by the Order.

8 The status of the parties

Sections 2 and 16 of the Unfair Contract Terms Act 1977, which deal with negligence and ss 3 and 17 which deal with contractual liability, apply generally whether the party against whom it is attempted to enforce the clause is a consumer, a business or whatever. In the case of ss 3 and 17, however, he must be a consumer or contracting on written standard terms (or on a standard form contract), which latter can include contracts between business parties.

Generally, the Act applies only where the party seeking to use a particular clause is a business.

The Consumer Transactions (Restrictions on Statements) Order 1976 only applies where the clause is to be applied against a consumer and only where the clause is used in the course of a business.

9 Unequal bargaining power

There are no statutory controls specifically concerned with unequal bargaining power, although this question is partially covered by the guidelines for determining reasonableness contained in Sched 2 to the Unfair Contract Terms Act 1977.

The common law on such matters, insubstantial though it is, is unaffected by the Act. Hence, particularly, though not exclusively, where the relevant contracting party is a consumer, relief might still be found under the common law against terms which are harsh or unconscionable, imposed where the parties were of unequal status.

Appendix 1

Unfair Contract Terms Act 1977

1977 c 50

As amended by the Sale of Goods Act 1979; and the Supply of Goods and Services Act 1982.

An Act to impose further limits on the extent to which under the law of England and Wales and Northern Ireland civil liability for breach of contract, or for negligence or other breach of duty, can be avoided by means of contract terms and otherwise, and under the law of Scotland civil liability can be avoided by means of contract terms.　[26 October 1977]

PART I

AMENDMENT OF LAW FOR ENGLAND AND WALES AND NORTHERN IRELAND

Introductory

1—(1) For the purposes of this Part of this Act, 'negligence' means the breach—

- (*a*) of any obligation, arising from the express or implied terms of a contract, to take reasonable care or exercise reasonable skill in the performance of the contract;
- (*b*) of any common law duty to take reasonable care or exercise reasonable skill (but not any stricter duty);
- (*c*) of the common duty of care imposed by the Occupiers' Liability Act 1957 or the Occupiers' Liability Act (Northern Ireland) 1957.

(2) This Part of this Act is subject to Part III; and in relation to contracts, the operation of sections 2 to 4 and 7 is subject to the exceptions made by Schedule 1.

(3) In the case of both contract and tort, sections 2 to 7 apply (except where the contrary is stated in section 6(4)) only to business liability, that is liability for breach of obligations or duties arising—

    (*a*) from things done or to be done by a person in the course of a business (whether his own business or another's); or

    (*b*) from the occupation of premises used for business purposes of the occupier;

and references to liability are to be read accordingly.

(4) In relation to any breach of duty or obligation, it is immaterial for any purpose of this Part of this Act whether the breach was inadvertent or intentional, or whether liability for it arises directly or vicariously.

Avoidance of liability for negligence, breach of contract, etc.

2—(1) A person cannot by reference to any contract term or to a notice given to persons generally or to particular persons exclude or restrict his liability for death or personal injury resulting from negligence.

(2) In the case of other loss or damage, a person cannot so exclude or restrict his liability for negligence except in so far as the term or notice satisfies the requirement of reasonableness.

(3) Where a contract term or notice purports to exclude or restrict liability for negligence a person's agreement to or awareness of it is not of itself to be taken as indicating his voluntary acceptance of any risk.

3—(1) This section applies as between contracting parties where one of them deals as consumer or on the other's written standard terms of business.

(2) As against that party, the other cannot by reference to any contract term—

    (*a*) when himself in breach of contract, exclude or restrict any liability of his in respect of the breach; or

    (*b*) claim to be entitled—

        (i) to render a contractual performance substantially different from that which was reasonably expected of him, or

        (ii) in respect of the whole or any part of his contractual obligation, to render no performance at all,

except in so far as (in any of the cases mentioned above in this subsection) the contract term satisfies the requirement of reasonableness.

4—(1) A person dealing as consumer cannot by reference to any contract term be made to indemnify another person (whether a party to the contract or not) in respect of liability that may be incurred by the other for negligence or breach of contract, except in so far as the contract term satisfies the requirement of reasonableness.

(2) This section applies whether the liability in question—

  (*a*) is directly that of the person to be indemnified or is incurred by him vicariously;

  (*b*) is to the person dealing as consumer or to someone else.

Liability arising from sale or supply of goods

  5—(1) In the case of goods of a type ordinarily supplied for private use or consumption, where loss or damage—

  (*a*) arises from the goods proving defective while in consumer use; and

  (*b*) results from the negligence of a person concerned in the manufacture or distribution of the goods,

liability for the loss or damage cannot be excluded or restricted by reference to any contract term or notice contained in or operating by reference to a guarantee of the goods.

  (2) For these purposes—

  (*a*) goods are to be regarded as 'in consumer use' when a person is using them, or has them in his possession for use, otherwise than exclusively for the purposes of a business; and

  (*b*) anything in writing is a guarantee if it contains or purports to contain some promise or assurance (however worded or presented) that defects will be made good by complete or partial replacement, or by repair, monetary compensation or otherwise.

  (3) This section does not apply as between the parties to a contract under or in pursuance of which possession or ownership of the goods passed.

  6—(1) Liability for breach of the obligations arising from—

  (*a*) section 12 of the Sale of Goods Act 1979 (seller's implied undertakings as to title, etc.);

  (*b*) section 8 of the Supply of Goods (Implied Terms) Act 1973 (the corresponding thing in relation to hire-purchase),

cannot be excluded or restricted by reference to any contract term.

  (2) As against a person dealing as consumer, liability for breach of the obligations arising from—

  (*a*) section 13, 14 or 15 of the 1979 Act (seller's implied undertakings as to conformity of goods with description or sample, or as to their quality or fitness for a particular purpose);

  (*b*) section 9, 10 or 11 of the 1973 Act (the corresponding things in relation to hire-purchase),

cannot be excluded or restricted by reference to any contract term.

  (3) As against a person dealing otherwise than as consumer, the liability specified in subsection (2) above can be excluded or restricted by reference

to a contract term, but only in so far as the term satisfies the requirement of reasonableness.

(4) The liabilities referred to in this section are not only the business liabilities defined by section 1 (3), but include those arising under any contract of sale of goods or hire-purchase agreement.

7—(1) Where the possession or ownership of goods passes under or in pursuance of a contract not governed by the law of sale of goods or hire-purchase, subsections (2) to (4) below apply as regards the effect (if any) to be given to contract terms excluding or restricting liability for breach of obligation arising by implication of law from the nature of the contract.

(2) As against a person dealing as consumer, liability in respect of the goods' correspondence with description or sample, or their quality or fitness for any particular purpose, cannot be excluded or restricted by reference to any such term.

(3) As against a person dealing otherwise than as consumer, that liability can be excluded or restricted by reference to such a term, but only in so far as the term satisfies the requirement of reasonableness.

(3a) Liability for breach of the obligations arising under section 2 of the Supply of Goods and Services Act 1982 (implied terms about title etc. in certain contracts for the transfer of property in goods) cannot be excluded or restricted by reference to any such term.

(4) Liability in respect of—

    (a) the right to transfer ownership to the goods, or give possession; or

    (b) the assurance of quiet possession to a person taking goods in pursuance of the contract,

cannot (in a case to which subsection (3a) above does not apply) be excluded or restricted by reference to any such term except in so far as the term satisfies the requirement of reasonablenesss.

(5) This section does not apply in the case of goods passing on a redemption of trading stamps within the Trading Stamps Act 1964 or the Trading Stamps Act (Northern Ireland) 1965.

Other provisions about contracts

8—(1) In the Misrepresentation Act 1967, the following is substituted for section 3—

    3. If a contract contains a term which would exclude or restrict—

        (a) any liability to which a party to a contract may be subject by reason of any misrepresentation made by him before the contract was made; or (*b*) any remedy available to another party to the contract by reason of such a misrepresentation,

that term shall be of no effect except in so far as it satisfies the requirement of reasonableness as stated in section 11 (1) of the Unfair Contract Terms Act 1977; and it is for those claiming that the term satisfies that requirement to show that it does.'.

(2) The same section is substituted for section 3 of the Misrepresentation Act (Northern Ireland) 1967.

9—(1) Where for reliance upon it a contract term has to satisfy the requirement of reasonableness, it may be found to do so and be given effect accordingly notwithstanding that the contract has been terminated either by breach or by a party electing to treat it as repudiated.

(2) Where on a breach the contract is nevertheless affirmed by a party entitled to treat it as repudiated, this does not of itself exclude the requirement of reasonableness in relation to any contract term.

10 A person is not bound by any contract term prejudicing or taking away rights of his which arise under, or in connection with the performance of, another contract, so far as those rights extend to the enforcement of another's liability which this Part of this Act prevents that other from excluding or restricting.

Explanatory provisions

11—(1) In relation to a contract term, the requirement of reasonableness for the purposes of this Part of this Act, section 3 of the Misrepresentation Act 1967 and section 3 of the Misrepresentation Act (Northern Ireland) 1967 is that the term shall have been a fair and reasonable one to be included having regard to the circumstances which were, or ought reasonably to have been, known to or in the contemplation of the parties when the contract was made.

(2) In determining for the purposes of section 6 or 7 above whether a contract term satisfies the requirement of reasonableness, regard shall be had in particular to the matters specified in Schedule 2 to this Act; but this subsection does not prevent the court or arbitrator from holding, in accordance with any rule of law, that a term which purports to exclude or restrict any relevant liability is not a term of the contract.

(3) In relation to a notice (not being a notice having contractual effect), the requirement of reasonableness under this Act is that it should be fair and reasonable to allow reliance on it, having regard to all the circumstances obtaining when the liability arose or (but for the notice) would have arisen.

(4) Where by reference to a contract term or notice a person seeks to restrict liability to a specified sum of money, and the question arises (under

this or any other Act) whether the term or notice satisfies the requirement of reasonableness, regard shall be had in particular (but without prejudice to subsection (2) above in the case of contract terms) to—

(a) the resources which he could expect to be available to him for the purpose of meeting the liability should it arise; and

(b) how far it was open to him to cover himself by insurance.

(5) It is for those claiming that a contract term or notice satisfies the requirement of reasonableness to show that it does.

12—(1) A party to a contract 'deals as consumer' in relation to another party if—

(a) he neither makes the contract in the course of a business nor holds himself out as doing so; and

(b) the other party does make the contract in the course of a business; and

(c) in the case of a contract governed by the law of sale of goods or hire-purchase, or by section 7 of this Act, the goods passing under or in pursuance of the contract are of a type ordinarily supplied for private use or consumption.

(2) But on a sale by auction or by competitive tender the buyer is not in any circumstances to be regarded as dealing as consumer.

(3) Subject to this, it is for those claiming that a party does not deal as consumer to show that he does not.

13—(1) To the extent that this Part of this Act prevents the exclusion or restriction of any liability it also prevents—

(a) making the liability or its enforcement subject to restrictive or onerous conditions;

(b) excluding or restricting any right or remedy in respect of the liability, or subjecting a person to any prejudice in consequence of his pursuing any such right or remedy;

(c) excluding or restricting rules of evidence or procedure;

and (to that extent) sections 2 and 5 to 7 also prevent excluding or restricting liability by reference to terms and notices which exclude or restrict the relevant obligation or duty.

(2) But an agreement in writing to submit present or future differences to arbitration is not to be treated under this Part of this Act as excluding or restricting any liability.

14 In this Part of this Act—

'business' includes a profession and the activities of any government department or local public authority;

'goods' has the same meaning as in the Sale of Goods Act 1979;

'hire-purchase agreement' has the same meaning as in the Consumer Credit Act 1974;

'negligence' has the meaning given by section 1 (1);

'notice' includes an announcement, whether or not in writing, and any other communication or pretended communication; and

'personal injury' includes any disease and any impairment of physical or mental condition.

PART II

AMENDMENT OF LAW FOR SCOTLAND

Scope of Part II

15—(1) This Part of this Act applies only to contracts, is subject to Part III of this Act and does not affect the validity of any discharge or indemnity given by a person in consideration of the receipt by him of compensation in settlement of any claim which he has.

(2) Subject to subsection (3) below, sections 16 to 18 of this Act apply to any contract only to the extent that the contract—

(*a*) relates to the transfer of the ownership or possession of goods from one person to another (with or without work having been done on them);

(*b*) constitutes a contract of service or apprenticeship;

(*c*) relates to services of whatever kind, including (without prejudice to the foregoing generality) carriage, deposit and pledge, care and custody, mandate, agency, loan and services relating to the use of land;

(*d*) relates to the liability of an occupier of land to persons entering upon or using that land;

(*e*) relates to a grant of any right or permission to enter upon or use land not amounting to an estate or interest in the land.

(3) Notwithstanding anything in subsection (2) above, sections 16 to 18—

(*a*) do not apply to any contract to the extent that the contract—

(i) is a contract of insurance (including a contract to pay an annuity on human life);

(ii) relates to the formation, constitution or dissolution of any body corporate or unincorporated association or partnership;

(*b*) apply to—

a contract of marine salvage or towage;

a charter party of a ship or hovercraft;

a contract for the carriage of goods by ship or hovercraft; or,

a contract to which subsection (4) below relates,

only to the extent that—

(i) both parties deal or hold themselves out as dealing in the course of a business (and then only in so far as the contract purports to exclude or restrict liability for breach of duty in respect of death or personal injury); or

(ii) the contract is a consumer contract (and then only in favour of the consumer).

(4) This subsection relates to a contract in pursuance of which goods are carried by ship or hovercraft and which either—

(a) specifies ship or hovercraft as the means of carriage over part of the journey to be covered; or

(b) makes no provision as to the means of carriage and does not exclude ship or hovercraft as that means,

in so far as the contract operates for and in relation to the carriage of the goods by that means.

Liability for breach of duty

16—(1) Where a term of a contract purports to exclude or restrict liability for breach of duty arising in the course of any business or from the occupation of any premises used for business purposes of the occupier, that term—

(a) shall be void in any case where such exclusion or restriction is in respect of death or personal injury;

(b) shall, in any other case, have no effect if it was not fair and reasonable to incorporate the term in the contract.

(2) Subsection (1)(a) above does not affect the validity of any discharge and indemnity by a person, on or in connection with an award to him of compensation for pneumonconiosis attributable to employment in the coal industry, in respect of any further claim arising from his contracting that disease.

(3) Where under subsection (1) above a term of a contract is void or has no effect, the fact that a person agreed to, or was aware of, the term shall not of itself be sufficient evidence that he knowingly and voluntarily assumed any risk.

Control of unreasonable exemptions in consumer or standard form contracts

17—(1) Any term of a contract which is a consumer contract or a standard form contract shall have no effect for the purpose of enabling a party to the contract—

(a) who is in breach of a contractual obligation, to exclude or restrict any liability of his to the consumer or customer in respect of the breach;

(b) in respect of a contractual obligation, to render no performance, or to render a performance substantially different from that which the consumer or customer reasonably expected from the contract;

if it was not fair and reasonable to incorporate the term in the contract.

(2) In this section 'customer' means a party to a standard form contract who deals on the basis of written standard terms of business of the other party to the contract who himself deals in the course of a business.

Unreasonable indemnity clauses in consumer contracts

18—(1) Any term of a contract which is a consumer contract shall have no effect for the purpose of making the consumer indemnify another person (whether a party to the contract or not) in respect of liability which that other person may incur as a result of breach of duty or breach of contract, if it was not fair and reasonable to incorporate the term in the contract.

(2) In this section 'liability' means liability arising in the course of any business or from the occupation of any premises used for business purposes of the occupier.

'Guarantee' of consumer goods

19—(1) This section applies to a guarantee—
- (*a*) in relation to goods which are of a type ordinarily supplied for private use or consumption; and
- (*b*) which is not a guarantee given by one party to the other party to a contract under or in pursuance of which the ownership or possession of the goods to which the guarantee relates is transferred.

(2) A term of a guarantee to which this section applies shall be void in so far as it purports to exclude or restrict liability for loss or damage (including death or personal injury)—
- (*a*) arising from the goods proving defective while—
  - (i) in use otherwise than exclusively for the purposes of a business;

    or
  - (ii) in the possession of a person for such use; and
- (*b*) resulting from the breach of duty of a person concerned in the manufacture or distribution of the goods.

(3) For the purposes of this section, any document is a guarantee if it contains or purports to contain some promise or assurance (however worded or presented) that defects will be made good by complete or partial replacement, or by repair, monetary compensation or otherwise.

Obligations implied by law in sale and hire-purchase contracts

20—(1) Any term of a contract which purports to exclude or restrict liability for breach of the obligations arising from—
- (*a*) section 12 of the Sale of Goods Act 1979 (seller's implied undertakings as to title etc.);
- (*b*) section 8 of the Supply of Goods (Implied Terms) Act 1973 (implied terms as to title in hire-purchase agreements),

shall be void.

(2) Any term of a contract which purports to exclude or restrict liability for breach of the obligations arising from—
- (*a*) section 13, 14 or 15 of the said Act of 1979 (seller's implied

undertakings as to the conformity of goods with description or sample, or as to their quality or fitness for a particular purpose);

(b) section 9, 10 or 11 of the said Act of 1973 (the corresponding provisions in relation to hire-purchase),

shall—

(i) in the case of the consumer contract, be void against the consumer;

(ii) in any other case, have no effect if it was not fair and reasonable to incorporate the term in the contract.

Obligations implied by law in other contracts for the supply of goods

21—(1) Any term of a contract to which this section applies purporting to exclude or restrict liability for breach of an obligation—

(a) such as is referred to in subsection (3)(a) below—

(i) in the case of a consumer contract, shall be void against the consumer, and

(ii) in any other case, shall have no effect if it was not fair and reasonable to incorporate the term in the contract;

(b) such as is referred to in subsection (3) (b) below, shall have no effect if it was not fair and reasonable to incorporate the term in the contract.

(2) This section applies to any contract to the extent that it relates to any such matter as is referred to in section 15 (2) (a) of this Act, but does not apply to—

(a) a contract of sale of goods or a hire-purchase agreement; or

(b) a charterparty of a ship or hovercraft unless it is a consumer contract (and then only in favour of the consumer).

(3) An obligation referred to in this subsection is an obligation incurred under a contract in the course of a business and arising by implication of law from the nature of the contract which relates—

(a) to the correspondence of goods with description or sample, or to the quality or fitness of the goods for any particular purpose: or

(b) to any right to transfer ownership or possession of goods, or to the enjoyment of quiet possession of goods.

(4) Nothing in this section applies to the supply of goods on a redemption of trading stamps within the Trading Stamps Act 1964.

Consequence of breach

22 For the avoidance of doubt, where any provision of this Part of this Act requires that the incorporation of a term in a contract must be fair and reasonable for that term to have effect—

(a) if that requirement is satisfied, the term may be given effect to notwithstanding that the contract has been terminated in consequence of breach of that contract;

(b) for the term to be given effect to, that requirement must be satisfied even where a party who is entitled to rescind the contract elects not to rescind it.

Evasion by means of secondary contract

23   Any term of any contract shall be void which purports to exclude or restrict, or has the effect of excluding or restricting—

(a) the exercise, by a party to any other contract, of any right or remedy which arises in respect of that other contract in consequence of breach of duty, or of obligation, liability for which could not by virtue of the provisions of this Part of this Act be excluded or restricted by a term of that other contract;

(b) the application of the provisions of this Part of this Act in respect of that or any other contract.

The "reasonableness" test

24—(1) In determining for the purposes of this Part of this Act whether it was fair and reasonable to incorporate a term in a contract, regard shall be had only to the circumstances which were, or ought reasonably to have been, known to or in the contemplation of the parties to the contract at the time the contract was made.

(2) In determining for the purposes of section 20 or 21 of this Act whether it was fair and reasonable to incorporate a term in a contract, regard shall be had in particular to the matters specified in Schedule 2 to this Act; but this subsection shall not prevent a court or arbiter from holding, in accordance with any rule of law, that a term which purports to exclude or restrict any relevant liability is not a term of the contract.

(3) Where a term in a contract purports to restrict liability to a specified sum of money, and the question arises for the purposes of this Part of the Act whether it was fair and reasonable to incorporate the term in the contract, then, without prejudice to subsection (2) above, regard shall be had in particular to—

(a) the resources which the party seeking to rely on that term could expect to be available to him for the purpose of meeting the liability should it arise;

(b) how far it was open to that party to cover himself by insurance.

(4) The onus of proving that it was fair and reasonable to incorporate a term in a contract shall lie on the party so contending.

Interpretation of Part II

25—(1) In this Part of this Act—
'breach of duty' means the breach—

(a) of any obligation, arising from the express or implied terms of a contract, to take reasonable care or exercise reasonable skill in the performance of the contract;

(*b*) of any common law duty to take reasonable care or exercise reasonable skill;

(*c*) of the duty of reasonable care imposed by section 2(1) of the Occupiers' Liability (Scotland) Act 1960;

'business' includes a profession and the activities of any government department or local or public authority;

'consumer' has the meaning assigned to that expression in the definition in this section'of 'consumer contract';

'consumer contract' means a contract (not being a contract of sale by auction or competitive tender) in which—

(*a*) one party to the contract deals, and the other party to the contract ('the consumer') does not deal or hold himself out as dealing, in the course of a business, and

(*b*) in the case of a contract such as is mentioned in section 15 (2) (*a*) of this Act, the goods are of a type ordinarily supplied for private use or consumption;

and for the purpose of this Part of this Act the onus of proving that a contract is not to be regarded as a consumer contract shall lie on the party so contending;

'goods' have the same meaning as in the Sale of Goods Act 1979;

'hire-purchase agreement' has the same meaning as in section 189 (1) of the Consumer Credit Act 1974;

'personal injury' includes any disease and any impairment of physical or mental condition.

(2) In relation to any breach of duty or obligation, it is immaterial for any purpose of this Part of this Act whether the act or omission giving rise to that breach was inadvertent or intentional, or whether liability for it arises directly or vicariously.

(3) In this Part of this Act, any reference to excluding or restricting any liability includes—

(*a*) making the liability or its enforcement subject to any restrictive or onerous conditions;

(*b*) excluding or restricting any right or remedy in respect of the liability, or subjecting a person to any prejudice in consequence of his pursuing any such right or remedy;

(*c*) excluding or restricting any rule of evidence or procedure;

(*d*) excluding or restricting any liability by reference to a notice having contractual effect,

but does not include an agreement to submit any question to arbitration.

(4) In subsection (3) (*d*) above "notice" includes an announcement, whether or not in writing, and any other communication or pretended communication.

(5) In sections 15 and 16 and 19 to 21 of this Act, any reference to excluding or restricting liability for breach of an obligation or duty shall include a reference to excluding or restricting the obligation or duty itself.

PART III

PROVISIONS APPLYING TO WHOLE OF UNITED KINGDOM

Miscellaneous

26—(1) The limits imposed by this Act on the extent to which a person may exclude or restrict liability by reference to a contract term do not apply to liability arising under such a contract as is described in subsection (3) below.

(2) The terms of such a contract are not subject to any requirement of reasonableness under section 3 or 4: and nothing in Part II of this Act shall require the incorporation of the terms of such a contract to be fair and reasonable for them to have effect.

(3) Subject to subsection (4), that description of contract is one whose characteristics are the following—

(*a*) either it is a contract of sale of goods or it is one under or in pursuance of which the possession or ownership of goods passes; and

(*b*) it is made by parties whose places of business (or, if they have none, habitual residences) are in the territories of different States (the Channel Islands and the Isle of Man being treated for this purpose as different States from the United Kingdom).

(4) A contract falls within subsection (3) above only if either—

(*a*) the goods in question are, at the time of the conclusion of the contract, in the course of carriage, or will be carried, from the territory of one State to the territory of another; or

(*b*) the acts constituting the offer and acceptance have been done in the territories of different States; or

(*c*) the contract provides for the goods to be delivered to the territory of a State other than that within whose territory those acts were done.

27—(1) Where the proper law of a contract is the law of any part of the United Kingdom only by choice of the parties (and apart from that choice would be the law of some country outside the United Kingdom) sections 2 to 7 and 16 to 21 of this Act do not operate as part of the proper law.

(2) This Act has effect notwithstanding any contract term which applies or purports to apply the law of some country outside the United Kingdom, where (either or both)—

(*a*) the term appears to the court, or arbitrator or arbiter to have been imposed wholly or mainly for the purpose of enabling the party imposing it to evade the operation of this Act; or

(b) in the making of the contract one of the parties dealt as consumer, and he was then habitually resident in the United Kingdom, and the essential steps necessary for the making of the contract were taken there, whether by him or by others on his behalf.

(3) In the application of subsection (2) above to Scotland, for paragraph (b) there shall be substituted—

'(b) the contract is a consumer contract as defined in Part II of this Act, and the consumer at the date when the contract was made was habitually resident in the United Kingdom, and the essential steps necessary for the making of the contract were taken there, whether by him or by others on his behalf'.

28—(1) This section applies to a contract for carriage by sea of a passenger or of a passenger and his luggage where the provisions of the Athens Convention (with or without modification) do not have, in relation to the contract, the force of law in the United Kingdom.

(2) In a case where—

(a) the contract is not made in the United Kingdom, and

(b) neither the place of departure nor the place of destination under it is in the United Kingdom,

a person is not precluded by this Act from excluding or restricting liability for loss or damage, being loss or damage for which the provisions of the Convention would, if they had the force of law in relation to the contract, impose liability on him.

(3) In any other case, a person is not precluded by this Act from excluding or restricting liability for that loss or damage—

(a) in so far as the exclusion or restriction would have been effective in that case had the provisions of the Convention had the force of law in relation to the contract; or

(b) in such circumstances and to such extent as may be prescribed, by reference to a prescribed term of the contract.

(4) For the purposes of subsection 3 (a), the values which shall be taken to be the official values in the United Kingdom of the amounts (expressed in gold francs) by reference to which liability under the provisions of the Convention is limited shall be such amounts in sterling as the Secretary of State may from time to time by order made by statutory instrument specify.

(5) In this section,—

(a) the references to excluding or restricting liability include doing any of those things in relation to the liability which are mentioned in section 13 or section 25 (3) and (5); and

(b) 'the Athens Convention' means the Athens Convention relating to the Carriage of Passengers and their Luggage by Sea, 1974; and

(c) 'prescribed' means prescribed by the Secretary of State by regulations made by statutory instrument;

and a statutory instrument containing the regulations shall be subject to annulment in pursuance of a resolution of either House of Parliament.

29—(1) Nothing in this Act removes or restricts the effect of, or prevents reliance upon, any contractual provision which—

> (*a*) is authorised or required by the express terms or necessary implication of an enactment; or

> (*b*) being made with a view to compliance with an international agreement to which the United Kingdom is a party, does not operate more restrictively than is contemplated by the agreement.

(2) A contract is to be taken—

> (*a*) for the purposes of Part I of this Act, as satisfying the requirement of reasonableness; and

> (*b*) for those of Part II, to have been fair and reasonable to incorporate,

if it is incorporated or approved by, or incorporated pursuant to a decision or ruling of, a competent authority acting in the exercise of any statutory jurisdiction or function and is not a term in a contract to which the competent authority is itself a party.

(3) In this section—

> 'competent authority' means any court, arbitrator or arbiter, government department or public authority;

> 'enactment' means any legislation (including subordinate legislation) of the United Kingdom or Northern Ireland and any instrument having effect by virtue of such legislation; and

> 'statutory' means conferred by an enactment.

30—(1) In section 3 of the Consumer Protection Act 1961 (provisions against marketing goods which do not comply with safety requirements), after subsection (1) there is inserted—

> '(1A) Any term of an agreement which purports to exclude or restrict or has the effect of excluding or restricting, any obligation imposed by or by virtue of that section, or any liability for breach of such an obligation, shall be void'.

(2) The same amendment is made in section 3 of the Consumer Protection Act (Northern Ireland) 1965.

General

31—(1) This Act comes into force on 1st February 1978.

(2) Nothing in this Act applies to contracts made before the date on which it comes into force; but subject to this, it applies to liability for any loss or damage which is suffered on or after that date.

(3) The enactments specified in Schedule 3 to this Act are amended as there shown.

(4) The enactments specified in Schedule 4 to this Act are repealed to the extent specified in column 3 of that Schedule.

32—(1) This Act may be cited as the Unfair Contract Terms Act 1977.

(2) Part I of this Act extends to England and Wales and to Northern Ireland; but it does not extend to Scotland.

(3) Part II of this Act extends to Scotland only.

(4) This Part of this Act extends to the whole of the United Kingdom.

SCHEDULES

SCHEDULE 1

SCOPE OF SECTIONS 2 TO 4 AND 7

1 Sections 2 to 4 of this Act do not extend to—
- (*a*) any contract of insurance (including a contract to pay an annuity on human life);
- (*b*) any contract so far as it relates to the creation or transfer of an interest in land, or to the termination of such an interest, whether by extinction, merger, surrender, forfeiture or otherwise;
- (*c*) any contract so far as it relates to the creation or transfer of a right or interest in any patent, trade mark, copyright, registered design, technical or commercial information or other intellectual property, or relates to the termination of any such right or interest;
- (*d*) any contract so far as it relates—
  - (i) to the formation or dissolution of a company (which means any body corporate or unincorporated association and includes a partnership), or
  - (ii) to its constitution or the rights or obligations of its corporators or members;
- (*e*) any contract so far as it relates to the creation or transfer of securities or of any right or interest in securities.

2 Section 2 (1) extends to—
- (*a*) any contract of marine salvage or towage;
- (*b*) any charterparty of a ship or hovercraft; and
- (*c*) any contract for the carriage of goods by ship or hovercraft;

but subject to this sections 2 to 4 and 7 do not extend to any such contract except in favour of a person dealing as consumer.

3 Where goods are carried by ship or hovercraft in pursuance of a contract which either—

(a) specifies that as the means of carriage over part of the journey to be covered, or

(b) makes no provision as to the means of carriage and does not exclude that means,

then sections 2 (2), 3 and 4 do not, except in favour of a person dealing as consumer, extend to the contract as it operates for and in relation to the carriage of the goods by that means.

4 Section 2 (1) and (2) do not extend to a contract of employment, except in favour of the employee.

5 Section 2 (1) does not affect the validity of any discharge and indemnity given by a person, on or in connection with an award to him of compensation for pneumoconiosis attributable to employment in the coal industry, in respect of any further claim arising from his contracting that disease.

SCHEDULE 2

'GUIDELINES' FOR APPLICATION OF REASONABLENESS TEST

The matters to which regard is to be had in particular for the purposes of sections 6 (3), 7 (3) and (4), 20 and 21 are any of the following which appear to be relevant—

(a) the strength of the bargaining positions of the parties relative to each other, taking into account (among other things) alternative means by which the customer's requirements could have been met;

(b) whether the customer received an inducement to agree to the term, or in accepting it had an opportunity of entering into a similar contract with other persons, but without having to accept a similar term;

(c) whether the customer knew or ought reasonably to have known of the existence and extent of the term (having regard, among other things, to any custom of the trade and any previous course of dealing between the parties);

(d) where the term excludes or restricts any relevant liability if some condition is not complied with, whether it was reasonable at the time of the contract to expect that compliance with that condition would be practicable;

(e) whether the goods were manufactured, processed or adapted to the special order of the customer.

SCHEDULE 3

AMENDMENT OF ENACTMENTS

In the Supply of Goods (Implied Terms) Act 1973 (as originally enacted and as substituted by the Consumer Credit Act 1974)—

(*a*) in section 14 (1) for the words from 'conditional sale' to the end substitute 'a conditional sale agreement where the buyer deals as consumer within Part I of the Unfair Contract Terms Act 1977';

(*b*) in section 15 (1), in the definition of 'business', for 'local authority or statutory undertaker' substitute 'or local or public authority'.

SCHEDULE 4

REPEALS

Chapter	Short title	Extent of repeal
56 & 57 Vict. c. 71.	Sale of Goods Act 1893.	In section 55, subsections (3) to (11). Section 55A. Section 61 (6). In section 62 (1) the definition of 'contract for the international sale of goods'.
1962 c. 46	Transport Act 1962.	Section 43 (7).
1967 c. 45.	Uniform Laws on International Sales 1967.	In section 1 (4), the words '55 and 55A'.
1972 c. 33.	Carriage by Railway Act 1972.	In section 1 (1), the words from 'and shall have' onwards.
1973 c. 13.	Supply of Goods (Implied Terms) Act 1973.	Section 5 (1). Section 6. In section 7 (1), the words from 'contract for the international sale of goods' onwards. In section 12, subsections (2) to (9). Section 13. In section 15 (1), the definition of 'consumer sale'.

The repeals in sections 12 and 15 of the Supply of Goods (Implied Terms) Act 1973 shall have effect in relation to those sections as originally enacted and as substituted by the Consumer Credit Act 1974.

Appendix 2

The Consumer Transactions (Restrictions on Statements) Order 1976

(SI 1976 No 1813)

[As amended by the Consumer Transactions (Restrictions on Statements) (Amendment) Order 1978 (SI 1978 No 127)]

Laid before Parliament in draft

Made - - -   *1st November 1976*

Coming into Operation in accordance with the provisions of Article 1

Whereas the Director General of Fair Trading made a reference, to which section 17 of the Fair Trading Act 1973 applies, to the Consumer Protection Advisory Committee:

And whereas a report on that reference has been made by that Committee to the Secretary of State, and pursuant to section 83 of that Act the report has been laid before Parliament:

And whereas the report states that the Committee would agree with the proposals set out in the reference if the proposals were modified in the manner specified in the report:

And whereas a draft of this Order has been approved by a resolution of each House of Parliament:

Now, therefore, the Secretary of State, in exercise of his powers under section 22 of the Fair Trading Act 1973, hereby makes the following Order:—

1 This Order may be cited as the Consumer Transactions (Restrictions on Statements) Order 1976, and shall come into operation as respects—

(*a*) this Article, Article 2 and Article 3(*a*), at the expiry of the period of 1 month beginning with the date on which this Order is made;

(b)   the remainder of Article 3, at the expiry of the period of 12 months beginning with that date; and

(c)   the remainder of this Order, at the expiry of the period of 2 years beginning with that date.

2—(1) In this Order—

'advertisement' includes a catalogue and a circular;

'consumer' means a person acquiring goods otherwise than in the course of a business but does not include a person who holds himself out as acquiring them in the course of a business;

'consumer transaction' means—

(a)   a consumer sale, that is a sale of goods (other than an excepted sale) by a seller where the goods—

  (i)   are of a type ordinarily bought for private use or consumption, and

  (ii)   are sold to a person who does not buy or hold himself out as buying them in the course of a business.

For the purposes of this paragraph an excepted sale is a sale by auction, a sale by competitive tender and a sale arising by virtue of a contract for the international sale of goods as originally defined in section 62(1) of the Sale of Goods Act 1893 as amended by the Supply of Goods (Implied Terms) Act 1973;

(b)   a hire-purchase agreement (within the meaning of section 189(1) of the Consumer Credit Act 1974) where the owner makes the agreement in the course of a business and the goods to which the agreement relates—

  (i)   are of a type ordinarily supplied for private use or consumption, and

  (ii)   are hired to a person who does not hire or hold himself out as hiring in the course of a business.

(c)   an agreement for the redemption of trading stamps under a trading stamp scheme within section 10(1) of the Trading Stamps Act 1964 or, as the case may be, within section 9 of the Trading Stamps Act (Northern Ireland) 1965;

'container' includes any form of packaging of goods whether by way of wholly or partly enclosing the goods or by way of attaching the goods to, or winding the goods round, some other article, and in particular includes a wrapper or confining band;

'statutory rights' means the rights arising by virtue of sections 13 to 15 of the Sale of Goods Act 1893* as amended by the Act of 1973, sections 9 to 11 of the Act of 1973, or section 4(1)(c) of the Trading Stamps Act 1964 or section 4(1)(c) of the Trading Stamps Act (Northern Ireland) 1965 both as amended by the Act of 1973.

(2) The Interpretation Act 1889 shall apply for the interpretation of this Order as it applies for the interpretation of an Act of Parliament.*

3 A person shall not, in the course of a business—

(*a*) display, at any place where consumer transactions are effected (whether wholly or partly), a notice containing a statement which purports to apply, in relation to consumer transactions effected there, a term which would—

(i) be void by virtue of section 6 or 20 of the Unfair Contract Terms Act 1977, or

(ii) be inconsistent with a warranty (in Scotland a stipulation) implied by section 4(1)(*c*) of the Trading Stamps Act 1964 or section 4(1)(*c*) of the Trading Stamps Act (Northern Ireland) 1965 both as amended by the Act of 1973,

if applied to some or all such consumer transactions;

(*b*) publish or cause to be published any advertisement which is intended to induce persons to enter into consumer transactions and which contains a statement purporting to apply in relation to such consumer transactions such a term as is mentioned in paragraph (*a*)(i) or (ii), being a term which would be void by virtue of, or as the case may be, inconsistent with, the provisions so mentioned if applied to some or all of those transactions;

(*c*) supply to a consumer pursuant to a consumer transaction goods bearing, or goods in a container bearing, a statement which is a term of that consumer transaction and which is void by virtue of, or inconsistent with, the said provisions, or if it were a term of that transaction, would be so void or inconsistent;

(*d*) furnish to a consumer in connection with the carrying out of a consumer transaction or to a person likely, as a consumer, to enter into such a transaction, a document which includes a statement which is a term of that transaction and is void or inconsistent as aforesaid, or, if it were a term of that transaction or were to become a term of a prospective transaction, would be so void or inconsistent.

4 A person shall not in the course of a business—

(i) supply to a consumer pursuant to a consumer transaction goods bearing, or goods in a container bearing, a statement about the rights that the consumer has against that person or about the obligations to the consumer accepted by that person in relation to the goods (whether legally enforceable or not), being rights or obligations that arise if the goods are

* References to the Act of 1893 and its amendments, and to the Act of 1889, are to be read as references, respectively, to the Sale of Goods Act, 1979, and the Interpretation Act, 1978: see the Interpretation Act, 1978, ss 17(2)(*a*) and 25(2).

defective or are not fit for a purpose or do not correspond
with a description;

   (ii) furnish to a consumer in connection with the carrying out of a
consumer transaction or to a person likely, as a consumer, to
enter into such a transaction with him or through his agency a
document containing a statement about such rights and obligations,

unless there is in close proximity to any such statement another statement
which is clear and conspicuous and to the effect that the first mentioned
statement does not or will not affect the statutory rights of a consumer.

5—(1) This Article applies to goods which are supplied in the course of a
business by one person ('the supplier') to another where, at the time of the
supply, the goods were intended by the supplier to be, or might reasonably
be expected by him to be, the subject of a subsequent consumer transaction.

  (2) A supplier shall not—

   (*a*) supply goods to which this Article applies if the goods bear, or are
in a container bearing, a statement which sets out or describes or
limits obligations (whether legally enforceable or not) accepted or
to be accepted by him in relation to the goods; or

   (*b*) furnish a document in relation to the goods which contains such a
statement,

unless there is in close proximity to any such statement another statement
which is clear and conspicuous and to the effect that the first mentioned
statement does not or will not affect the statutory rights of a consumer.

  (3) A person does not contravene paragraph (2) above—

   (i) in a case to which sub-paragraph (*a*) of that paragraph
applies, unless the goods have become the subject of a
consumer transaction;

   (ii) in a case to which sub-paragraph (*b*) applies, unless the
document has been furnished to a consumer in relation to
goods which were the subject of a consumer transaction, or
to a person likely to become a consumer pursuant to such a
transaction; or

  (iii) by virtue of any statement if before the date on which this
Article comes into operation the document containing, or
the goods or container bearing, the statement has ceased to
be in his possession.

John Fraser
Minister of State, and
Department of Prices and
Consumer Protection.

1st November 1976

Appendix 3

Council of Europe Resolution [76] 47

on Unfair Terms in Consumer Contracts and an Appropriate Method of Control

(Adopted by the Committee of Ministers on 16 November 1976 at the 262nd meeting of the Ministers' Deputies)

The Committee of Ministers,

Considering that the aim of the Council of Europe is to achieve a greater unity between its member states;

Convinced of the need to increase the legal protection of consumers in order to strengthen their power;

Considering that the inclusion of unfair terms in contracts for the supply of goods and services and that the absence of appropriate legislation in this field place consumers in a position of inferiority which is prejudicial to their interests;

Considering that consumers are with increasing frequency offered contracts for the supply of goods and services on terms which seldom protect their interests adequately and which they have no true power to amend;

Considering that for these reasons consumers should be afforded protection against unfair terms of contract,

I Recommends governments of member states:

1 to introduce legal or other instruments which are effective to protect consumers against unfair terms in contracts relating to the supply of goods or services, in particular against unfair terms in contracts based on standard texts and in other contracts where the consumer has little, if any, possibility of negotiating or influencing their content;

2 to lay down, as a principle in relation to the contractual situations described in paragraph 1, that any term or combination of terms which

causes a balance of rights and obligations under the contract as a whole contrary to the interests of consumers is to be regarded as unfair and to draw the appropriate consequences therefrom;

3 to take, strengthen or maintain, as appropriate, measures which are apt to prevent the inclusion in such contracts of terms which are inconsistent with the mandatory rules of law, or of other terms which are regarded as unfair in relation to consumers;

4 to take measures or strengthen the existing measures to protect consumers from inadequate or misleading presentation of the contents of such contracts and in particular to ensure that, where necessary, all the terms of such contracts are readily and comprehensibly available to consumers before they consent to them;

5 to provide for an appropriate method of control relating to unfair contract terms drawn from the principles set out in the appendix to this resolution. The method of control adopted shall be based on all or part of principles I, II or III therein;

6 to consider the extension of the principles of paragraphs 1–5 to contracts relating to immovable property;

II   Invites governments of member states to inform the Secretary General, after the expiration of a period of five years, of the steps which they have taken in consequence of this resolution and of the experience they have acquired in implementing it, so that the Committee of Ministers may decide whether the questions dealt with in this resolution should be re-examined in the light of the needs apparent at that time in the field of consumer protection.

SYSTEM OF CONTROL PRINCIPLES

I

1 A procedure should be available under which the question whether terms contained in standard contract forms are unfair may be considered on the initiative of interested persons, organisations representing the interests of consumers, trade or professional associations or public bodies. The views of such persons and bodies may be presented during the procedure.

2 Whether or not the standard contract form is amended under paragraph 1, any individual contract concluded on the basis of the standard form may nevertheless be subject to a procedure for hearing disputes.

II

1 Any interested person, organisation representing the interests of consumers, trade or professional association or public body should be able to submit terms contained in standard contract forms—whether or not

revised under Principle I—to a procedure before a judicial body or another appropriate body, which shall be designated or created by each state, so that this body may examine them in order to determine whether any term contained therein is unfair. Such a body may act of its own motion. If some official body has been established in connection with Principle I, that body shall not be competent for the purposes of this paragraph.

2 Decisions taken under the procedure referred to in paragraph 1 should, as far as possible, apply to the terms of all standard contract forms of the same type and should, in appropriate cases, be published.

III

A procedure should be available for the speedy introduction of legislative measures designed to render unlawful the use in contracts of unfair terms.

IV

1 A simple, rapid and cheap judicial procedure, as part of the consumer protection policy and especially against unfair terms of contracts, should be set up which could be easily available for consumers.

2 In this context, measures should be taken to encourage the amicable settlement of individual disputes.

Appendix 4

Cases

Hughes v Hall and Hall

QUEEN'S BENCH DIVISION
DONALDSON LJ, BINGHAM J
5 FEBRUARY 1981

A Scrivener QC and *A Taylor* for the appellant
K Jackson for the respondents

DONALDSON LJ. These are two appeals by case stated from the decisions of Magistrates who were confronted with charges against the two respondents alleging offences under Article 3(d) of the Consumer Transactions (Restrictions on Statements) Order 1976, as amended by section 23 of the Fair Trading Act 1973.

The facts which gave rise to these offences were that both respondents were involved in a secondhand car business, and they sold cars in circumstances in which the purchasers were given documents which included the magic phrase 'sold as seen and inspected'.

It was argued before the Magistrates that the giving of such a document did not offend against the Order to which I have referred and the Magistrates came to the conclusion that that submission was well founded.

In order that the Magistrates' conclusion and my view may be understood, it is necessary to refer first of all to the Order. The relevant paragraph is paragraph 3(d), and it provides that:

'A person shall not, in the course of a business—— ... (d) furnish to a consumer in connection with the carrying out of a consumer transaction or to a person likely, as a consumer, to enter into such a transaction, a document which includes a statement which is a term of that transaction and is void or inconsistent as aforesaid, or, if it were a term of that transaction or were to become a term of a prospective transaction, would be so void or inconsistent.' The reference to the document being 'void as aforesaid' is a reference to an earlier part of the paragraph as amended by

158

section 6 of the Unfair Contract Terms Act 1977. The other thing which is to be said before leaving paragraph 3(d) is that it is important to notice that it applies to a document furnished not only in connection with or as part of a transaction, but to a document including a term which *might* have been included in the contract' and, if so included, would have been void under section 6 of the 1977 Act.

The use of the word 'void' perhaps is not as happy as it might have been, because the effect of section 6 of the 1977 Act is perhaps not to avoid the term but to prevent the term having the effect contemplated by the section.

Section 6(2) of the Unfair Contract Terms Act 1977 provides that as against a person dealing as consumer, liability for breach of the obligations rising from (a) sections 13, 14 or 15 of the Sale of Goods Act 1893, or (b) sections 9, 10 or 11 of the Supply of Goods (Implied Terms) Act 1973, cannot be excluded or restricted by reference to any contract term.

The Magistrates said this: 'We were of the opinion that the defendant would be guilty if he had furnished a statement which is void by virtue of section 6(2) of the Unfair Contract Terms Act, 1977.' That conclusion thus far is accepted by both parties. They go on to say that 'The statement "sold as seen and inspected" would be void if its effect was to exclude the consumer's legal rights.' I think perhaps subject to adding 'under the Sale of Goods Act' that too would be accepted by both parties.

Then they say: 'Each document containing this statement is both exclusive and conclusive as evidence of its own terms.' For my part I would agree with that, in the sense that you cannot normally adduce evidence as to what the parties individually meant by the use of words, although you may well be able to adduce evidence as to the background against which the words are used, such as, for example, in this case, a motor car transaction.

They then go on: 'The consumer's legal rights would not be avoided because the term used is too vague, it does not express clearly what its intention is, and if construed strictly, against the respondent's interests, and without extrinsic evidence, it would not enable the respondent to avoid civil liability. The term would not, therefore, be void by virtue of the above Act, and accordingly we upheld the submissions of no case to answer and dismissed the two informations.'

It is that last conclusion which lies at the heart of this appeal. It is said by counsel for the respondent that the Magistrates are not only right in saying that the term is too vague, but that it would have no effect anyway. If the car was sold by description, it would make no difference to the purchaser's right, that the implied warranty of description was negatived. He could rely upon the express terms of the contract.

He says again that if the buyer in fact examines the goods before the contract is made, then there is no warranty as to merchantability as regards defects which that examination ought to have revealed. Similarly he says in relation to section 14(3) of the Act, that there is no implied warranty of fitness for a particular purpose, unless the buyer expressly or by implication had made known to the seller the particular purpose for which the goods are bought. If the purchaser did make the purpose known, then this clause will not affect the matter one way or another.

For my part I do not accept these submissions. I think that if a clause was included in the contract 'sold as seen and inspected', *prima facie* and subject always to what else might be expressly said in the contract, that would negative a sale by description. It would be a sale of a specific object as seen and inspected. That would exclude the implied warranty under section 13 of the Sale of Goods Act, and whether or not or how much it left in the way of an express obligation would depend upon the rest of the contract. For example it would still be open to the purchaser to complain that he got a different car from the one he had seen and inspected. But in my judgment he would lose some of his rights, even if he might still have other rights. This to my mind is quite sufficient to create an offence under this Act, because anything which has that effect would be voided by section 6 of the Unfair Contract Terms Act.

For these reasons I think that the Magistrates were incorrect.

I have not expressly referred to their suggestion that it was too vague. It must be implicit in what I have said that it is not too vague. The clause has to be considered in the context of people who buy and sell secondhand cars, and not in the context of marine insurance brokers. In the context in which it is used, I have no doubt as to what it should be understood as meaning.

I would allow the appeal.

Woodman v Photo Trade Processing Ltd

EXETER COUNTY COURT
CLARKE J
3 APRIL 1981

7 May. The following judgment was read.

CLARKE J. In this arbitration pursuant to Order 19 of the County Court Rules, Photo Trade Processing Ltd ('PTP') now seek to set aside the award of Mr Registrar Lowis dated 26 June 1980. They also ask for a new trial.

By that award the Learned Registrar had upheld the claim of the Plaintiff, Mr Woodman, in which he alleged that PTP had lost certain photographic films which in June 1979 he had entrusted to a shop in Exeter named Dixons for developing and printing. Dixons at all times were agents for PTP. The loss of Mr Woodman's films was undisputed, but by way of defence PTP sought to rely upon a clause in their contract with the Plaintiff limiting their liability to the replacement of the lost films with new ones.

In the course of the arbitration the Plaintiff submitted that the alleged clause was of no effect because it did not satisfy the requirement of reasonableness laid down by the Unfair Contract Terms Act 1977 ('The Act'). In upholding that submission the Learned Registrar in his judgment specifically considered and applied the various tests of 'reasonableness' set out in Section 11 and Schedule 2 of the Act, those matters having been drawn to his attention in the course of argument. Before me, however, Mr Meeke for PTP submitted that the terms of Sections 6 & 7 of the Act make Schedule 2 inapplicable to the type of contract in issue in this case. Hence, he argued, there was an error of law on the face of the arbitration award, thereby opening the discretion to set aside the award. (*Mayer* v *Pearce* 1958, 3 All ER 213). Mr Tench appearing for Mr Woodman (or, to be more accurate, for his personal representatives in view of Mr Woodman's death since the arbitration) agreed with that proposition.

I accept that Schedule 2 does not apply. The only relevant provision is Section 11; Subsection (1) of which requires that the clause should be 'a fair and reasonable one to be included having regard to the circumstances which were, or ought reasonably to have been, known to or in the contemplation of the parties when the contract was made.' There is a specific consideration to which I will refer later in Section 11 (4), but otherwise the question of what is 'fair and reasonable' is at large and undefined in the Act.

In considering that wide question of what is 'fair and reasonable' the 'guidelines' set out in Schedule 2 for other types of contract would be among the matters necessarily needing consideration in this case. But Mr

Meeke submitted, and Mr Tench accepted that the Learned Registrar, by treating Section 11 (1) and 11 (4) and Schedule 2 of the Act as if they were exhaustive of the matters to be considered, might have construed the question of reasonableness too narrowly. Accordingly I exercised my discretion to set aside the award and proceeded to a re-hearing. It is right to say, however, now that I have heard full argument, that I do not think that the Registrar did omit any relevant consideration.

For the purpose of the re-hearing both parties agreed to accept the facts as set out in the Learned Registrar's award without calling any further evidence. I will not repeat those facts except to the extent that I find it necessary to refer to them for the purpose of my decision.

The missing items are alleged to be 23 out of a reel of 36 exposures on 35mm film which Mr Woodman had, by arrangement, taken of a friend's wedding, intending to give them to those friends as a wedding present. He did not, however, reveal the subject matter of the photographs when he handed them in to Dixons, nor did he give any special instructions. All he got back were 13 of the negatives with prints therefrom. This suggests that the 23 negatives somehow became separated and lost during the processing rather than in Dixons shop, but in any event it would (unless explained) constitute a breach of the inevitable implied term that PTP would exercise reasonable care. By Section 1 (1) of the Act such a breach is classified as 'negligence'. No explanation was offered as to how these films could have become lost without fault.

The clause relied upon by PTP, and held by the Learned Registrar to have become incorporated in the contract between the parties, was printed on a card measuring $4\frac{1}{2}$ inches square, exhibited on the front of the Dixons shop counter. This card was not produced in evidence, but in view of the number of words which the Registrar held to have been printed upon it, I conclude that the lettering must have been fairly small. I regard myself as bound by the Registrar's finding of fact that that notice was 'adequately displayed' to Mr Woodman; but having regard to the quantity of advertising material usually displayed in photographers' shops I am not surprised that Mr Woodman says he did not see it. I would not wish this judgment to be regarded as any indication that a card of this size would constitute adequate notice except in exceptional circumstances.

The important part of the notice read as follows:

'All photographic materials are accepted on the basis that their value does not exceed the cost of the material itself. Responsibility is limited to the replacement of films. No liability will be accepted, consequential or otherwise, however caused.'

I accept that such a clause, if upheld under the Unfair Contract Terms Act, would be sufficient to exclude liability for any loss including loss by negligence on the part of PTP. It is therefore a 'contract term or notice' within the meaning of Section 2 (2) of the Act which raises the requirement of reasonableness.

Evidence was given before the Registrar that similar exclusion clauses were 'standard practice throughout the trade.' In their defence PTP plead that it is 'the custom among photographic processors.' In the course of argument Mr Meeke submitted that firms did exist who would, at a cost, carry out film processing and accept liability for their work, but there was no evidence before the Registrar of any such alternative. Specialist firms may exist, but I am bound to conclude on the evidence that Mr Woodman had no realistic alternative.

An analysis of the clause in question in this case shows that it preserves liability for what may be called the 'tangible loss', namely the value of the film itself, but it excludes liability for the intangible value of the picture itself. That intangible value would vary enormously. A few, such as an owner's photograph of his house or garden, could be rephotographed without difficulty. Most would be in the nature of holiday photographs the loss of which would cause at least disappointment. In some cases, such as the wedding photographs in the present case where no other photographer attended, real distress would be caused by their loss. A few photographs, such as a picture of a loved-one shortly before death, would be almost priceless to grief stricken relatives. In the circumstances of the present case I conclude that virtually all photographs handed in at Dixons would be of a personal nature rather than for any commercial or industrial use, so the consequence of loss are emotional rather than economic.

The consequences of loss to Mr Woodman consisted of his disappointment in having failed his friends' expectations rather than the disappointment of being unable to see the photographs themselves, but such consequences are all of the same nature. They are all losses of expected enjoyment. On the evidence I conclude that it was foreseeable to PTP that Mr Woodman would suffer some loss of enjoyment if they lost his films.

Mr Meeke classified loss of enjoyment as 'Solatium' for which, he argued, the law provides no right to damages. Therefore, he submitted, the clause only denies a remedy which the law does not allow anyway. Certainly such non-pecuniary loss was generally regarded as irrecoverable until recent years, but since the somewhat similar case in Scotland of *Diesen* v *Sampson* (1971 SLT 49), and since *Jarvis* v *Swan Tours* (1973 QB 233) in England, damages for distress, disappointment and annoyance have been recoverable, at least where the principle object of the contract was to provide pleasure. I have borne in mind Mr. Meeke's submission that those cases are distinguishable, but in my view thay are not. The whole object of this contract was to transform the films into pictures which would be likely to have at least some pleasure value. I conclude therefore that the clause in question does purport to shut out claims that are recoverable in law.

It was argued that the translation of distress and displeasure into terms of money for the purposes of a damages claim is a difficult task. That may be true, but quantification is equally difficult, for example, in the pain and suffering element of personal injury claims, except to the extent that the law has evolved a framework of conventional sums.

I now turn to consider the 'requirement of reasonableness' in relation to the clause in question. I was asked, particularly by Mr Meeke and to some extent by Mr Tench, if I found this particular clause to be unreasonable, to go further and suggest what type of clause would be reasonable. To some extent I must consider the reasonableness of alternatives in order to throw light upon the reasonableness of the clause in question. But I must stress that it is no part of my function to lay down what type of clause PTP should use. That must be for them to decide.

PTP argue that the clause they use is reasonable, and for the benefit of the public and themselves, because it enables them to operate a cheap mass-production technique. No evidence was adduced as to the extent of their cost savings as a result of the absence of claims and the absence of checking mechanisms to prevent loss, but I suspect that it amounts to more than the 'few pence' on every film suggested by Mr Tench. In these cost-conscious days I accept that a cheap mass-production service is desirable, and it is probably good enough for the vast majority of ordinary photographers who could well complain if they have to pay more in order to protect the interests of a minority whose pictures are of greater value.

The Act, however, does not require me to consider only what is reasonable for the majority of the public. I have to consider whether the term in this particular contract is fair and reasonable 'having regard to the circumstances which were, or ought reasonably to have been, known to or in the contemplation of the parties when the contract was made.' Dixons did not know what I would call the 'picture value' of Mr Woodman's photographs, but I conclude that it ought reasonably have been within their contemplation that:

(1) His photographs might have a high 'picture value', and
(2) He might be entrusting the film to them because he had no alternative.

I was told that there are, as yet, no reported authorities on the Unfair Contract Terms Act itself; but I was referred to three cases which provide some guidance.

Firstly there is *Peek* v *North Staffordshire Railway* (1863 10 HLC 493), a decision on Section 7 of Railway and Canal Traffic Act 1854 which permitted transport undertakings to impose conditions limiting their liability if adjudged by a Court to be just and reasonable. The clause under scrutiny in that case excluded all liability for loss or injury to various categories of fragile goods 'unless declared and insured according to their value.' It is a clause less onerous to the customer than that in the present case to the extent that PTP excluded liability without any option of declaring and insuring a special risk. And yet the House of Lords found the North Staffordshire Railway clause to be unreasonable.

Three main reasons emerge for the decision in Peek's case:
1. because it excluded liability for the consequences of negligence as well as mere accident,
2. because the railway was in a monopoly situation which realistically forced the customer to agree to their terms of business, and
3. because the only alternatives offered to the customer were either total exclusion of liability or insurance at a fixed rate which the Court regarded as so exorbitant as to compel customers to accept exclusion of liability.

Peek's case is complicated by the obligation laid upon common carriers to carry for reasonable remuneration; but it has strong bearing upon the present case because PTP, by adopting the same terms as the rest of the trade, also offers its customers no choice.

The present case is also similar because of the exclusion of liability for negligence as well as accident, but I do not regard this feature with the same degree of horror as did the House of Lords in Peek's case. The mischief is the same in that the trader is enabled to drop his standards with impunity, but the pressures of public opinion upon traders to maintain standards are stronger than they were in 1863. Furthermore it must be less objectionable to exclude liability for negligence where the items are comparatively small in value. A common carrier may handle cargoes of immensely greater value than any photograph.

The exclusion clause in the present case is marginally more reasonable than that in Peek's case because it at least preserves liability for the 'tangible value' of the films. But it is less reasonable in that it offers no insurance facility whatsoever. Insurance is a matter that I am specifically required to consider by Section 11 (4) of the Act. No doubt PTP could insure, but in the circumstances of this particular trade where no claims are likely to be really heavy, it would be more reasonable to satisfy claims out of their resources boosted by increased charges to their customers.

If there is to be insurance, it would have to be remembered that only the customer knows the 'intangible value' of his films. A system could be devised whereby a customer discloses the insurance value of his films when he hands them in for processing, but I do not regard insurance as a requirement of reasonableness in the film processing trade. The customer cannot buy a replacement photograph with his insurance moneys. What he really wants is some assurance that the processor will take extra care not to lose his more precious pictures.

Next I was referred to *Levison* v *Patent Steam Carpet Cleaning Co Ltd* (1977) 3 AER 498, where Lord Denning, MR, anticipating the introduction of the Unfair Contract Terms Act, held that a limitation of liability clause was unreasonable because the cleaning company had not specifically drawn it to the attention of the customer and advised him to insure. Comparing that with the present case, Mr Woodman's attention was not specifically drawn to the exclusion clause, nor was he advised to procure his own insurance (not that insurance would readily be available to him in such circumstances).

Thirdly I was referred to *Schroeder Music Publishing Co Ltd* v *Macauley* (1974) 1 WLR 1308 where Lord Diplock, dealing with a contract alleged to be an unreasonable restraint of trade, posed as a test of fairness the question of 'whether the restrictions are both reasonably necessary for the protection of the legitimate interests of the promisee and commensurate with the benefits secured to the promisor under the contract.'

Applying that test to the present case, I think that PTP do have a legitimate interest in keeping their costs down in order to remain competitive in the trade. But it cannot be regarded as reasonably necessary to protect that interest by compelling everybody, including the few who have high value photographs, to take their chance with the PTP mass-promotion system. For the majority of customers the lower prices resulting from excluded liability may be a commensurate benefit, but even then the balance is uncertain because he does not know the extent of the risk he runs to get those lower prices.

No evidence was offered as to the frequency with which films are lost during the PTP process. However, on this particular contract with Mr Woodman the balance must be to his disadvantage because of the importance of his particular photographs.

I conclude therefore that the clause in question is unreasonable having regard to almost all the criteria mentioned in the three authorities I have referred to. I have also considered the criteria set out in Schedule 2 of the Act, but in the circumstances of this case they seem to add nothing new, except only to the extent that account should be taken of 'alternative means by which the customer's requirements could have been met.' It is the feasibility of those alternatives which I must now consider.

Mr Tench suggested three possible alternatives, one of which was that PTP should accept all liability for negligence but exclude it for 'mishap.' This would certainly be reasonable from the customer's point of view, provided that the burden of proving 'mishap' falls upon PTP once the customer has proved the loss of films entrusted to them. But there would be few such 'mishaps' and in practice it would be virtually equivalent to the acceptance of full liability. As such I think it leans unreasonably against PTP.

A further suggestion by Mr Tench was that there should be some standardised level of compensation for the loss of 'picture-value' in every case. For example, 10 times the film cost or processing cost. I was referred to the 'Code of Practice for the Photographic Industry,' and paragraph 47 of that code states 'The Consumer may be informed of the reasonable compensation offered in the event of a film being lost or damaged by the processor or retailer.' This appears to envisage some sort of pre-arranged formula for compensation (another example of which is paragraph 76 which suggests a 'refund' as appropriate where developing and printing work is considered unsatisfactory because of an irreparable defect). However, I do not think that such a system, by itself, can be fair and reasonable in this trade because of the degree of uniformity in film costs and processing charges. In some industries servicing charges vary widely according to the delicacy or amount of work needing to be done, and in those instances compensation calculated as a multiple of servicing charges would achieve a sort of rough justice. But photographic film is reasonably uniform in price, and the developing and printing process is more or less uniform in cost. Compensation as a multiple of either figure would therefore also fall within a narrow range, and what is fair to the bulk of customers would be less than fair to a minority.

The Code of Practice appears to recognise this difficulty in that paragraph 49 adds a further recommendation for the benefit of that minority. This paragraph reads:

'The Retailer will advise the laboratory if an order being placed for processing is of exceptional value or importance, before the order is accepted, provided he has been informed by the consumer. There may be a special service combined with a higher price.'

The authors of the Code therefore do envisage the need for additional care in some cases, and it is that element that is totally lacking in the PTP terms of business. The so-called 'Special Service' was Mr Tench's third suggestion. He called it a 'two-tier system' of a normal service with total exclusion of liability and a special service at a higher charge with full acceptance of liability.

Even if such a special service were to provide for a standardised level of compensation at an appropriately high level to suit the needs of the minority, such a system has all the benefits to the customer of giving him a choice. It presents him with an alternative where he can reasonably expect more than normal care to be taken of his photographs.

But it is not necessarily the case that PTP should have to set up such a special service for themselves. If Mr Meeke is right and specialised laboratories do exist who accept liability and who are accessible to the general public, then PTP only have to refer their customers who want it to that laboratory. Such a system would certainly require that the choice be brought to the attention of all customers. Furthermore the Special Service option would have to be identified (ie name and address) and made convenient so that the customer is not indirectly compelled to accept the normal service.

Not many customers would opt for such a special service at a higher price (although Mr Woodman might well have been among that few if he had had the option) and I conclude that it would still leave ample scope for PTP to continue its low-cost mass-production technique for ordinary holiday photography.

In the light of the Code of Practice I reach the conclusion that some such form of two-tier system is not only reasonable but practicable. Accordingly PTP (on whom the burden lies under Section 11 (5) of the Act) have failed to persuade me that the clause which they applied to Mr Woodman's contract satisfies the statutory test of reasonableness.

It remains for me to consider the question of damages. It seems to me that the disappointment and distress suffered by Mr Woodman was quite exceptional and yet well within the range of what was foreseeable to PTP. I would not differ from the view of the Learned Registrar that the sum of £75 is appropriate.

Southwestern General Property Company Limited v Josef Marton

QUEEN'S BENCH DIVISION
CROOM-JOHNSON J
6 MAY 1982

Thayne Forbes for the plaintiff
Peter Langan for the defendant

CROOM-JOHNSON J On 15th May 1979 the plaintiffs sold by auction some land to the defendant. The defendant sought to rescind the contract on the grounds of innocent misrepresentation. The plaintiffs accepted his action as a repudiation of the contract, resold to another buyer for £4,400 less than the defendant had agreed to pay and they now claim that sum from him. The defendant says that he was induced to buy by innocent but false representations made by the plaintiffs in the auctioneers' catalogue. It should be made quite clear straightaway that he has expressly disclaimed any suggestion that there was deliberate misrepresentation by the plaintiffs. The plaintiffs deny that any representations made by them were false and they say that the conditions of sale which were set out in the auctioneers' catalogue preclude the defendant from relying on any representations, even if they were false. The plaintiffs also deny that any such representations as were made induced the defendant to make his purchase. The defendant's reply to all that is that the conditions of sale in the catalogue were unreasonable and therefore of no effect.

The description in the auctioneers' catalogue was of lot 82, and began, 'Long Leasehold Building Land'. It then goes on to describe the position as 'Land between 36 & 38 Oakwood Road, Hampstead Garden Suburb.' There is then a not to scale plan, and the remainder of the particulars read as follows: 'Held on lease for a term of 99 years from 25.3.1970 at a ground rent of £26 per annum. The Freeholders' Surveyors have stated that their clients would sell the freehold for £520, subject to contract. Planning Consent was granted in January 1968 for the erection of a house & garage. This consent has lapsed. Planning Consent was refused in May 1972 because the proposed house is out of character with the existing development in this part of the Hampstead Garden Suburb Conservation Area.' There is also added a short sentence about something else which is wholly immaterial.

The matters which are complained of by the defendant are the first sentence, 'Long Leasehold Building Land', and the two sentences dealing with the planning consent which was granted in January 1968 and the planning consent which was refused in May 1972.

The actual grounds upon which the planning consent had been refused in 1972 by the Borough of Barnet, who were the planning authority, reads that 'the proposed house because of its height, bulk, size and design is out of character with the existing development in this part of the Hampstead Garden Suburb Conservation Area.' The words about height, bulk, size and design are not included in the auction particulars, but no complaint is, or could be, made of their omission. The description of the planning consents or refusals which were in the particulars were not otherwise complete. The application which was refused on 3rd May 1972 had been made by a Mr Ross, a director of the plaintiffs who had owned this plot of land since 1971. What is not mentioned in the particulars in the catalogue is that Mr Ross then put in an appeal against the refusal of his application by Barnet. The appeal was heard by an inspector of the Department of the Environment, and before him the planning authority of Barnet had put in a statement, as they were entitled to do. They set out the reasons, which I have read, for their own refusal of the application. They then set out a number of the representations which had been made by committees, conservation advisory committees, local residents' associations and local residents individually, protesting at the suggestion of building on this vacant plot of land in Hampstead Garden Suburb.

Part of the protests referred to in this statement were that the Hampstead Garden Suburb Conservation Area Advisory Committee considered that, 'in any case, a house on this site would be out of place since it would amount to infill development and the present gap, allowing a glimpse of Big Wood, is an essential part of the local amenities which should be preserved.' After setting these out in the statement Barnet went on to say: 'It seems somewhat unlikely that the Local Planning Authority would give favourable consideration to any future application for a dwelling sited on the appeal site, which is now situated within a designated Conservation Area, as the existing open site provides a pleasant break in the street scene along Oakwood Road with a view through to Big Wood, an essential part of the local amenities which ought to be preserved. The proposed infill development would be detrimental to the visual amenities of the occupiers of nearby residential properties, the street scenes and views to and from Big Wood.'

Earlier in the statement Barnet had explained that the application had been refused, 'because the proposed development is considered to be out of character with the existing development in this part of the Hampstead Garden Suburb Conservation Area.'

The inspector from the Ministry dismissed Mr Ross's appeal. He gave three grounds. The first was the proposed three-storey house. By virtue of its design and size and so forth, it would, 'unacceptably dominate and oppress the small 2-storey neighbouring artisan cottages.' There was another reason in connection with its design which he added. The second ground was: 'although the planned treatment of the front elevation would be likely to blend with the neighbouring properties, the pitch and shape of the roof ... would strike a jarring note in the harmony of the street scene.' So far he had very much followed Barnet's own reasons for refusing the application, but he also rejected the application and dismissed the appeal on a wider ground, a third point, which read as follows: 'the proposed dwelling would mostly fill the comparatively large rural gap between Nos. 36 and 38 Oakwood Road thus virtually sealing off the view of Big Wood from Oakwood Drive. This would significantly reduce the rustic quality of this part of the road which it is the aim of the Conservation Area to retain.'

In the particulars in the catalogue at auction there was no reference to Mr Ross's appeal, and there was no reference to the wider grounds upon which the inspector dismissed his appeal.

Although it is not really material to anything I have to decide in this case, it is an agreed fact, which has been put before me by counsel, that Barnet has over the years taken up a particular position with regard to the in-filling of this vacant site. I was told by counsel that, after Mr Ross's appeal was dismissed, there was an application in February 1981 which Barnet again dismissed, giving as one of its reasons the in-filling of the open space which had been there referred to by the inspector and that again in 1982 there had been a yet further refusal which was on the same grounds as that in 1981, although that application is possibly going to be the subject of appeal.

The defendant says that the statement in the particulars, 'Long Leasehold Building Land' and the two sentences dealing with the planning applications in January 1968 and May 1972, together represented that the property could be used for building, provided that the house was regarded as suitable by the planning authority of Barnet. That is the way in which his particulars of misrepresentation are pleaded in his defence. What that means, when looking at the wording of the particulars, really is that the representation was that, if the proposed house was in character with the existing development, the property would be able to be used for building. He says that that representation was false, in view of the attitude which had been taken up by Barnet and the grounds upon which the inspector in 1972 had refused the appeal. The plaintiffs say, on the other hand, that both parts of those particulars, the reference to 'Long Leasehold Building Land' and the reference to the planning application, were true. They say that this was indeed building land, because the lease which was being sold gave the lessee the right to build, and indeed so it did; it gave the lessee liberty to erect one private detached dwelling-house on the property, to be built and completed to the approval of the lessor, and it also stipulated of course that any such dwelling-house had to be approved by the planning authority. 'Building land' is not a term of art: it may mean different things at different times, but in my view it is not sufficient to say that it is building land and properly so described simply because it is lawful as between the lessor and the lessee. There may be, for example, considerations of planning which come into building land, and, if somebody offered land for sale as building land which was legal as between the lessor and the lessee but it was nevertheless in a green belt, it could not properly be described as building land. The meaning of the expression 'building land' must depend upon the context in which it is used and in my view the proper meaning depends on how the phrase would strike someone who was reading the words in the circumstances in which they were intended to be read. People who are buying at auction are plainly concerned with matters of planning. The defendant submits that the words 'Long Leasehold Building Land' mean land capable of being used for building, and I think that his submission upon that is correct.

The sentences in the particulars dealing with the planning applications are accurate, say the plaintiffs, even though they are incomplete. The plaintiffs say, quite rightly, that they imply that the purchaser, if he wishes to build upon this particular plot, must get planning consent, but the words as they are set out convey the impression that, subject to a correct type of design being submitted, planning consent would be obtained. What was not included was the information of the inspector's grounds and the fact that it was somewhat unlikely that Barnet itself would give its consent, and these were clearly matters which would affect the market price of the land at auction.

The answer to the first question is that the words of description—those three sentences in the particulars—read together did represent that the land could be used for building if the purchaser submitted an application to build in a way which was in character with the existing development, and I conclude that the representation was therefore false.

The second question is: Did Mr Marton rely upon it? He gave evidence. He is a builder living in south London, but he was not looking here for something for a commercial transaction. He was looking for something where he might build a house in Hampstead for himself and his family to live. He got the catalogue from the auctioneers only the day before the auction. Lot 82 interested him, and he came to the conclusion from what he had read that planning permission had been refused simply because the house in the application was out of character. He thought that he could build a house which was in character and which would get permission. He went to look at the land with his wife in the time which he had, and they liked it. He went to the auction and his bid was successful. As he had only collected the catalogue the day before, and been to see the house on the morning before the auction, he said that he did not have time to make searches and enquiries. At the auction were some representatives of the auctioneers. He having come to the conclusion that, as the refusal had been because the design was out of character, the application would be successful if he submitted something which was in character—and these were his words—he would be able to build. It is not relied upon by the defendant that he received any assurance from the auctioneers' representatives, but the fact is that he did talk to them and said that after he had had a discussion with them he was 'double-sure', as he described it, '105 per cent sure', that what he had concluded as the result of reading the particulars in the catalogue was correct. He did read condition 13 in the catalogue. Condition 13, to which I shall revert later, said among other things that 'any intending Purchaser must satisfy himself by inspection or otherwise as to the correctness of each statement contained in the Particulars.' He said that he saw that, but as to that he satisfied himself by speaking to the auctioneers' representatives.

So far as this action is concerned, I have put on one side any conversation he had with the auctioneers' representatives. It is whether or not he relied on the particulars in the catalogue which matters here. The fact that he confirmed his reliance through other sources is irrelevant. The reliance, if any, which he placed upon the particulars in the catalogue does not have to be the only reliance, providing it is one of the matters upon which he did in fact rely, and I accept his evidence when he said that that is what he did. Therefore the second question is answered in favour of the defendant.

I now therefore come to the conditions of sale which were included in the catalogue and upon which the plaintiffs rely. The first is a general condition, 9 (i). It reads as follows: 'The property is believed to be and shall be taken as correctly described and any incorrect statement error or omission found in the Particulars or Conditions of Sale shall not annul the sale or entitle the Purchaser to be discharged from his purchase.' That is as far as is relevant.

Condition 9 (v) reads: 'No objection or requisition shall be raised as to the permitted user of the property for the purposes of the Town and Country Planning Act 1971 or any Act or Acts for the time being amending or replacing the same or as to any other matters arising under the said Act or any Rules or Regulations made or arising thereunder', and then these are probably the most significant words, 'the Purchaser shall take the properties as they are under the said Acts, Rules and Regulations.'

Condition 13 is quite obviously designed to avoid the effects of the Misrepresentation Act 1967. It is in two parts:

'(a) All statements contained in the foregoing Particulars are made without responsibility on the part of the Auctioneers or the Vendor and are statements of opinion and are not to be taken as or implying a statement or representation of fact', and then, I think, come the words that most matter, 'and any intending Purchaser must satisfy himself by inspection or otherwise as to the correctness of each statement contained in the Particulars.

(b) The Vendor does not make or give any representation or warranty in relation to the property nor has the Auctioneer or any person in the employment of the Auctioneers any authority to do so on his behalf.'

Arising out of the need to satisfy himself under condition 13 (a), there were special conditions attached to lot 82. These special conditions are really dealing with matters like requisitions and title, but they begin by giving the name, address and telephone number of the vendors' solicitors from whom enquiry can be made by the intending purchaser if he wishes. Special condition 8 reads, so far as is material: 'The property is sold subject to any development plan town planning scheme or any proposal or resolution for the acquisition thereof by any competent authority without any obligation on the part of the Vendor to disclose the same whether or not the Vendor has Notice thereof.' There might be some doubt as to whether special condition 8, on its strict interpretation, applies to the facts of the present case, but it is quite clear and it is not contested that the three general conditions are sufficient in one way or another to exclude liability for the representation which I have found was made, unless those conditions are to be avoided by section 3 of the Misrepresentation Act 1967. Section 3, as now replaced by section 8 of the Unfair Contract Terms Act 1977, reads as follows: 'If a contract contains a term which would exclude or restrict—(*a*) any liability to which a party to a contract may be subject by reason of any misrepresentation made by him before the contract was made; or (*b*) any remedy available to another party to the contract by reason of such a misrepresentation, that term shall be of no effect except in so far as it satisfies the requirement of reasonableness as stated in section 11(1) of the Unfair Contract Terms Act 1977; and it is for those claiming that the term satisfies that requirement to show that it does.'

The test of reasonableness set out now in the Unfair Contract Terms Act 1977, section 11, is in sub-section (1) and reads, as far as is relevant, in this way: 'In relation to a contract term, the requirement of reasonableness for the purposes of this Part of this Act, section 3 of the Misrepresentation Act 1967 ... is that the term shall have been a fair and reasonable one to be included having regard to the circumstances which were or ought reasonably to have been, known to or in the contemplation of the parties when the contract was made.'

The question therefore is: Were these conditions fair and reasonable to be included under sub-section (1) of section 11? Were they or ought they reasonably to have been known to or in the contemplation of the parties when the contract was made? The onus of proof in this matter is on the plaintiffs.

The plaintiffs say, first, that these were auction particulars and, though they must be reasonable for each separate contract which results from the inclusion of different properties in that catalogue, yet the circumstances of sales by auction required that such exception clauses and disclaimers should be made. The defendant's answer to that is that these are particulars which are in the catalogue and come from the vendors themselves and are matters peculiarly within the vendors' knowledge. The plaintiffs then say that the defendant was told by condition 13 (a) to make his own enquiries and by the special conditions was given the information of people from whom he could make them. That is correct. Against that it might be said that people do attend auctions at short notice, as Mr Marton did, when there is simply not time, as in his case, to make the enquiries, either of the vendors' solicitors or of the planning authority.

The third submission of the plaintiffs was that people like the plaintiffs selling land like this at auction are not catering only for people like Mr Marton: they are offering their land to anybody, which may include all sorts of buyers, including property speculators who buy land without enquiry simply on their nose for good bargains. What I have to consider is whether these conditions were reasonable to incorporate in a contract, not with property speculators in which they might very well be reasonable, but in a case such as a householder like Mr Marton who is very clearly concerned, if he wants to buy for himself, with planning matters. The defendant's submissions on this question of reasonableness are that the planning history of this property was something peculiarly within the knowledge of the plaintiffs, they had owned the land since 1971 and that the people who had made the 1972 application through their director had appealed it and had lost the appeal on the grounds which were not disclosed in the particulars. The defendant also says that the representation which was false was central to the purpose for which the defendant was buying the land, namely, to erect a dwelling-house. The very nature of the sale was to sell the land as building land, and the attitude of the local planning authority was some indication, even at that time, that what was being offered as building land was not likely to be building land at all.

The words of section 11 of the Unfair Contract Terms Act are very wide. I have to deal with this contract, with the parties to this contract and the circumstances in which this contract was made. The conclusion I have come to is that the plaintiffs have not satisfied me that these are terms which are fair and reasonable and have been included in the contract between the plaintiffs and defendant at the time of this auction. These terms, if they were included, would exclude liability for a failure to tell the purchaser more than only a part of the facts which were among the most material to the whole contract of sale. In the result the plaintiffs are unable to rely upon the conditions in the auctioneers' catalogue, and there must be judgment for the defendant.

Index

Advertisements—
  innocent publication of, 87–8
  statutory rights, and, 81, 83
  void exclusion clauses, and, 81
  wording used in, 79, 108
Agency, concept of, 37
Agents—
  forwarding, acting as, 49
  negligent acts by, 40
  third parties, and, 38
  vicarious immunity of, 38–9
Arbitration clauses, 35
  Northern Ireland, in, 35
  Scotland, in, 35
Arbitrator, reasonableness, and, 111

'By-pass' provision, 86–8

Catalogues, wording in, 79
Conditions—
  condition, warranty, distinction
    between, 20, 35
  disability, and, 5
  foreigners, and, 5–6
  hire of plant, and, 14
  illiteracy, and, 5
  implied, 35
  limiting, 21
  warranty, condition, distinction
    between, 20, 35
Consumer protection—
  contravention, of regulations, 92–3
  safety of products, and, 92
  supply of goods, and, 92–3
Consumer trade practices—
  misleading, 78
  undesirable, control of, 77

Consumer Transactions (Restrictions
    on Statements) Order 1976—
  compensation, and, 86
  enforcement of, responsibility for, 86
  manufacturer, subsequent consumer
    transaction, and, 85
  offences, in breach of, 86–7
  sue, right to, under, 86
  third parties, consumers' rights
    against, 79–80
Contract—
  acceptance—
    beyond ability to refuse, 8, 9
    free choice, exercise of, and, 9
    signature, and, 15
    ticket machine, automatic, through
      agency of, 7, 8, 10
  affirmation of, 56–9
  bargaining power, inequality of, 70, 131
  breach of, 33, 45–7, 51–61, 99–101,
    108, 129–30
    other cases, in, 99–101
    Scotland, in, 99–101
  consumer—
    dealing as a, 108–9
    Scotland, in, 108–9
  country, proper law of, parties'
    preference as to, 122
  course of dealing, regular, 11–13
  'declaration of intent', 59–60
  documents, contractual, 3, 9
  equipment, installation of, and, 102
  excluding terms, in, 3, 33
  failure to perform, 59
  'fair and reasonable', in a, 66
  fiduciary duty, breach of, and, 47
  'fundamental term', in, 51–61
    breach of, 'deviation cases', and,
      52, 58

Contract—*contd*
  implied contract, 37–8
  indemnity clause, and, 23–4, 29, 30
  inequitable contracts, 66
  insufficiency of notice, of terms of, 5
  'invitation to treat', 10
  liability, in, *see under* Liability
  limiting terms, in, 3, 33
  misperformance, and, 25, 56, 59
  offer, and, 10
  oral, 4, 12, 17, 48–50, 55
  parties, 'understanding of the', 14
  persons, not party to a, 36–7
  receipts, notices on, 4, 5
  repair, maintenance, and, 102
  replacement of, by another, 11
  'risk note', and, 4, 12
  secondary contract, evasion by means
    of, 107
  services, and—
    implied terms, and, 95
    price of, 93
    provision for, 93
    skill, used in performing, 93, 95
    time, for performance of, 93
  standard form, onerous terms in,
    69–70
  sue, to, party to contract only, 40
    Scotland, in, 40–1
  telephone conversation, and, 10–11
  terms of—
    display of, on premises, 3
    obliteration of, on tickets, 5
    putative, 3
    unavailability of, 6
    unusual terms, 7–8, 51
    'written standard terms', 98–9,
      129–31
      Scotland, in, 'standard form
        contracts', and, 98–9, 129–30
    see also Liability, Negligence
Contractual documents—
  acknowledgment, as, 3
  cheque book, as, 4, 9
  receipt, as, 3, 4
  ticket, admission, as, 3, 4

Damages—
  breach of contract, and, 33
  claim for, 22
  contract price, limiting damages to,
    115
  further heads of, 24

Damages—*contd*
  goods delivered, and, 22
  goods not delivered, and, 22
  insurance, and, 33, 37
  misrepresentation, and, 16
  pre-estimate of likely loss, 33
  terms, limiting damages, 33
Defences—
  'by-pass' provision, and, 86–8
  mistakes, for, 87
  reasonable precautions, as a, 87
Detinue, 25–6
'Deviation cases', breach of
  fundamental term, and, 52, 58
Disability, terms of contract, and, 5, 17
Disclaimers, trade descriptions, and, 88
Documents—
  blank documents, signing of, 17
  common law precedent, and, 22
  failure to hand over, 11, 12
  fraud, misrepresentation, and, 16,
    46–7
  innocent misrepresentation, 16
  misunderstanding of, non est factum
    plea, 16–17
  signature, contents of document
    bound by, 16
  signing of, 15–17
  statutory rights, unlawful exclusion
    of, 82–3
  Unfair Contract Terms Act 1977,
    drastic effect of, 22
  wording in, 79
  written statements in, 83
Doorstep sellers, 84
Duty of care, 22, 70, 96

Exclusion clauses—
  agents, and, 38–9
  ambiguous clauses, 19
  arbitrator, 111
  avoidance of, 10
  construction of, 27, 29, 31–2, 58
  'contra proferentum' rule, 19, 21, 34
  contracts, clauses effectively
    incorporated into, 3
  contractual terms, 3
  control of—
    England, in, 3
    Scotland, in, 3, 40, 53
    course of dealing, and, 11–15
    damages, excluding right to, 34
    estoppel, 35

Exclusion clauses—*contd*
 excluding wording of, 3, 21, 55
 exemption, varieties of, 3, 21, 55
 forbidden clauses, 80–1
 general rules, 28
 'goods', meaning of under Act, 94
  Scotland, in, 94–5
 indemnity clauses, 23–4, 29–30,
  105–7, 114
 injury *see under* Personal injury
 ineffective clauses, 22, 91, 97, 102,
  108, 122
 insurance policies, and, 20, 21, 34,
  121
 interpretation of, 19–41
 judicial hostility to, 21–2
 'latent defects', 21
 liability *see under* Liability
 limiting condition, 21, 34
 linked agreements, 91
 misrepresentation, 16–17, 50–1,
  117, 121, 130
 negligence *see under* Negligence
 notices, written, 94
 reasonableness, 61, 69, 101, 103,
  108, 129
  'competent authority', ruling of,
   110
  prime rules of, 110
   Scotland, in, 110
  quality of goods, and, 22, 81, 102,
   104
  requirement of, 110–17
  road transport, and, 92
   Scotland, in, 101, 108, 177
  unequal bargaining power, and,
   171
 'sold note', 12
 special exclusions, 33–6
 specified exclusions, 121–2
  Scotland, in, 121
 technical expressions, legal meanings,
  20
 third parties, 36–41
  Scotland, in, 40–1
 tickets, issue of by machine, 7, 8, 10
 time limits, imposition of, 34
 two constructions of negligence, 27
  new construction of, 53
 Unfair Contract Terms Act 1977,
  drastic effect of, 22
 unlawful clauses, 77, 88, 130
 unreasonable clauses, 65, 69

Exclusion clauses—*contd*
 void clauses, 90, 130
 warranty, exclusion of, 20
 wording, precise of, 21, 26–8

Fiduciary duty—
 breach of, liability for, 47, 68
Fraud—
 contract, and, 16
 extravagant condition, 71
 liability for, 46
 mis-statement, fraudulent, 118
'Fundamental breach', of contract,
  45–6, 51–61
 termination by, 108
'Fundamental term', in contract, 51–61
 breach of, 52, 58

Goods—
 carriage of, 37–40, 122
 carrier of, 37, 39–40, 46, 122
 clause, excluding right to, 34
 consumer, supply to, 77
 consumer use, for, 105
  Scotland, in, 105
 contract description, relevance of, 35,
  52, 60
 damage to, 22, 122
 damages—
  goods delivered, for, 22, 48
  goods not delivered, for, 22
 defective packing, 22
  quality of, 22
 description, 52
  incorrect description, 83
 hire of, 102
 lease of, 102
 obligation as to title, change of law,
  and, 101–3
  Scotland, in, 102–3
 quality of, 22, 81, 102, 104
 repossession of, 91
 right to reject, 34, 35
 sale of—
  by description, 82–3, 101–2
  right to complain, 22
  statements, written, and, 83–4
 statutory rights, suppliers failure
  to advise consumer, 77, 81, 85
 stolen, exclusion clause, and, 39,
  45–6
 subsequent consumer transaction and
  supplier, 85

178   INDEX

Goods—*contd*
  Supply of Goods and Services Act
    1982, reasonableness and, 103
      Scotland, not applicable in, 103
  supply of, to consumers, 77
  trading stamps, and, 103–4
    Scotland, in, 103
Guarantees—
  definition of, 104
    Scotland, in, 104
  guidelines for, 85
  verbal, 104
    Scotland, 104
  see also Manufacturers

Hire, conditions of, 14
Hire purchase contracts—
  conditions, in, 20, 35, 53, 94
  consumers' rights, obligations as to,
    83–4, 109
  extortionate credit bargains, 65
  debtor, protection of, 90
  finance houses, and, 84
  'fundamental breach of contract',
    and, 55–6
  goods—
    definition of, 94
      Scotland, in, 94–5, 109
  'linked transactions', 91
  'regulated agreements', 90
  terms, implied, exclusion of, 93
Housing—
  builders liability, 92
    Scotland, in, 92
  repairing leases, exclusion of terms,
    92

Illiteracy, terms of contract, and, 5, 17
Indemnity clauses, 23–4, 29, 30,
  105–7, 130
Inequitable contracts, 66, 68
Interlocutory injunction, 67

Liability—
  breach of contract, for, 129
  business, 95
  clauses limiting, 34
  common law, at, 31
  'contra proferentum rule', and, 19
  contract, in, 23, 25–6, 97, 112–3
  contractual, 25
  delictual, (Scotland), 16
  economic loss, and, 97
  fiduciary duty, breach of, and, 47, 68

Liability—*contd*
  fraud, for, 46
  indemnity for, 29–30
  late delivery, and, 25
  misperformance, and, 25
  negligence, for, 22–3, 26–9, 31, 95,
    129
    Scotland, in, 129
  outside negligence, 26
  tort, in, 23
    Post Office exemption, 123
  tortious, 25, 96
Linked agreements, exclusion clauses
  in, 91

Manufacturers—
  consumers, obligations to, 79–80, 86
  guarantees—
    control on the use of, 130
    definition of, 104
      Scotland, in, 104
    negligence, faulty goods and, 96
    Office of Fair Trading, guidelines
      by, 85–6
    undesirable restrictions in, 85
    verbal, 104
      Scotland, in, 104
    wording used in, 84–5, 131
'Material breach' of contract,
  (Scotland), 53, 99
Misperformance and liability, 25
Misrepresentation—
  innocent, 16
  reasonableness, and, 16, 17, 50–1,
    117–21, 130
    Scotland, in, 16, 110, 117
Moloney report, extract from, 84

Negligence—
  Act of God, and, 33
  construction of clause, and, 29
  'contra proferentum' rule, and, 19
  contracts, and, 4
  contractual, 25
  common duty of care, breach of, 96
  common law precedent, and, 22
  courts, exclusion clauses, and, 26
  damage resulting from, 26–7, 37, 39
  damage to property, 96–7
  death, and, 96
  definition of, 96
  duty of care, 22, 70, 96
  economic loss, and, 97
  employee's liability, and, 96

Negligence—*contd*
exclusion clauses, two constructions of, 27
faulty goods, and, 96
fraud, and, 16–17
holiday camps, and, 96
liability, in, 22–3, 26–9, 31, 95, 129
Scotland, in, 129
misrepresentation, and, 16–17
personal injury, and, 23, 96, 129
restraint of princes, and, 33
servants, agents, by, 40
sports stadia, and, 96
tortious, 25, 96
Notices, display of—
advertisements, in, 79
catalogues, in, 79
terms, use of, in, 80–1
offences, and, 80–1
statutory rights, and, 81
trade premises, on, 79
trade vehicles, on, 79
unlawful, 80
consumers' rights, and, 80–1
see also Exclusion clauses

Office of Fair Trading—
guidelines published by, 85–6

Parties, status of, 131
Passengers, carriage of, 21, 122
Patents—
contracts relating to, 92
determination of, 92
Personal injury, 3, 6–7, 9, 94, 96, 105, 122, 129

Reasonableness, 61, 69, 71, 103, 108, 129
see also Exclusion clauses, Misrepresentation
'Regulated agreements', 91
Rental agreements, 'linked transactions', and, 91
Risk, assumption of, 97
Scotland, in, 97
'Risk note', 4, 12

Sale of goods—
businesses, between, 115
Scotland, in, 109
by description, 82–3, 101–2
see also Goods

Scotland—
arbitration clauses, 85
assumption of risk, 97
contract—
'material breach', of, 53, 99
other cases, in, 99–101
'standard form' contracts, 98–9, 129–30
consumer, dealing as a, 108–9
delictual liability, 16
duty of care, breach of, 96
employee's liability, 96
exclusion clauses, control of, 1, 40, 53
fraud, 16, 117
goods—
consumer use, in, 105
definition of, 94–5
hire purchase, 109
hired, 94
guarantee—
definition of, 104
verbal, 104
misrepresentation, 16, 110, 117
negligence, liability for, 129
reasonableness, 16, 101, 108, 117
specified exclusions, 121
sue, to, party to contract only, 40–1
Supply of Goods and Services Act 1982, not applicable in, 103
title, obligations as to, change in law, and, 102–3
trading stamps, supply of goods and, 79, 103
Secondary contract, evasion by means of, 107
'Sold note', 12
'Standard form of contract', onerous terms in, 69–70
Statutory rights, 81–83

Third parties, exclusion clauses, and, 36
Time limits, imposition of, 34
Trade descriptions—
disclaimers, and, 88
false, 88
Trading stamps, supply of goods and, 79–81, 93, 103

Unconscionable bargains—
'poor and ignorant persons', and, 65–6
sale, undervalue of, 65
unequal status of parties, 131
victim of, independent advice to, 65

INDEX

Unenforceable contracts, 66
Unfair Contract Terms Act 1977 *see under* Exclusion clauses
Unlawful exclusion clauses, 77–88, 131

Vicarious immunity, 38

Void clauses, 90, 130

Warranty, condition, distinction between, 20
Weights and measures authorities— Order, responsibility for enforcing, 86